DATE DUE

MY 27 '99			
OC 20 '99			
MY 18 '00			
MR 1 4 '01			
SE 29 '05			

DEMCO 38-296

BRAZILIAN LEGACIES

Perspectives on Latin America and the Caribbean

THE CHAINS OF INTERDEPENDENCE
U.S. POLICY TOWARD CENTRAL AMERICA, 1945–1954
Michael L. Krenn

A HOLY ALLIANCE?
THE CHURCH AND THE LEFT
IN COSTA RICA, 1932–1948
Eugene D. Miller

QUISQUEYA LA BELLA
THE DOMINICAN REPUBLIC IN HISTORICAL AND
CULTURAL PERSPECTIVE
Alan Cambeira

BRAZILIAN LEGACIES
Robert M. Levine

THE HAUNTING PAST
POLITICS, ECONOMICS AND RACE IN CARIBBEAN LIFE
Alvin O. Thompson

BRAZILIAN LEGACIES

Robert M. Levine

M.E. Sharpe
Armonk, New York
London, England

Library of Congress Cataloging-in-Publication Data

Levine, Robert M., 1941–
Brazilian legacies / Robert M. Levine.
p.   cm. — (Perspectives on Latin America and the Caribbean)
Includes bibliographical references and index.
ISBN 0-7656-0008-0 (alk. paper). —
ISBN 0-7656-0009-9 (pbk. : alk. paper)
1. Brazil—Civilization—20th century.
2. Brazil—Social conditions.
3. Brazil—Social life and customs.
4. Life skills—Brazil.
I. Title.
II. Series.
F2537.L472 1997
981.06—dc20
96–38568
CIP

Printed in the United States of America

The paper used in this publication meets the minimum requirements of the
American National Standard for Information Sciences—
Permanence of Paper for Printed Library Materials,
ANSI Z 39.48-1984.

BM (c)   10   9   8   7   6   5   4   3   2   1
BM (p)   10   9   8   7   6   5   4   3   2   1

For Joey
b. São Paulo, 24 May 1985

Contents

Acknowledgments

Research for this project was funded by a grant from the North–South Center of the University of Miami, Coral Gables, and from the annual stipend for Brazilian studies provided by the Brazilian-American Chamber of Commerce in Miami. I am grateful to Davi Camargo Bom Meihy, Jeff Lesser, Cristina Mehrtens, Quélia Quaresma, Peter M. Beattie, E. Richard Downes, and, as always, José Carlos Sebe Bom Meihy, for their help, suggestions, and comments. Responsibility, of course, falls entirely to me, especially since many of the observations in this book are based on my long personal experience in Brazil, starting in early 1961 when I spent a week in Rio de Janeiro while returning from a semester's overseas undergraduate study program in Argentina, and recurring on a regular basis subsequently.

Manaus○

Belém○

Fortaleza○

Recife○

Salvador○

Brasília○

Belo Horizonte○

Nova Iguaçu○

São Paulo○ Rio de Janeiro○

Santos○

Curitiba○

Porto Alegre○

Brazilian cities with a population of more than 1 million, 1997

BRAZILIAN
LEGACIES

Introduction

Brazil, the largest and most populous country in Latin America, has long fascinated outsiders, although often for inaccurate reasons. Until recently, foreigners often saw Brazil as a land of coffee and parrots, Carnival and the Amazon, the samba-land of Hollywood's 1930s *Flying Down to Rio*. Waldo Frank, a well-meaning writer who traveled through South America in 1942, maintained that Brazil was a nation of "archetypal forest-dwellers," since 85 percent of Brazil's people had African blood, and out of the Brazilian forest a "new world culture" was emerging.[1]

The real Brazil is far different, of course, although to be sure it has produced an original and vibrant culture of its own. It is a manufacturing giant; food production is dominated by large agro-industrial businesses; and it boasts one of the most sophisticated cultural environments in the world. Brazil is a country of not only rain forests but concrete jungles teeming with energy and choked with traffic, as well as population blends of rich and poor, immigrant and migrant, old and young.

Its diverse population includes more persons of African descent than any country except Nigeria, and more Japanese than anywhere outside of Japan. More descendants of Arab peoples live in Brazil than anywhere outside the Middle East. Large numbers of Brazilians have ancestors from places as disparate as Italy, Jamaica, Poland, Germany, Switzerland, Korea, and the Confederate States of America. The largest Roman Catholic nation on earth, Brazil is also home to millions of evangelical Protestants as well as Buddhists, Muslims, Mormons, European spiritists, Sephardic and Ashkenazic Jews, and followers of a pantheon of animist religions brought to Brazil on the slave ships from Africa but still very much alive today.

3

Its successes range from its relaxed racial ambience to the quiet professionalism of its international diplomats. Brazil's exuberant soccer team won the world's imagination as it marched in 1994 to the *tetra,* the unprecedented fourth-time capture of the World Cup. Brazil has become known for its exports of its music, orange juice, shoes, and textiles, although fewer know that Brazil has also become a world leader in the sale of soybeans, passenger airplanes, minerals, and armaments. When frosts damaged Brazilian coffee plantations in 1994, world prices rose immediately. Outsiders also now know about the plight of Brazil's native peoples and abandoned street children. News about angry urban violence halved the annual number of international tourists to Rio de Janeiro since 1989 from 400,000 to 200,000, although tourism has picked up in other parts of the country, especially to the beautiful beaches of the northeastern coast.

Brazilians have reversed their former isolation. Mercosul, the Southern Cone's Common Market, has opened borders and spurred tourism, stimulating commerce as well. More than ever, Brazilians have become world travelers. An estimated 60,000 Brazilians visit Orlando each year; thousands more go to Western Europe, the Middle East, the rest of the United States, and Asia. Brazil exports not only soccer stars but musicians, dance groups, automobile racers, and soap operas; it also sends abroad university-educated men and women—obtaining entry into foreign countries by any means at their disposal—seeking to accumulate enough capital to return home with an economic stake for their families. There are Brazilian colonies in Tokyo, Riyadh, Los Angeles, Middleton (Wisconsin), Miami, Toronto, Paris, and scores of cities elsewhere. Brazil has forged two-way links with the world.

Brazilian Legacies is an interpretive essay that explains the historical reasons for the country's present-day condition. Given that Brazil is a vast country whose regions are as different from one another as far-flung regions in Russia, Canada, and the pre-interstate-highway United States, some of the discussion about "Brazilian culture" or "Brazilian life" may not apply universally. As a national entity, however, Brazil dominates its subcontinent, extending to the borders of nine Latin American neighbors. As such, common themes that make Brazil what it is today merit analysis.

Historians search the past for clues to the present and possible future. In so doing, this book probes Brazil's legacies: past forms of government that included colonial rule, a postindependence monarchy, a federal republic, and various spells of military dictatorship. It examines the realities of Brazil's complex social world, the role of insiders and outsiders. It delves into the inner motivations of the "Brazilian way." It considers both the world of luxury and accomplishment and the netherworld of poverty and underdevelopment. Two chapters focus on the tools that needy Brazilians have used to survive and, in more drastic cases, the mechanisms employed to fight back beyond coping. The concluding chapter takes stock of Brazil today and looks for reasons for optimism as the next century rapidly approaches.

Starting Points

Brazilian Legacies, then, explores how Brazil works and looks to the historical past for explanations of why things are as they are today. To overcome such historical constraints, one must understand their origins and their nature. Another premise is that much of what has been written about Brazil skates along the top of Brazilian life, shying away from probing beneath the surface.[2] Studies of how Brazil's underground economy works are few even though most scholars would agree that a substantial part of every nation's economic activities operates "off the books." There are many other questions that we tend to overlook. Why do some desperately poor people turn to crime, while others toil with dignity against great hardship? Why does democracy often increase, not decrease, the amount of corruption in government? What role do holidays and festivities play in the lives of people living on substandard wages, without any hope of upward mobility?

More than half of Brazil's people live outside the vibrant core of national life. The book's emphasis falls not so much on these people as on the system that has caused this situation as well as the strategies these marginalized folk have employed to cope. How the Brazilian system works, and how it moves individuals to act, will be the principal theme of this study. The task is difficult because a slender line separates deference from defiance, authority from rebellion. The analysis may seem critical, but it is based on a profound admiration for those aspects of Brazilian life that stem from the characteristic Brazilian mix of tolerance, competence, and decency, traits that we all should emulate.

Notes

1. Paul J. Carter, *Waldo Frank* (New York: Twayne Publishers, 1967), 134–35.
2. Many social scientists have deplored the scarcity of studies of themes that are hard to pin down. Florestan Fernandes, Charles Wagley and Marvin Harris, and Emílio Willems, for example, all called for further examination of the question of how class differences in cities are reflected at the cultural level. See Ruben George Oliven, "Culture Rules OK: Class and Culture in Brazilian Cities," *International Journal of Urban and Regional Research* 3 (March 1979), 29–48; Charles Wagley and Marvin Harris, "A Typology of Latin American Subcultures," *American Anthropologist* 57 (1955), 428–51; Emílio Willems, "Urban Classes and Acculturation in Latin America," in E.M. Eddy, ed., *Urban Anthropology. Research Perspectives and Strategies* (Athens: University of Georgia Press, 1968); Florestan Fernandes, "O Homem e a Cidade-metropole," *Educação e Ciências Sociais* 5 (1959), 23–44.

1

The Legacy of Color

First and foremost among the contrasts between Brazil and its neighbors has been its subcontinental size, making Brazil after the breakup of the Soviet Union the fourth largest country in the world, behind Canada, the United States, and China. Although its population has long been enormously diverse, Brazil's national culture preserved its homogeneity. Unlike Peru, Bolivia, Paraguay, Mexico, and Haiti, where millions do not speak the official language, Portuguese prevails from the rain forests to the southern Brazilian pampa.

Brazil was not always acknowledged as a land of significant potential. It was claimed for the Portuguese Crown in 1500 by the navigator Pedro Álvares Cabral when he ventured westward into the Atlantic looking for winds to blow him around the coast of West Africa en route to India. For centuries, Brazil remained less important to Lisbon than Portugal's Far Eastern and African commercial trading posts. Its plantations were worked at first by enslaved native labor and later by Africans, imported to work the plantations and mines. Working conditions were so bad that slaves lived an average of only seven years after landing in Brazil. After 1695, the discovery of large gold deposits in the mountainous interior created an influx of European prospectors. Most of the mined bullion was shipped back to Portugal, and the capital of the colony was moved south to the soaring but filthy city of Rio de Janeiro, the nearest seaport with access to the mines.

By 1800, Brazil's population was two-thirds African in origin. Many of the rest were mixed-race peoples living as sharecroppers in the countryside or clustered in shabby towns and unimpressive cities. Brazil had no printing press until late in the colonial period, no universities, few schools. To

European naturalists invited by the Crown in the early nineteenth century after Napoleon's military aggression had forced the royal family to take refuge in Portugal's New World colony, Brazil was a tropical paradise and place of natural wonders. Yet for most of the people who lived there it was a disquieting paradise.

The basis for much of the concern was the separation between the privileged Portuguese families and the rest of the inhabitants, eventually referred to as the *povo*—the common people. Even after the upper classes enlarged their membership by admitting (through marriage) persons of Dutch, English, and other European origins, the gap that separated the privileged from the rest was ethnic, religious, and racial. The elite were European, Roman Catholic, and light-skinned; the rest included some less fortunate Portuguese but otherwise were non-Caucasian, or indigenous, or people of a vast array of mixed racial categories. For generations, intellectuals worried that Brazil would never become civilized because of what they saw as the retrograde nature of the national population. "Our workers are lazy," said nineteenth-century Senator and Viscount Alfredo d'Escragnolle Taunay. "[They] have little love for the place in which they reside."[1] European immigrants were recruited and subsidized because landowners believed them to be ideal, compared with what they considered to be the racially inferior stock of most Brazilians. The attitudes shown by Brazilians of European origin toward nonwhites were usually the same as those held by visiting foreigners. Harvard naturalist Louis Agassiz traveled in Brazil in 1868 and concluded that racial mixture had produced a people "physically and morally degraded, a mongrel crowd as repulsive as mongrel dogs."[2] Given this view, shared in substance by educated Brazilians, who were of predominantly European origin, it is no surprise that social status in Brazil emerged as a function not of wealth or occupation but of family name. Status has also been largely a matter of race, which, despite frequent denials, has always correlated strongly with status and power.

On the other hand, there was a historical basis for a fluid social structure and for opportunities for some nonwhites to improve their lot. Unlike its neighbors, all former colonies of the Spanish Crown, Brazil has traveled along a path of historical evolution that has contributed to these differences. Because Brazil had no agricultural, sedentary indigenous population to enslave, Portugal's New World colony, although it used African slaves for plantation and mine labor, did not develop the same tradition of peasant Indian villages, for all practical purposes enslaved by economic reality, that was found in Peru and especially Mexico. Whereas Mexico City and Caracas and Lima and Havana were stately, modern cities, highly organized and glitteringly prosperous, Brazilian cities developed far more modestly, and rural elites were not always wealthy. More often than not, they lived in simple, even austere estate houses and consumed a diet not very different from that fed to their slaves. There were few schools and fewer cultural institutions, and there was little prospect for improvement. The effect of this was in some ways to reduce the distance between rich and poor; the scarcity of European settlers, moreover, produced a climate that was conducive to racial mixing and over the years contributed to a system of social distinctions that were in some ways softer than those found in the more rigorously hierarchical Spanish American lands.

Brazilian lore subscribed to the legend that three principal races—the European, the Indian, and the African—had formed the *povo*. From the beginning, relations between members of different racial groups in Brazil were complex, in part because the imbalance between female and male newcomers from Europe fostered frequent mixed unions. As a result, of all the New World colonies, Brazil was the largest in which people of mixed origin eventually made up a significant proportion of the population. In response, officials sought to gain effective control over the colony and the nation by reinvigorating the racial hierarchy that separated whites from freedmen. Lighter skin always brought with it advantages. From the beginning, Africans and blacks of unmixed African origin were relegated to the bottom of the social ladder, mixed groups to the middle, and whites always at the top except for recent immigrants. Widely held attitudes assumed that "whitening" *(branqueamento)* would purge Brazil of the taint of the blood of lesser races, and over the years Brazil's many colonization schemes aimed at recruiting Caucasians, preferably from northern Europe. Those who came tended to be Italians, Spaniards, and Portuguese, as well as Poles and Japanese in the early twentieth century. The settlers became indentured agricultural workers until they paid off their debts, but, unlike the Brazilian-born free labor force, usually managed within a generation to acquire land for themselves or to find stable lives in the cities.

By the nineteenth century, Brazil had developed one of the most relaxed racial milieus in the world. Since so many Brazilians were descended from racially mixed ancestry, one thing persons could do was to claim membership in a more acceptable racial category. The 1872 census, Brazil's first formal nationwide count, classified 20 percent of the population as black and another 42 percent as mixed. After that the percentages for blacks and mixed races dropped considerably. Since Brazilian custom frowned on labeling individuals biologically, it became possible to change one's category, especially if one's skin was lighter than that of other family members. There were practical rewards for doing this: the national bias continued to hold that white was best and black worst, with the nearer to white the better.

Still, the presence of a potentially unruly large underclass threatened well-to-do Brazilians and led to elaborate measures to maintain law and order. As early as 1850, Rio de Janeiro employed 800 professional inspectors, subdelegates, and delegates with police powers. These officials could arrest, judge, and sentence those accused of crimes. Active also was a permanent military police force of 400 men, uniformed and housed in barracks, as well as cavalry and infantry. The military police watched for potential disturbances of the peace, and acted principally to intimidate. There was extensive surveillance. Behavior considered threatening to public order was prohibited. The stereotypes imposed on blacks reflected a mixture of traits that were disparaged and others that were feared. More than anything else, black men were feared as potentially violent, and, as a result, they were prohibited by law from brawling in public or from practicing *capoeira,* an African ritualistic dance done by barefoot slaves. Performed later to rhythmic music, *capoeira* during the nineteenth century evolved into a martial art, sometimes assisted by daggers, razors, stones, and clubs, practiced by groups or gangs known as *maltas* or *badernas. Capoeira* practitioners often belonged to *candomblé* sects, making them even more menacing in the eyes of the police.

Unlike most of the Spanish American republics except for Argentina, Brazil's native population by the nineteenth century was mostly invisible to inhabitants of the coast where most of the population resided. Indians lived in the distant forests, and were considered primitive savages, although intellectuals for a time romanticized them as part of a nineteenth-century effort to discover Brazil's roots. José de Alencar's 1865 novel of hope and disappointment told the story of Iracema ("America" spelled partially backwards), a "brown virgin of ardent love," an Indian maiden whose love affair with a Portuguese conquistador produced a child who, tellingly, died.[3]

Mulatos (mulatto men) came to be considered unstable, *mulatas* (mulatto women) as sexually desirable. Dark-skinned people were generally deemed slothful, prone to violence, uncontrollable, and stupid, and were invariably excluded from desirable housing, employment, and social opportunities. Distrust in turn led authorities to enact new measures for social control. The government encouraged scientists to study the latent characteristics of Brazil's racial types. The first attempts were based on anthropological physiognomy, which was popular in Europe at the time. The imperial government sent the official Commission of Exploration to Ceará in 1859 to examine and classify indigenous subjects according to angle of facial profile, skull size, and "life marks," believing, for example, that a greater facial angle attested to greater intelligence. Reformed in 1876, Rio de Janeiro's National Museum, an early center of anthropological studies and public exhibitions, sponsored expeditions to examine native culture, collecting life masks, skulls, and artifacts.

Popular works of fiction, especially the Visconde de Taunay's *Inocência* (1872) and José de Alencar's *Senhora* (1875) disseminated their authors' view that character could be revealed through appearance. The armed forces weighed, measured, and studied recruits to determine ways to predict stamina and successful military performance, all on the basis of now-discredited but then highly touted theories of eugenics. This self-assured confidence in the possibility of predicting (and therefore preventing) criminal behavior gradually lost favor, although as late as the 1930s forensic scientists working for the government tried to use fingerprint types to predict unstable character.

Although economic standing was arguably more important than any other factor in bestowing status in Brazilian society, race mattered for persons of color. The story of the mulatto Rebouças clan illustrates how race was a Brazilian fact of life. The clan originated in the marriage during the 1780s between Gaspar Pereira Rebouças, a poor immigrant tailor from northern Portugal (possibly of New Christian origin; his ancestors may have been among the thousands of Jews forcibly converted in Portugal in 1497 at pain of expulsion), and Rita Brasília dos Santos, a freed slave described as "of comely appearance" and with a dark complexion. White men greatly outnumbered white women in Brazil then, and such marriages were not uncommon, in part because of Roman Catholic Church pressure to legitimize sexual unions. The children and grandchildren of these marriages played eminent roles not only in Brazilian independence but in the technical modernization of their country in the second half of the nineteenth century, especially as each successive generation "whitened."

At least four of their nine children took light-skinned *mulatas* or whites as spouses. A son, Antônio Pereira Rebouças, became a lawyer and a leader in the independence movement in Bahia, and later a deputy to the National Assembly in Rio de Janeiro. He was honored during his lifetime—the emperor conferred on him the title of Knight of the Imperial Order of the Cross—yet he was also dogged by racial prejudice, including at least one vicious, racially motivated attack, when enemies in Sergipe accused him publicly of fomenting a rebellion of slaves against white landowners. After his exoneration from the charges, he remained silent, both publicly and privately, a decision that his astute biographer, Leo Spitzer, sees as the key to the success of his social adaptation. André Rebouças, who studied engineering in Paris before being named head of the construction project to build new docks on the Rio de Janeiro waterfront, was paid more than a third less than the British engineer who replaced him. Throughout his life he received racial insults, anonymous threats, and even letters written to his white friends attacking them for associating with mulattos, although Rebouças received even worse treatment when he visited the United States in 1873 for a few weeks. After abolition, for which he worked diligently, he settled in Africa, first in Mozambique and later in the Transvaal (he left Lourenço Marques because he could not bear to see how Africans were mistreated by European colonials there); then he moved again to Capetown, reputed to be more "liberal" in race relations. He departed again, in 1893, settling in Funchal, in the Madeira Islands, a spot midway between his Brazilian and African worlds. He became impoverished and took ill, and in May 1898, on the tenth anniversary of the abolition of Brazilian slavery, he threw himself over a cliff.[4]

Slave emancipation in 1888 brought little change to the lives of blacks, whose stubborn resistance to legal bondage had ultimately led planters to abandon the slave system. There was no effort to improve the lot of former slaves, as happened in the United States with Radical Reconstruction. Some Brazilian leaders favored such a program, but nothing much was done. One exception was the establishment of the Black Guard, an organization formed out of street *capoeira* gangs (along the lines of a social brotherhood) to defend Princess Isabel, signer of the emancipation decree, and to protect the interests of blacks against planters and republicans. It soon was disbanded, however. Members of the Guard broke up republican rallies and harassed opponents of the monarchy. Authorities feared further Black Guard violence, and many members were arrested in police sweeps and shipped off to the notorious prison camp on Fernando de Noronha Island. Property owners, especially those dependent on cheap manual labor, feared that ex-slaves in general would abandon the countryside for the cities. As a result, municipalities enacted punitive legislation forcing beggars to register and be licensed, and broadening the legal definition of vagrancy so that persons encountered within urban limits could be arrested simply if they did not belong there. Life even for the 3 million free blacks at midcentury and after was trying, psychologically as well as economically. They lived in what was euphemistically termed "honorable poverty," and they were restricted to manual trades or artisanship.

Over the decades, the condition of being a slave influenced patterns of behavior, speech, and attitudes. Blacks and mulattos were forced to conform to expectations about them as lazy or slothful, untrustworthy, unusually expressive with their eyes, and childlike—exactly the same stereotypes expected of blacks in the United States. They were believed to be musical and to be capable of exaggerated sexual prowess. Until as late as the 1950s, all lower-class Brazilians, most of whom were dark-skinned, were expected to avoid eye contact on the street with their betters and to step respectfully off the curb if affluent persons approached them on a narrow sidewalk. A few voices disagreed with the racial attitudes of the day. The Sergipe-born physician and educator Manoel Bonfim took issue in 1905 with the prevailing lament over racial mixture. Looking at Latin America's relative backwardness, Bonfim condemned the effects of colonialism and the legacy of economic dependence upon forced labor and slavery. "Social parasitism," he said, was to blame: the Spanish and Portuguese heritage that justified stripping away the riches of its colonial possessions. Bonfim was ignored, however, until the 1930s, and forgotten again until 1993, when his book was republished as a curiosity.[5] Brazil's racism was always expressed openly, at least the 1950s, when it became officially unpopular and became more muted in application. Hollywood's Orson Welles, invited in 1941 to host a birthday celebration broadcast for dictator Getúlio Vargas, was told that he could not bring a black friend into the studio. Welles's attempts to film *It's All True,* an anthology film with segments about Brazilian Carnival and the plight of northeastern raft fishermen, was criticized in a secret letter from Welles's production manager to the Brazilian police, complaining about Welles's "insistence on emphasizing the unsavory Negro element and mixture of the races."[6]

Society's polarized view has influenced the way in which the poor have been seen as good but weak, unprotected, untrustworthy, and childlike. In turn, the rare efforts of minority groups to organize have been dismissed because of the deep-seated belief that class-based interest groups carry the seeds of disorder and agitation. Historically, there are no meaningful instances of one put-upon group lending solidarity to another. This was the fate of the politically timid Frente Negra (Negro Front) groups of the 1930s, of the tiny (and ineffective) black power groups of the 1970s, and in general of the women's movement not only during the military dictatorship but after. Others in the "better" classes were sometimes more direct. The Algerian-French writer Albert Camus, on a visit to Brazil in August 1949 at the invitation of the French Embassy, quoted a well-known Brazilian upper-class poet with whom he had been required to dine. The poet assured Camus that things were bad in Brazil, that "there's no luxury here; we're poor, miserable," while tapping affectionately on the shoulder of the liveried chauffeur who was driving his enormous Chrysler through the streets of dazzling Rio de Janeiro, which Camus noted was at the same latitude as Madagascar.

As happened in most countries emerging during the twentieth century, many blamed the poor for their own plight. "Strange to say it is the privileged rural man," a Ministry of Agriculture report in 1942 said, "to whom the soil gives everything, who is the worst nourished."[7] Even sociologist Josué de Castro, hounded throughout his career for being an advocate of reform to aid the hungry, observed that the issue was not lack of food, but "bad dietary habits growing out of a routinized deformation of the healthy nutritive instinct" and "taboos and dietary restrictions of all kinds" that make the prevailing type of diet in Brazil one of the most precarious in the world.[8] Reminiscing about his role in 1942 during planning for the creation of the Federal University of Bahia, Thales de Azevedo, himself a graduate of the Bahian Faculty of Medicine in 1927, recollected that the debate over the existence of superior and inferior races was very much alive, and that a scholarly article in a medical journal by a Rio de Janeiro–based physician, Dr. Américo Valério, claiming that some races were, in fact, medically superior to others, was accepted by some.[9] Nor did the notion completely die out by the 1990s. A sociology professor at São Paulo's Catholic University Law School teaches in his classes the same principles, which he defends as a "question of logic."

Slavery's Legacy

In no other country in the world did African slavery have such an enormous impact as in Brazil. At the beginning of the nineteenth century, two out of every three Brazilians were of African origin. Slavery, knowledgeable historians agree, "molded the contours of Brazilian life" and strongly influenced its evolution.[10] Studies of slave culture have been done mostly by ethnographers and anthropologists, examining such themes as transference of African culture to Brazil, linguistics, slave family life, sexuality, and morality. Slaves, of course, formed a coerced labor force, and all the subsidiary ethnographic themes taken together cannot outweigh the central point that Brazil was marked by the brutality of the slave system. Afro-Brazilians attempting to escape from the slave system or to assert communal autonomy were repressed cruelly or massacred.

Most rural slaves were engaged in sugar raising or mining, in year-round backbreaking labor. They worked under hazardous conditions and were subject to poor diets, inadequate clothing and housing, harsh discipline, and frequent punishment. The effect on the slaves themselves was cauterizing: many died early, and slave women suffered from low fertility. The slave trade favored men over women, with an overall ratio in Bahia from 1600 to 1830 of 3 : 2 and, on sugar estates, closer to 2 : 1. Slave society typically had a low percentage of children and an excess of men. The annual rate of natural decline of the slave population was perhaps 3 percent a year, forcing planters to rely on the continued slave trade to replenish their human working stock. Fueled by resurgent prospects for agricultural profits between 1780 and the 1830s, the slave system actually expanded during those years, with new male slaves continuing to outnumber female slaves by a 3 : 2 ratio. Since this was accompanied by an overall increase in the Brazilian population, new sources of food production were required, providing work for slaves and the free rural poor.

These conditions, in turn, contributed to the ways that planters viewed slaves. Slave women were taken at whim by their masters, or turned into prostitutes for their owners' profit. Whites during the eighteenth and early nineteenth centuries believed that intercourse with a black virgin girl was a remedy for syphilis. Slave owners considered it a waste of time to promote family life to achieve natural population growth among slaves. It was more efficient to cull from among young male slaves selected in Africa for their strength and stamina, in the slave auction pens of the port city of Salvador da Bahia de Todos os Santos than to have to worry about caring for Brazilian-born slave children *(crioulos),* half of them female, until they were able to work as adolescents. Moreover, mature male slaves could produce enough sugar in fourteen to twenty-four months to equal their purchase cost. Good businessmen, planters utilized slaves "to maximum production by keeping down costs and maintaining an intensive work schedule. For the planter to double his investment, an adult slave had to live for only five years under such conditions."[11] Slaves imported to Brazil before the nineteenth century usually died before reaching thirty years of age. Women as well as men were forced to perform dangerous work on the plantations. *Moedeiras* fed the cane through the milling rollers, with the constant risk of being pulled into the machinery; other workers hoisted buckets filled with the cane juice by pulleys and poured them into the cauldrons spilling over with boiling liquid.[12]

The conditions under which the slaves were forced to work shocked visitors. The sugar-making process was like the modern assembly line, with technology determining the pace of the work, the speed of the mill, the heat of the cauldrons, and pace of the cutting. The labor was exhausting and enervating. Heat was intense; slave workers were always tired. Injuries were common, even for skilled slaves. Profits depended not only on cost-effective methods of maintaining labor but also on good timing. Sugar production depended upon skills in cutting, carting, milling, boiling, and drying. Planters who simply worked slaves to death were foolish. They had to give slaves rest periods, and the religious calendar obliged them to give holidays to their workers on saints' days and other Catholic festivals. Slaves were whipped in the fields but not around the mills. When slaves met their quotas, they could rest or devote themselves to raising garden crops and even sell the surplus in local markets, or to the mill owner. Some slaves saved enough money to buy their liberty. After all, overseers knew that angry slaves could engage in sabotage, to which the complex sugar mills were highly vulnerable, or revolt.

The free population of blacks and racially mixed individuals continued to grow on the fringes of slaveholding. Some of these people engaged in small-scale agriculture; other were householders; still others artisans, fishermen, or rubber gatherers. The composition of these free peoples varied from region to region. Especially as economic patterns changed (the exhaustion of mines in Minas Gerais, for example, and the decline of northeastern sugar production, the free rural poor adopted diversified ways of surviving. Thus new terms were born, describing degrees of dependence on land relationships (*colono,* an indentured rural agricultural worker, often an immigrant), or levels of perceived backwardness (*caipiras* and *matutos,* varieties of rustics). Overall, however, Brazil's peasantry bore no collective folk memory of the past. It grew alongside the institution of slavery and was connected to it; it was fixed to the land, and forced to remain docile. Some former slaves and free blacks refused to work for day wages, feeding the elite's preference for immigrant labor. In São Paulo as well as many other former slaveholding regions, many employers refused to negotiate with freed slaves after emancipation. Planters turned to foreign immigrants, but within a generation the demands made by European workers so upset landowners that they began to return to use of blacks as laborers.

The ways that Brazilians saw themselves reflected their thoughts about race. Ironically, Brazilians sometimes boasted of African blood though they showed no trace of such lineage physically, as long as their social status was not threatened. Others who could have claimed mestizo origins, like the writers Mário de Andrade and Jorge de Lima, were considered white because of their intellectual status. Even in recent times, among ordinary Brazilians, nonwhites (Afro-Brazilian spokesmen use the term "Negro" for all non-Caucasians except Asians) have remained unrepresented in areas involving decision making. Dark-skinned persons have rarely if ever reached the highest levels of industry, business, the professions, or the government, although during the past two decades inroads have been made in the middle and upper-middle ranks of the professional armed forces. Blacks have achieved success only in athletics and entertainment. Slaves after emancipation in 1888 were left to their own devices in a competitive society in which immigrant labor was prized and black and racially mixed Brazilians deprecated. The expression "money whitens" does not hold completely true even today, because, in the few cases where blacks have succeeded professionally or accumulated decent incomes, they have not gained the same measure of social access as whites.

Traditional attitudes have proved long-lived. Mixed-race *mulatas* were long ignored in Brazilian beauty pageants, while the embodiment of Brazilian attractiveness remained the white woman with skin tanned at the beach, not naturally dark. Coffee-colored women were described bluntly: *"Morena da cor do pecado"* ("Morena, color of sinning"), the newsmagazine *Istoé*'s headline went, atop a 1993 story about actress Luiza Thomé, born in Itapipoca in the interior of Ceará.[13] In the 1990 census, 44 percent of the population were classified as blacks or *pardos,* a term connoting dark skin, an indication that the ideal excluded nearly half of the population.

Brazil's legacy from its decades of slavery was unique in comparison to that of other places in the hemisphere where slavery had flourished. Brazil in the early 1800s approached Haiti in the high proportion of slaves to overseers, but although slave rebellions did occur in Brazil, they never erupted into revolution, as occurred in the French Caribbean colony. In the United States in 1776, slavery was an embarrassment that mocked the Declaration of Independence, and as a contentious issue embroiled American politics down to and beyond Lincoln's Emancipation Proclamation, which was promulgated not so much as a moral imperative as a practical weapon to guarantee the preservation of the Union. In Brazil, although abolitionists took voice after midcentury and slavery as a system was frequently debated in parliament, slavery was not fully abolished until 1888, when the system had become moribund.

Until the 1960s, historians in the United States tended to describe slavery as if it were a historical institution that lacked a history. This was true, and continued to be true in many ways, for Brazilian historians of Brazilian slavery, who concentrated on broader, theoretical issues (means of production, affinity for resistance), not on the evolution and variety of the institution over time. In some places (the tobacco-growing colonies of Virginia and Maryland; the mines of Minas Gerais), slaves lived in small groups, geographically separated; in other places (on rice and indigo plantations in South Carolina, for example, and on the ranches of the upper São Francisco River), slaves lived by themselves, with owners frequently absent. Writings a generation ago assumed that slaves were consistently mistreated, much more so than in Latin America. We now know that in Brazil (and in Jamaica), slave deaths exceeded births, making it much more important to import constantly new slaves from Africa. Slaves in North America lived much longer and produced many more surviving offspring. Only 6 percent of the 10 or 11 million Africans carried to the Americas between the sixteenth and nineteenth centuries went to what became the United States, but the number of slaves in the United States tripled between 1810 and 1860. Slave reproduction counted for far lower numbers in Brazil not only before 1850, when ships brought in a regular supply of robust new slaves, but after 1850, when the importation of slaves had largely ceased.

Brazilian blacks who chafed at the reality underlying the racial myth had to practice a high degree of discretion and to appear not to be complaining. This was the case of the São Paulo–based Frente Negra associations of the 1930s and 1940s (which failed because they functioned in a political vacuum, under Getúlio Vargas's dictatorship), and the small group of São Paulo black intellectuals who published the magazine *Niger* in the 1950s. Opponents accused these groups of being racist themselves, since they took pride in their heritage and therefore threatened the unwritten understanding in Brazilian society that the country should "whiten" itself. The country's few black intellectuals struggled with lack of outlets for their work, and São Paulo's strong cultural hegemony acted to misconstrue the message of prewar black intellectuals. This was because, since published *paulista* blacks tended to advocate social integration as a solution to their sense of alienation because of color, black and *mulato* intellectuals in other parts of Brazil, especially in the North, found it even harder to break into print and therefore were unable to communicate their views. Lino Guedes, the first black poet to probe slavery's legacy, was not very well known.

In 1951, the São Paulo sociologist Florestan Fernandes, himself a light-skinned *mulato,* published a book on race relations in Brazil in collaboration with the French scholar Roger Bastide. Designed, in Fernandes's words, to "raise consciousness," the book succeeded, encouraging other important studies on a subject long ignored by Brazilian social scientists. Looking back twenty-five years later at his pioneering work, Fernandes made some telling points about how the study had been organized and how it had been received. Fernandes and Bastide had written mostly about blacks, leaving aside the more problematic category of mulattos (persons of mixed race, the word coming from "mule").

Black protest in Brazil, to Fernandes in 1979, represented "innocuous nonconformity," and as a result remained suffocated within its own milieu. Raising black consciousness led nowhere, but instead brought a new form of frustration more corrosive and more pernicious than its predecessors. Violence can be avoided, he warned, but the fermentation of racial tensions among what he termed the "Negro masses" will continue and grow. The term *baiano* (a Bahian black) came to be substituted in the South for the generic negative term "Negro." The Afro-Brazilian was "no longer a spectator on the fringes of life and history." The "bad image" was losing the demoralizing character that it had for so long. On the other hand, successful blacks fretted, seeking to convince whites that they were acceptable. They attempted to influence others by emphasizing their high, privileged standard of living and their "faultless character." They sought to reeducate whites in their moral appraisal of blacks, but they created "neither the game nor its rules." This left them to a "merry-go-round of illusions" that sapped their talent. They were too timid, the sociologist declared.[14]

By the postwar period, serious observers of race relations in Brazil had conceded that although Brazil's multiracialism was unique, the country had not escaped social stratification by race. The many research projects carried out under the auspices of the United Nations Educational, Scientific, and Cultural Organization (UNESCO), headed first by race specialist Arthur Ramos and later by Manuel Diegues Júnior, showed that darker skin meant lower social status even though there were no definitive racial lines. Evidence of racial discrimination was unmistakable, although Roger Bastide and Florestan Fernandes's study of São Paulo concluded that racial barriers in Brazil were "not of the same kind as in the U.S."[15] Few people, however, paid heed to the academic debate. Image-makers, textbook authors, and journalists clung to the old racial democracy myth, insinuating that anyone challenging it was some sort of a communist. At the other end of the spectrum, a few lone black voices arose in angry protest. The debate remained muted throughout Brazil's military dictatorship from 1964 to 1978, although the two most outspoken militants on the race issue, Guerreiro Ramos and Abdias do Nascimento, joined many others in opposition to the regime in exile, giving them, to some degree, a platform as well as a comparative vantage point with which to judge Brazilian race relations. Most blacks, however, remained outside of the debate. Some, including Carolina Maria de Jesus, the *favela* dweller whose published diary in 1960 had become Brazil's all-time best-selling book, found kind words to say about the military regime's economic record and its programs to improve public health, as well as its propaganda efforts to remind the nation that all Brazilians, regardless of race, should work together.[16]

By the mid-1960s, the American black power movement, brought back to Brazil by soccer players and musicians who had traveled abroad, had begun to have a cultural impact among blacks, encouraging blacks to take pride in their appearance (Afro and Jamaican hairstyles became suddenly popular) as well as distinctive dress. This new black consciousness movement in itself demonstrated the weakness of the "multiracial" interpretation of race relations in Brazil, since the new leaders of the movement insisted on the term "Negro" for all Brazilians not labeled white, the same characterization as in the United States. A few blacks gained success electorally, especially Benedita da Silva, a Pentecostal social activist who successfully entered politics despite an unadorned lower-class upbringing and little financial backing. Michael Jordan, Magic Johnson, and the other members of the 1992 Olympic basketball squad (the first "Dream Team") became as popular among Brazilian youths, white and black, as they did in Europe. Interracial advertisements featuring Pelé with the blond television star Xuxa (he allegedly had a sexual dalliance with her when she was sixteen) began to appear in print and on television, although the overwhelming number of advertisements continued to feature light-skinned models, with the traditionally disproportionate percentage of Nordic types.

Congresswoman Benedita da Silva's story illustrates that in exceptional cases, the centuries-old barriers faced by black women have started to crumble. The thirteenth child born to a washerwoman in a Rio de Janeiro favela, she began working as a servant at age ten and eventually became a community activist and the first black woman elected to the national legislature. Still living in the urbanized portion of one of Rio's notorious favelas, in 1992 she missed election to Rio de Janeiro's mayorship in 1992 by a margin of fewer than 100,000 votes, losing to César Maia, a conservative white candidate running on a mildly progressive platform. Once she lost, however, the media, never comfortable with her as a political player, backed away, never casting her in the role of a spokesperson or role model as likely would have happened in the United States. When she was elected to the Senate in October 1994, a Brazilian newsletter distributed internationally mocked her frizzy hair, saying that she would have to "pack a large stock of combs and brushes designed for Negroes," accompanied by a stereotyped, mocking cartoon caricature that in the United States would have aroused protest.[17] Barriers against permitting blacks, and especially black women, to the inner sanctums of the political culture remained very high.

Black militancy, foreign to Brazil's racial climate, entered the picture sporadically and late, during the 1970s. The agents of change were young black organizers of black-pride movements, centering on the Afro-Brazilian Carnival associations, in Salvador. João Jorge Santos Rodrigues, the thirty-six-year-old leader of Olodum, the most openly militant *bloco africo* (black Carnival organization) in Salvador, created an uproar during the early 1990s by speaking forcefully against racism. A black from Salvador who first worked boxing groceries in a supermarket, then became a laborer in a petrochemical plant, and by 1993 was studying law, Rodrigues has claimed that "[T]here is an invisible wall separating blacks and whites in Brazil." Racism in Brazil, he adds, "is worse than in South Africa."[18]

Contradictory images lingered into the 1990s. One, a positive image, said that the country was democratic, white, and destined for greatness. This was the Brazil of the television ads: blond, European Brazil. The other, the negative image, lurked beneath the surface, although it was spelled out in the newspapers: the Brazil of crime, of favelas, of the poor. This Brazil was peopled with blacks who were dirty and uneducable, holding back progress. Dark-skinned actors appeared in ads mostly to warn against AIDS and cholera, or in other stereotyped ways. Brazil's racism, Rodrigues said, was hypocritical because it was officially denied. Brazil's concept of racial democracy, moreover, presupposed that blacks knew their place and stayed in it.

Racial intermarriage remained a touchy subject. Over the centuries, most of the sexual unions between men and women from different racial and ethnic groups that produced the dozens of terms and classifications describing the mixed offspring took place outside marriage. In most instances, the woman was a slave or a member of an indigenous tribe, or was a mixed-race *mulata*. Today, four-fifths of marriages in Brazil are endogamous, and only a tiny portion of these take place between persons of widely differing colors. Ninety-three percent of mixed marriages in 1980 were between persons of white and tan skin, or between browns and blacks. The racial democracy myth lingered.

Brazil's first antidiscrimination law, the Afonso Arinos Law, was enacted in 1951, outlawing racial discrimination in public accommodations— a response to a Brazilian hotel's refusal to provide a room for the visiting African American dancer Katherine Dunham. Employment advertisements for entry-level positions, however, continued to stipulate the need for "good appearance," a euphemism for white or near-white skin and stylish clothing. In 1985 the law was toughened, and its provisions extended to cases of marital-status bias. The 1988 constitution elevated discrimination on the basis from a misdemeanor to a felony. Little else changed, and there were no cases of enforcement in cases of housing or other de facto discrimination. Academic specialists in social relations continued to avoid the subject: characteristically, the only publication in Brazil to address the question of housing discrimination on the basis of race was *Estudos Afro-Asiáticos,* a Rio-based journal primarily concerned with foreign racial issues.

Brazilian blacks have been so powerless that networks of mutual assistance have been limited to the ready exchange of information; real opportunities for work or better conditions have been rare. The major difference may be the lack of parallel institutions in the black community. The Negro Front and other black-consciousness groups have all suffered from a relatively small number of adherents, ignored except for the barest of occasional lip service from social progressives, reviled (and frequently suppressed) by conservatives in power, and with little influence in the black community, too poor to devote energy or resources to institution building.

Many Brazilians until at least the 1950s continued to accept the premises of the first intellectual generation of the Old Republic (1889–1930) that blamed miscegenation for the malaise of that regime. During the late nineteenth century, most elite Brazilians agreed with Spencerian notions of race differences, although a handful of intellectuals, notably Sílvio Romero, declared Brazilian society to be unique and strong in its racial mix. A generation later, Paulo Prado's influential *Retrato do Brasil* damned mestizos with faint praise. Yes, he said, there have been notable examples of intelligent mixed-race Brazilians, but the population as a whole is physically feeble and vulnerable to disease and to vices.[19] The leading spokesman for this position was the eminent conservative Oliveira Vianna (1883–1951). However, during the 1920s and after, Gilberto Freyre, a sociologist and social historian trained at Columbia University, used the same essentially racist arguments to praise the legacy of racial mixture among Africans, Indians, and Portuguese. Vianna argued that the masses were incapable of governing themselves because they were racially inferior and, as a result of that inferiority, caught up in a social pathology that made them prone to passivity, clannishness, lack of social cohesion, and violence. As a result, Vianna advocated state authoritarianism and the continuation of the paternalistic framework of elite relations with the common people.[20]

One of the distinctions of the Brazilian racial experience has long been the fact that Afro-Brazilians as well as all other non-Caucasian groups and racial mixtures live in two cultures, although blacks and mulattos make up more than half of the national population. In the Caribbean, by contrast, African cultural memories (even if adapted or even invented) dominate, permitting even poor blacks to participate in "mainstream" culture. In Brazil, Afro-Brazilians live under a national culture that considers their cultural memories to be primitive and atavistic.

Change

Change has been piecemeal. Presidential candidate Fernando Henrique Cardoso during his 1994 campaign remarked while on a visit to the Northeast that his family had a "foot in the kitchen," a phrase referring to the landowners' old habit of impregnating kitchen slaves or servants. Intellectuals and some organizations identified with black consciousness across the country protested Cardoso's gaffe. Most listeners, however, did not consider the comment to be demeaning.

Changes also affected the small groups—as yet unconnected to any national movement—seeking to raise black consciousness. Shortly after the murder by police vigilantes of a group of sleeping black children in front of Rio's venerable Candelária Church in July 1993, a group of African Americans from Los Angeles traveled to Rio to attend a conference on the Black Diaspora that had been organized by the Rio de Janeiro Institute for the Research of Black Culture. The Americans marveled at the thick foundation of history and culture that infused the conference debates—universal knowledge, for example, about the seventeenth-century *quilombo* (maroon society) of Palmares, the free community of escaped slaves.[21] Yet Brazilian black consciousness groups remained small in number, with a few thousand members out of an estimated total nonwhite population exceeding 70 million. Membership in black groups remained limited mostly to black professionals, intellectuals, and students, not the poor. Leadership positions, moreover, were monopolized not only by members of the middle class but by persons with comparatively light-hued skin.

This analysis, however, uses North American racial definitions of "black" and "white." Although there is evidence that individuals of color in Brazil are moving in this direction as well—using the word "Negro" to connote anyone not considered "white" by society—there nevertheless is truth to the assertion that the "mulatto escape hatch" and other mechanisms for tolerance have worked in recent decades to open opportunities for persons of mixed racial backgrounds. The number of Brazilians of mixed racial backgrounds who have broken out of the lowest classes is growing, and although there are few persons of very dark skin in any positions of importance, there seems to be an unwritten acknowledgment in the larger cities that skin color and racial phenotype are not really very important. Because of this, combined with the melting pot created by the assimilation of Asians, the descendants of European and Middle Eastern immigrants, and assisted by the sophisticated, inclusive national media, one finds less overt awareness of racial distinctions in everyday life in Brazil than practically anywhere in the world. This is an enormously positive attribute, and one that merits appreciation by those in societies that have legislated racial equality but which in practice remain segregated physically and psychologically.

Another characteristic of Brazilian life is that for historically complex diverse reasons, members of Brazil's underprivileged population—although they, like everyone else, live increasingly in conditions menaced by crime and violence—do not harbor the same kinds of "in-your-face" hostility and rage as do the inhabitants of the inner cities of North American cities. This is not to say that living hand-to-mouth in poverty does not inflict damage. Yet Brazil does have a network of helping institutions, although they are not well funded. For centuries the Casas de Misericordia have offered help to indigents. Charitable individuals have paid school costs for children like

Carolina Maria de Jesus in forsaken Sacramento as early as the 1920s; and today foreigners are surprised when they hear that a family with five or six children of their own has "taken in" a baby left by a neighbor or by a passer-by unable to provide for it.

It remains to be seen whether the continued menace of drug violence in city slums and the continued shortage of public funds to provide adequate schools and health care facilities will mar the decades-old live-and-let-live quality of Brazilian life. Foreigners have interpreted the poor's lack of complaining about dealing with conditions as docility, but they have overlooked the fact that therapeutically this circumstance has a healthy side as well. Is it better to work for improved conditions in an atmosphere of suppressed animosity and rage, as more and more is the case in the United States, or in an atmosphere in which interpersonal relations are tempered by a still-present cordiality and apparent good-naturedness?

Notes

1. Alfredo d'Escragnolle Taunay, "Artigos de Propaganda," III, *Bulletin 24* (September 1886), 4.

2. Prof. and Mrs. Louis Agassiz, *A Journey in Brazil* (Boston, 1868), 139, 298.

3. José de Alencar, *Iracema: A Legend* (Rio de Janeiro: 1865); Renata R. Mautner Wasserman, *Exotic Nations: Literature and Cultural Identity in the United States and Brazil, 1830–1930* (Ithaca, NY: Cornell University Press, 1994), 208.

4. Leo Spitzer, *Lives in Between: Assimilation and Marginality in Austria, Brazil, West Africa, 1780–1945* (Cambridge: Cambridge University Press, 1989), 121; see also 101–26.

5. Manoel Bonfim, *A América Latina: Males do Origem* (1905; reprint, São Paulo: Topbooks, 1993).

6. Myron Meisel and Bill Krohn, in *New York Times,* 10 October 1993, H27.

7. Statement, Information Service, Brazilian Agricultural Ministry, 17 February 1942. See Albert Camus, *Diário de Viagem* (São Paulo: Distruibadora Record, 1985).

8. Josué de Castro, *Geography of Hunger* (Boston: Little, Brown, 1952), 296–97.

9. Maria Palácios, "Entrevista com Thales de Azevedo," *Revista da FAEEBA* (Salvador), 1:1 (Janeiro–Junho 1992), 125–38, 126; Thales de Azevedo, interview with author, Salvador, May 13, 1990. See also Luiz Antonio de Castro-Santos, "Power, Ideology, and Public Health in Brazil, 1889–1930," Ph.D. dissertation, Harvard University, 1987.

10. Stuart B. Schwartz, "Recent Trends in the Study of Brazilian Slavery," in S.B. Schwartz, *Slaves, Peasants, and Rebels: Reconsidering Brazilian Slavery* (Urbana: University of Illinois Press, 1992), 2.

11. S.B. Schwartz, *Slaves,* 42.

12. S.B. Schwartz, *Slaves,* 63, n. 7.

13. *Istoé* (São Paulo), 30 June 1993, 84.

14. Florestan Fernandes, "The Negro in Brazilian Society," in Warren Dean, ed., *Reflections on the Brazilian Counter-Revolution: Essays* (Armonk, NY: M.E. Sharpe, 1981), 107–13.

15. Roger Bastide and Florestan Fernandes, 2nd ed., *Brancos e Negros em São Paulo* (São Paulo: Companhia Editora Nacional, 1971), 294.

THE LEGACY OF COLOR 25

16. Carolina Maria de Jesus, unpublished diary entry, 1 September 1966, courtesy of Vera Eunice de Jesus Lima.

17. "Brasil Faxletter," 10 August 1994, 2. Courtesy of Thomas Holloway.

18. Interview, João Jorge Santos Rodrigues, *Veja,* 10 June 1993, 7–9.

19. Paulo Prado, *Retrato do Brasil: Ensaio sobre a Tristeza Brasileira* (1926; 2nd ed.: São Paulo: IBRASA, 1981), 138–39.

20. Jeffrey D. Needell, "Race and the State: Oliveira Vianna, Gilberto Freyre, and the Role of Afro-Brazilians in the Brazilian Polity," paper presented at the American Historical Association annual meeting, Washington, DC, 29 December 1992.

21. Mabie Settlage, "From the Diaspora," E-mail on AFRO-LATAM, 25 October 1994.

2

Social Realities

The Upper Classes

Traditionally, Brazil had two hierarchical classes. On top sat the upper class of property owners as well as merchants, bureaucrats, and officials; virtually everyone else belonged to the *povo*—the common people. There were divisions within each group, of course. Only men born in Portugal were appointed to high positions, so in time Brazilian-born members of the gentry chafed at their second-class status and ultimately opted for independence from Portugal. Soon after independence, French culture (as well as influences from Italy, Germany, Great Britain, and the United States) surpassed Portuguese culture in status. Brazilians came to consider their own dialect and traditions preferred to those of the mother country. Members of Brazil's upper classes accepted and imitated the forms of cultural expression imported from abroad and at the same time tended either to denigrate or to romanticize native Brazilian culture. By the end of the nineteenth century, moreover, Portuguese culture was identified mainly with immigrants from Portugal, mostly peasants and petty merchants. Brazilian high culture during the belle époque was rigorously French, emphasized by the creation of the Brazilian Academy of Letters with its forty immortals, housed in a building named the Petit Trianon—the same name as its counterpart in Paris. The Brazilian elite spent millions to build opera houses, theaters, statuary, arches, and to widen streets to approximate the great European boulevards. Upper-class culture was sophisticated, multilingual, and cosmopolitan. Still, as late as 1970, an influential literary critic estimated that high culture reached only some 50,000 persons out of 90 million Brazilians.

Given the survival of colonial-era attitudes deprecating manual labor ("Work," went a popular saying, "is for dogs and Negroes") and the legacy of slavery, the old system prevailed. Nineteenth-century European liberalism—conservative in the modern understanding of the term—provided the rationale for this. Liberalism provided a rationale for Brazilians to oversee the colonial order; but by 1831 it was used to justify suppression of radicals. The elite maintained not only slavery but the colonial-era patron-client system. Up through independence, elite youths were trained at Portugal's University of Coimbra, mostly in civil law. They became bureaucrats, magistrates, or judges, and they held very similar social attitudes, although the social system that prevailed in rural Brazil varied from region to region. Social homogeneity alone, José Murilo de Carvalho observes, would not have been sufficient to weld a unified elite, as Brazil's many upper-class-led rebellions especially during the regency period, 1831–40, demonstrated.[1] Brazil's modern ruling elite emerged from the plantocracy that had dominated the Empire but now also included industrialist and urban professionals. Technology had brought about the transition. The most successful sugar producers in the late-nineteenth-century Northeast convinced their state legislatures to back immense foreign loans to pay for the construction of sugar refineries, first *engenhos centrais* and then *usinas*. Sugar production then became an agro-industrial enterprise, and the most successful of the former planters broadened their activities, in part through their clan and business networks *(panelinhas)* and in part by seeking out change when it stood to benefit them personally. By the First World War, Brazilian sugar producers were industrialists and businessmen, as linked as ever to the old traditional families of the region but much more diversified in their activities. The upper-class entrepreneurs joined by marriage the families of the older aristocracy of families, many of whom had enjoyed titles of nobility under the monarchy. Membership in these families facilitated access to political opportunities, to business and to social success. Culturally they were predisposed to deprecate what they considered to be the uncouth culture of the Brazilian people—historian Vianna Moog called the tendency *mazombismo*—preferring, instead, imported European expression. They sent their children to private schools modeled after schools in Paris or London; sometimes they spoke at home in English or French, or hired European governesses to teach them; and they traveled back and forth to the fashionable cities of the Continent. They valued the kind of society in which their privileges and special rights were guaranteed.

Rural elites were descendants of the old landowning families, joined by merchants and bureaucrats in their employ literally or figuratively. Many had become *coronéis* (colonels), local bosses. Allied with incumbent political machines at state and national levels, they dominated everything in their jurisdictions and therefore were able to deliver votes on demand at election time. The rural plantocracy shared the values of the national elite and frequently was connected to it through extended family networks. Often they lived quite simply, consuming the same diet as their employees and servants, and living in fairly rustic surroundings.

Not as closed as, say, Europe's aristocracy, Brazil's elite opened its doors not only to wealth but through marriage, especially if the groom was a foreigner of desirable social standing. Recruits to the upper class had to be Caucasian, as might be expected, and nominally Roman Catholic. Even so, Brazil was always a highly stable society, and on the whole very few persons managed to win acceptance into the upper class if they did not originate there. Persons who acquired great affluence, especially if they were immigrants, were considered *arrivistas* (upstarts); it was suspected that they were unscrupulous, that they had no traditional Brazilian values. The established upper-class families, after all, guarded their reputation for sobriety, and it was not true that they were especially decadent in spite of the reputation for decadence attributed to the declining plantocracy in the Northeast and in the older coffee-growing regions of the Center-South, especially around Rio de Janeiro and in the Paraíba Valley. Members of Brazil's upper classes often spoke several languages well (French and English almost always), sailed frequently to Europe, and performed in public with social grace if not flair.

Not all upper-class families were wealthy, but they knew the rules. Visiting sociologist T. Lynn Smith marveled at what he considered to be the upper-class capacity for being "better equipped educationally, emotionally, and temperamentally for the maximum enjoyment of a luxurious mode of living than others." Contributing to this, according to Smith, was the fact that because of concentration of property and wealth, the relative absence of middle-class groups in some parts of the country, the lack of skilled labor, and "the ease with which a vegetative existence can be carried on," not only is poverty maintained but rigid adherence to long-established cultural practices has muted tensions between classes. Smith offers a backhanded compliment: "Until recently the aspiration to land-ownership was a rare phenomenon among Brazil's millions of rural workers. On the other hand, hundreds of thousands of Brazilian *caboclos, matutos,* and *sertanejos* would feel deprived of their rights if interfered with in building a hut of wattle and daub, *pau-a-pique,* or thatch with a thatched roof on the spot of their choosing. They do have standards," he added. Brazil's rich and powerful, in other words, can be comfortable in their luxury because the masses are satisfied with the little they have.[2] New times altered the relaxed nature of the traditional upper-class families. After the 1930s, members of a "new" upper class, considered ostentatious and extroverted, gained social prominence. Brazilian playboys (the Guinles, Baby Pignatari, and others) earned international fame for fast living and tended to be lionized in the gossipy society pages of Brazilian daily newspapers. Out of this group came the Brazilian equivalents of the glitterati of the French Riviera and Beverly Hills, exquisitely dressed and jetting around the world first-class. Not all recruits to the elite, however, were socially prominent or careerist. The 1930 Revolution brought into positions of influence a new generation of elite members, some military leaders. The grandfather of President Fernando Henrique Cardoso (1995–), for example, was a field marshal during São Paulo's constitutionalist revolt in 1932 and his grand-uncle was war minister during Vargas's provisional government.

The internationalization of the moneyed elite and decades of unstable political conditions tested upper-class loyalty to Brazil. Many members of the elite saw their allegiances waver not only culturally but fiscally. Between 1976 and 1985, an estimated $10 billion in capital flight was transferred out of Brazil legally, not counting other transfers of cash accomplished extralegally, sometimes through *sacadores,* or dollar shippers. At least another $10 billion or so has likely left the country since then. Brazilians from automobile racing champion Emerson Fittipaldi to São Paulo politician Paulo Maluf, a masterful pseudo-populist who amassed great wealth while in office, have purchased lavish homes in South Florida.

Brazil's powerful elite stratum shaped the ways in which social relationships operated. Rural sociologist Archibald O. Haller explains:

> In rich democracies it may make some sense to restrict the definition [of elites] to office holders in government, unions, and big business. In Brazil, this doesn't ring true. The question is how Brazilian national and major regional economic and political decisions are made and who makes them. Prestigious politicians, whether in office or not, are involved in the decision-making process—unless they are exiled or otherwise muzzled. Certain bishops count, whether proscribed or not. So do some of the generals and few prestigious professors of prestigious universities.[3]

Many Brazilian elites, in turn, have exercised power without holding important posts; important officeholders often have been in fact "stooges for real elites who may or may not hold office." Many business leaders, agriculturalists, military men, and others are not elites in the sense the term is used elsewhere. The difference is that in terms of power Brazil is historically and openly an unequal society. There are in-elites and out-elites. Informal networks—*panelinhas*—facilitate the transfer of influence within cliques whose members support one another. While not all members of the top 1 or 2 percent in the highest socioeconomic stratum hold power, practically all elites emerge from it.

The Middle Classes

The late anthropologist Charles Wagley traced Brazil's middle class back to the early nineteenth century, when a need arose for a permanent group of scribes, clerks, and workers in similar occupations, now termed white-collar. In small towns and cities, such jobs opened up as well, although somewhat later.[4] Immigrants who managed to establish themselves in cities after extricating themselves from the indentured obligations to work on the land to pay off their ocean passage—often over a period of years—were likely to enter business, another avenue into the middle class. As time passed, the increasing complexity of government and commerce created the need for specialists: accountants, engineers, managers, and technicians of all kinds. These people came to form a new upper-middle class, usually sharing the same values as the upper classes and in some cases as affluent, but lacking the social pedigree of the members of the elite. From the 1970s to the mid-1990s, this "new" middle class had extraordinary success in somehow riding the waves of hyperinflation and actually emerging on sounder economic footing, due among other reasons to opportunities for creative currency dealings, to generous tax investment incentives, and to propitious real estate investment sometimes based on privileged information.

The term "middle class" when used in Brazil connotes something very different from "middle class" in North America. In the United States and Canada, even many of the wealthiest members of society resist the "upper-class" label, preferring to be designated as middle class to avoid the disparaging connotation of being members of an elite in a supposedly egalitarian society. In Brazil, the distinction is less clear-cut, probably because its middle class either aspires to elite status or accepts elite values. Newspapers, for example, defer to *colunáveis*—habitués of the society pages—in ways long considered passé in the United States, although coverage of the antics of Donald Trump, Leona Helmsley, and the Kennedys is based less on their lineage than on their wealth and their exercise of power.

A huge difference separates the lives of Brazilians in the higher range of the middle class from those lower down. Anxiety about downward mobility, about falling into the true working class, and about having to use public schools and state health clinics preserves the system. Indeed, some of the most conservative values in Brazilian society come from the middle class. Both groups, moreover, enjoy the advantages of living in a country with a depressed wage scale. Each employs household maids, not only the wealthy upper-middle class but members of the salaried middle class as well.

Kinship groups are extremely important for middle-class families. In a milieu where state administrative agencies often lagged badly in providing needed services, and where a distended bureaucracy, expanded even more during the 1930s as a way to enlist the political support of the urban middle class, required the use of personal contacts to cut through red tape, not only *parentelas* but *panelinhas* (networks of contacts) reigned supreme.

In most societies, upward mobility for people born into the middle class is generally more difficult than it is for lower-class individuals. The number of available positions in the social structure is inversely proportional to the level of the positions; the higher the level, the fewer the opportunities. Breaking into managerial or other well-paid positions usually requires formal education and specialized expertise, and in Latin America, as everywhere else, there are unwritten rules governing social acceptability. When middle-class Brazilians did achieve upward mobility, it was usually over a short distance, especially from the lower-middle stratum. Most stayed at the same level as their parents.

The "new," or upper-middle, class embraces members of the professions, retail merchants, bureaucrats, technicians above a certain level, small landowners, and small manufacturers. These people have their own clubs, their neighborhoods, and their own style of life. Commercial employees, teachers, and lower-level bureaucrats belong to the lower-middle class. When salaried men and women attempt to compete with the fast-track affluence of the upper-middle class, buying on credit to keep up appearances, trouble often occurs, just as anywhere else. Yet tens of thousands of other Brazilians in this categories have thrived. The difference seems to be a family's access to income other than salary. Salaries for technical and managerial positions, as well as earnings for professionals, are high but do not keep up in the long run with inflation; during recessionary periods, salary earners often are hurt although not nearly as badly as helpless elderly people living on pensions whose worth has eroded to virtually nothing. Those in the "new" middle class who have prospered, able to afford international travel, ownership of expensive apartments and houses (usually more than one), frequently traded-in automobiles, fashionable clothing, and expensive private schools and clubs, are those who supplement family income with income from foreign bank accounts, stocks, and especially rent from real estate holdings. The material opulence of the upper classes has reached this "new" middle class as well, although on a smaller scale, attested to by Brazilians' continuing love of consumer electronics, cellular telephones, fax machines, videocassette recorders (VCRs), and imported merchandise of all kinds.

The telling characteristic of this new upper-middle class is defined by its sources of income. The lower-middle class lives from salaries and wages, and thereby is particularly vulnerable to inflation and economic instability. The upper-middle class earns income from investments in properties, apartments, stocks; its members often have foreign bank accounts, or they may store away jewelry, artwork, and anything else that can be converted to cash if necessary. Children in this group when they marry often receive two condominium apartments as gifts—one from each family; the newlyweds then rent out one of them as an immediate source of supplementary income. In smaller cities, or among families with fewer assets, the gift often is something less costly than an apartment: a car that can be turned into a taxicab, for example, which is then leased to three different drivers for eight-hour shifts.

Even though members of Brazilian middle-class groups share the same pressures and stresses as any comparable group around the world, several favors have combined to give them characteristics that are admirable. Social clubs and extended families more than neighborhoods lend cohesion and provide useful support networks in times of need. Perhaps because they did not reject elite values, middle-class families have inherited the elite's cultural tastes. The result is that members of Brazilian middle-class families are far more likely to read good books, to enjoy high as well as popular culture, and to be well informed about world affairs. Whereas thirty years ago the Brazilian weekly newsmagazines casually plagiarized features from *Time, Newsweek,* and other foreign sources, today *Veja, Visão,* and *Istoé* not only hold their own but often surpass their foreign counterpart magazines in cultural content as well as in hard-hitting investigative reportage. The "dumb and dumber" mentality has not affected Brazilian culture nearly as much as it has that of the United States. Brazilian university students from the middle classes for the most part are better prepared for their studies, more worldly, and more independent than are U.S. students. The level of creativity and competence achieved in Brazilian society despite its insufficiencies is striking and worthy of praise.

Significantly below the "new" middle class in options are families dependent entirely on salaries. These families lack an economic base in small property (in contrast to the counterpart group in the post–World War II United States). Families in this sector are constantly in debt, and they live in substandard housing, often cramped apartments or small, unattractive rented houses. Members of this middle-class sector depend on education to provide opportunities for their children to reach higher living standards, but those in need of education are invariably the ones most damaged by the poor state of public education. At the free secondary and university level, most places are occupied by students of upper- or "new" middle-class background; 73 percent in the case of a study of *ginásio* students in São Paulo.[5] Politically, members of the middle classes are traditionally the most conservative in Brazil, because they fear the radical slogans of affluent progressives and are terrified of falling in economic level into the lower classes below. They are also practical: they value honesty in government, but they know that jobs and favors, even for necessities, are often obtained not by waiting patiently for one's turn but by seeking a *jeito,* a private facilitation, through the use of connections, or *pistolãoes.*

Members of the next group in descending order, the lower-middle class, usually lack the necessary contacts to obtain *jeitos.* These people are the country's artisans, technical workers, public school teachers, retail employees, taxi and bus drivers, and lower-level bureaucrats. Although they may be highly skilled—say, the stonemasons who construct intricate, lovely mosaic sidewalks in stone using primitive tools and working under terrible and unsafe conditions—their counterparts in Europe or in the United States earn ten times their wages. These people travel by bus, not private automobile; they do not have air conditioning in their homes; they eat simply; they are unable to take vacations or send their children to private schools. Because there are virtually no scholarships based on merit, and because members of this lower-middle class tend to be (but not always are) of darker skin complexion than their social betters, they have virtually no opportunities to rise any higher than they are already.

One way of estimating the total numbers of Brazilians in the middle and upper classes is to consider the figures, released by the government's economics data institute, that of 150 million citizens in 1993, only 30 million participated in the market economy. The size of this large group of people—three times the population of Belgium and six times that of Denmark—suggests that beneath the level of people working for a living and earning enough to pay for something more than basic foodstuffs, fares, and rent, there is an abyss that defies comprehension.[6]

A gulf in quality of life, opportunities for employment, shared values, and general welfare has separated the middle classes from the vast majority of the Brazilian population. The middle classes have long championed the need to protect society from perceived breakdowns of the moral and social order.[7] Perhaps for these reasons, and because the middle classes were overwhelmingly of European origin in contrast to the mixed-race and black Brazilians of the *povo,* middle-class values have been consistently conservative, even though middle-class families without independent sources of income have suffered hardships during times of depression, recession, or hyperinflation. One of the frustrations experienced by middle-class employees, in a country with a perennially youthful profile owing to its very high birthrate, was that seniority in employment and years of experience on the job have been only rarely rewarded. That unions have little power worsens the plight of workers on the job fifteen or twenty years or longer, invaluable workers but paid only barely more than entry-level. Brazil's tacit agreement to maintain wage repression means that middle-class employees can rarely hope to better their lives through hard work. Middle-grade workers are rewarded according to their value to their employers but marginally.

The Lower Classes

Except for intermittent eruptions of violence for food or to protest fare raises or other imposed hardships, the lower class for the most part has remained silent. This enormous heterogeneous population, encompassing most Brazilians in every generation, has included myriad graduations ranging from working-class families living in hard circumstances, to the semi-employed, to the propertyless urban and rural helpless indigents. It has included those whose indigence was linked to fluctuations in the cost of staples and to economic and demographic hardships, as well as others cast into poverty by infirmity or old age or, in the case of millions of children, lack of sufficient family support. During the 1930s, the stream of migrants departing from the stagnant rural hinterland had become a flood, with the exodus of hundreds of thousands from the land seeking industrial jobs in the South. Land area under cultivation shrunk while city slums ballooned. In 1993, an estimated 65 million Brazilians earned less than the family income needed for decent food and shelter. The vast gulf between rich and poor was the second largest in Latin America, after Panama. For the first time in history, migrant families who had trekked south to the industrial zones of São Paulo and Rio de Janeiro were beginning to abandon the hope of finding jobs; tiring of having to live in the street or in three-sided cardboard shanties under bridges and pedestrian overpasses, some of the families, if they could, began to return to the Northeast.[8] The poor were not as docile as they might have been. Immigrant communities and some urban neighborhoods organized formal or semiformal self-help groups, ranging from burial societies starting during the nineteenth century to the *comunidades de base* (Catholic base communities) of the 1960s, dedicated to literacy training and raising of social consciousness. Women textile operatives in São Paulo during the unsettled period of the First World War failed to win help from anarchist labor union organizers, who considered women weak and in need of protection (and who therefore tried to expel them from the labor movement), but they employed their own devices to fight for their rights. These ranged from strikes to less disruptive (but sometimes equally effective) tactics of quitting abusive jobs and spreading information about factories that employed harsh foremen or that punished workers for insufficient output.

The rigid social system instructed all Brazilians at the bottom how to behave deferentially. In preserving the psychology of paternalism and rewarding in meager ways those living up to the stereotype of the good-natured and uncomplaining *povo*, the myth was preserved intact until the 1980s, when outbursts of physical aggression frightened the complacent to the core, driving them further behind their walls of protection. Chances for upward mobility have been limited sharply not only by disparaging stereotypes about the lower classes but by a remarkable (for a country as rich as Brazil) lack of opportunities for training. At the height of São Paulo's industrial boom, fueling what economists called Brazil's pre-OPEC "economic miracle," only 18 percent of São Paulo's 735,000 full-time workers in the industrial sector were skilled. Nor did policymakers give priority to human factors. São Paulo, Brazil's "promised land" for migrants, the center of the boom, saw real wages fall, infant mortality rise, life expectancy decline, and many other indexes of the quality of life dwindle as well.[9] The results of decades of neglect are tragic. Homeless boys follow well-dressed people in the streets, tugging at their clothing to beg for handouts. Some emit a foul odor: their own clothing is filthy, and they find it difficult to wash. "I know I stink," said an adolescent beggar to a tourist: "I can't help it."[10]

The Rural Poor

Most of Brazil's rural population have been tied to the plantations, ranches, and *fazendas* that have dominated the countryside.[11] The most destitute among the Brazilian population have traditionally been rural families deprived of land ownership by the persistence of traditional patterns of land concentration and lacking opportunities for education, training, or decent employment. The diet of this "lower-lower" class has traditionally been monotonous and barely adequate. Animal protein has come from occasional dried beef or salt cod; the staple dish has long been rice and beans, although the success of soybean exporting after the 1970s led many farmers to shift from black beans (*feijão preto*) to soybeans, therefore driving up the cost of the healthiest part of the peoples' diet to a point beyond affordability. Illiterate, plagued by disease, and unable to find regular work, rural families have lived for generations close to starvation. They expend exhausting efforts simply to survive: reducing household consumption to a minimum, exploiting family labor to the fullest, and procuring sources of supplemental income.[12] The higher proportion of income a family has to spend for food, generally the lower its standard of living. The families with the highest incomes among the lower classes were found in a survey to be households with from four to seven working members. When families break up, or shrink in size, hardship looms. The pattern whereby in rural Brazil nearly everyone except the powerful owners of the land lived harsh lives, not just the landless peasants, emerged early. A 1942 study of residents of sugarcane plantations in São Paulo by anthropologist Harry W. Hutchinson found that while agricultural laborers had to spend 67 percent of their incomes on food, the foreman had to spend 53 percent and the chief of the plantation 35 percent. Things were even worse for urban slum-dwellers: a study (1934) by the pioneering Brazilian nutritionist Josué de Castro of 500 lower-class families in Recife showed that 71.6 percent of income had to go for food and 18.9 percent for housing. In cities, of course, the gap between the poor and those higher on the socioeconomic ladder was much greater than in the countryside. Castro's study, called communistic by conservative opponents of his work, revealed that daily earnings of all gainfully employed members of the 500 working-class families he interviewed in Pernambuco's capital averaged less than 28 cents per family.[13] The great majority of Brazilians have tended to remain within their respective regions for most of their lives despite migrations. Just as elsewhere, at the national level, during most periods of time, we are dealing with a self-selecting minority whose notions about the spatial dimensions of their own society are unique to them. Thus Euclides da Cunha, the war correspondent whose telegraphed dispatches about the assault on Canudos during the 1890s brought the backlands to the readers of the São Paulo newspaper for which he worked, had a national vision of the "Brazil" he was writing about; the settlers under siege, most of them backlanders who had never seen the coast, understood something entirely different when they referred to their world, whose boundaries were spiritual. For them Brazil was an abstraction, a distant place; their homes were real, in a tiny valley remote from anything they did now know personally.

Problems arise when one attempts to characterize most places as rural or urban. It is misleading to mistake the social organization for society. To be sure, large towns and cities are urban; plantations, ranches, and other sparsely populated hinterland areas are surely rural. We are forced to choose: census categories codify arbitrary definitions, and data are organized to suit. Most rural people live in villages and make their living on the land. Villages are home and community, and residents tend to stay there. Some leave, driven away by trouble or by climatic hardship, but on the whole comings and goings are limited. Residents of a village know their neighbors very well. The village also functions as a social center to which they are closely connected even when they are physically distant. Migrants halfway across Brazil from their villages of origin congregate in weekly outdoor markets in Rio de Janeiro or São Paulo, conveying news, gossiping, always bound by their village ties. The floods of migrants during the postwar decades, in fact, have blurred if not eradicated the great rural-urban differences that long characterized Brazilian society, just as the impact of satellite technology has brought urban (and international) influence to those who are not motivated to leave for the cities.

Rural poverty has remained a historical condition, not a temporary circumstance. The rural poor have rarely participated in the market economy, since they have rarely had cash. Millions have lived as *agregados*—landless peons—permitted to grow garden crops in exchange for heavy labor for the landowner. Whatever cash was acquired was spent on medicine, mostly of the home-brewed kind, and on burial expenses. Corpses in some places were wrapped in banana leaves, to save the coast of a cloth shroud, and children were customarily buried in the ground without coffins, the wooden box rented just for the burial ceremony and then returned to the funeral home. Lower-class women, especially the black *baianas,* dressed in flowing white robes, and accumulated bangles and sometimes silver or silverplate jewelry, which they wore to adorn themselves, and which were sold upon their deaths to pay for their funerals and simple wooden markers.

The dramatic social legislation of the Vargas era never extended in any meaningful way to the countryside. The rural poor remained tied to the land by traditional patron-client relationships that left them squatters, living in substandard housing, and dependent on the landowner (often the local *coronel*) for everything. The system did provide some protection for the rural workers, and, in Charles Wagley's words, "a sense of *noblesse oblige* and paternalism on the part of the employed, a survival from the times of slavery and the monarchy."[14] Lacking other kinds of help in hard times, when floods came, or drought or disease, or a precipitous fall in the price of the locally produced staple, rural families had no recourse but to pack up their few miserable possessions and migrate elsewhere, despite a lifetime of association with their patron. Even worse, in recent decades corporate management of plantations and food processing has severed the traditional patron-client ties. Workers receive wages—when there is work to do. Older, higher-level workers are regularly dismissed, time clocks are installed, and indifferently enforced regulations take the place of paternalistic concern.[15]

What most rural Brazilians have experienced is typified by the case of the Cariri Valley village of Barro, in Ceará. Desperately poor, Barro was locked into a system of monocrop production, mostly cotton. Land ownership in Barro was extremely concentrated, and wealth more so.[16] Tracing changes in patron-client relations on the site since 1897, researchers found nine different phases, from the patron as monopolistic wielder of local power supplying access to land and cash or credit for his clients, classic *coronelismo* (1897–1905), through modified forms of *coronel* rule: state intrusion in 1907 with the arrival of a revenue agent (soon murdered at the orders of coronel Zé Inácio, the local boss); to the patron as an intermediary of the state; to (1975) the state as an antagonistic alternative to the local patron; and, finally, after 1975, to the state as patron.[17] *Coronel* domination was highly paternalistic. The "Mayor's" role, and the clearly moral definition of relationships, was described years later by an octogenarian resident of Barro:

> Zé Inácio had very few resident sharecroppers. Everyone had his own piece of land. But everyone would help the Mayor at planting and at harvest time. No, he wouldn't pay anyone directly. Everyone would help with the harvesting and would receive a small part of the crop and all they could eat and drink—especially drink!—while working. Of course, if anyone wanted to, he could receive payment in money. Why would anyone have wanted to? It wouldn't have made any sense. They would help the Mayor and whenever they needed help the Mayor would help them. He took care of those who helped him like a father would. You could ask any favor of him. He was the government, the bank and the marketplace all in one.[18]

The system survived under different guises until the 1930s, when Zé Inácio died. Over the decades he had been able to deal with the state through intermediaries and to hold power by delivering the rural vote in his district through a combination of coercion and reward. Over time, however, patron-client relations became depersonalized. The relationship of the rural worker and sharecropper changed, becoming contractual, no longer based on mutually accepted (if unwritten) rules. With the disappearance of the local boss, Barro, still a poor community, lost any degree of autonomy it might have had as people from outside the area swiftly took control of major parts of the marketing of local production. The opening of a railhead in a neighboring village abruptly affected the local economy, with mixed results. Goods manufactured outside now became more readily available in Barro, but purchasers had to have cash to pay for them. Impersonal wage labor became more common. Patrons now dominated through brokerage, not through any combination of personal wealth and power. The new *coronel,* Justino Alves Feitosa, was not the richest man in the region but, as a well-connected bureaucrat, the one who controlled state resources. He determined who would receive credit and who would have access to water. He selected wage laborers for state construction projects. He was a broker, accepting cash and in kind for his services. "It is doubtful that the rural masses saw his role in this way, but the realization was not long in coming," remark Soiffer and Howe.[19] If dealings between patrons and clients in Barro had long been dominated by a "moral economy" relationship, patrons sought to emphasize the economically rationalized aspects of their relationships at exactly the same time that clients needed to reply on informal mechanisms. This proved to be disastrous for rural workers, and contributed to lowered morale and a feeling of helplessness among the lower classes, increasingly blocked from possibilities of advancement through personal means. The influx of cash credit as bank loans and other state programs favored large producers, and small producers were squeezed out. The state imposed minimum wage regulations but also provided tax and other incentives for landowners to make production more efficient. In areas like Barro across the country, agricultural land formerly used to grow beans and corn and other food crops were turned to soybean production, highly profitable as an export crop, but providing no sustenance to local residents. Still, in spite of a deterioration in patron-client relations, the psychology survived.

On the other hand, original artisanship began to disappear—hammock-making, weaving, pottery, and wood and leather crafts. In their place came items brought into Barro, often of cheap plastic, manufactured in southern Brazil or in Asia. The town population swelled as families abandoned their rural residences. With the move to the city came the complete loss of patronage. Those who wandered to the coast or to the industrial south to seek jobs had to leave behind even the godparents of their children. Circumstances stripped them of even the most elemental forms of protection they and their parents had been able to marshal.

Things did not stand still, even in distant places. Consider the accounting of a veteran migrant in Soure on the Amazonian island of Marajó:

> We have been well in Soure. My married son lives in a house on my plot; we fish together. We came 17 years ago. Things were different then. Building a canoe was easier because the good wood was easy to find and cheap—we just had to go and get it. There were only 3 or 4 of us foraging. Not now: all of the land has been bought up, and you have to pay for everything you need. Wood is expensive. You need a bank loan to be able to build a boat. You can get work if you know how to be a mason, or carpenter, or whatever but the people coming in now don't know how to do these things. They only know how to fish. They have no "pull" to get government jobs. They keep coming; they never stop.[20]

We know that families living in plantation regions, or in the traditional, dispersed rural settlement pattern, frequently confronted many of the pressures and institutions characteristic of peasant life. The rigid dualism of women's roles (as sainted mothers in the home, or as prostitutes in the street) hindered relaxed behavior and forced women to remain on their pedestals. Ladies, according to Gilberto Freyre, bloomed early. Girls from the elite were sent at age eight or nine to boarding schools run by nuns (or, in the larger cities, run by Protestant or Roman Catholic educators); they returned home at age thirteen or fourteen to continue their training in the womanly arts (dancing, embroidery, French, sometimes English, music). By now they dressed like ladies; timidity and docility were considered graces. They attended balls and concerts, heavily chaperoned; fluttered their fans flirtatiously; and waited for the parents or agents of prospective husbands to negotiate with the girls' parents for their hands. An English traveler described the results of some of these matrimonial matches:

> Sometimes the "future husband" was a pleasant surprise—a pale youth of twenty-three or twenty-five, a ruby or an emerald sparkling from his forefinger, his moustaches perfumed, his hair smooth, oily . . . a hero who had escaped from some bright German oleogravure or from the pages of a novel. And romantic love developed between the contracting parties. Other times the "future husband" was some fat, solid, newly-rich Portuguese, middle-aged, his neck short and his hands coarse. Perhaps a very fine person—inside; but what a death-blow for a sentimental girl of the fifties. And yet she often accepted him—the potbellied one—such a marriage being nothing more than a business partnership.[21]

Girls bore children as soon as they married. Most were mothers by the time they were fifteen, or earlier. For many, the blush of adolescence passed quickly. Like women of all classes, most were drained by frequent childbirth, and many died of infection or other consequences of unhygienic health care.

The mass of the rural population fared much worse. People relieved themselves into the same rivers where they bathed. People from "better" families undressed in crude bathhouses made from coconut palm fronds, but they still dipped in sewage-filled waters. Dirt and foul odors were everywhere. Carcasses of dogs, cats, and even mules and horses rotted outdoors in the heat. The capital city of Rio de Janeiro had no street cleaning, no light, no air, no sewers; flies and mosquitoes and rats multiplied unchecked. In Rio and other large cities, night wastes were sometimes thrown out of windows to the street, or gathered by slaves in barrels *(tigres),* carried on the slaves' heads to be dumped into rivers, the seashore, or alleys. Flocks of vultures, buzzards, and other carrion birds were everywhere. Not that the elite did not try to impose cleanliness, at least for themselves: Freyre found a full one-third of the factories in Brazil under the Empire to be soap factories. Saint-Hilaire noted the apostolic simplicity with which hosts were provided with basins and towels to wash the feet before going to bed. This was to reduce the dangers of hookworm and other parasitic infections in a country where most poor people walked barefoot.

Other pressures of life included the stress of being trapped in credit cycles fostered by the necessity to buy provisions on credit from stores owned by the local landowner; they also included obligations to work for local patrons in exchange for protection. Nuclear families remained the main productive unit; rural families were connected through marriage, fictive kinship (godfather- and godmotherhood), mutual aid, and religious observances.[22] When changes came, especially when rural society came to be buffeted by the winds of outside influences, including the incursion of government bureaucracy and the arrival of radio and television, rural populations, like it or not, became integrated into the national and world society. This process of integration into the wider economic world produced highly uneven results. I remember entering by jeep the bleached cream and chalk town of Palmares in Pernambuco's *zona da mata,* along the banks of the Una River, southwest of Recife in 1970. It was dusk on Saturday, and the streets were deserted except for a throng of people in the town square. Some were local residents. Others were people from outlying places who had come to Palmares for the weekly outdoor market, or to buy supplies or drink in the bars. Dust covered everything. People were dressed in rudimentary clothing, some fashioned by hand from burlap sacking. This lent a primitive air not unlike that attributed to the backlands *caboclo* as described by Euclides da Cunha seventy years before in *Os Sertões.* Men and women stood clustered in small, separate groups, hunched down to steady themselves; others sat in narrow doorways. A few old men squatted, whittling small pieces of wood. Silences were punctuated only by the sound of people spitting on the ground. As far as I was concerned, Palmares's square could have looked the same a hundred or two hundred years earlier. Its economy was more depressed than usual, since its *usina* (refinery) had shut down three years earlier. There was an air of being cut off from the rest of the world, of timelessness. There were no vehicles in sight, only a few horses and mules tethered to trees. The gathering darkness obscured any advertising signs or other artifacts of modern life. Then I noticed a glowing light in a corner of the square, and a black wire stretching from its location to a shabby building on the other side of the street. That building was the town hall; the wire was carrying electricity to a color television set placed in the plaza, surrounded by a dense crowd of watchers, many of them children. When I inched my way to see what the people were watching and finally approached the set, I was stunned: these disconsolate, humbly clad villagers were watching a relay transmission of CBS's Walter Cronkite narrating the descent of an Apollo space capsule on its return trip from a lunar landing.

The electricity was being produced by a generator, and I could not tell whether the poor image was caused by its flickering output or from a bad satellite relay. The bystanders did not seem to notice. They watched without emotion, as if this was as old hat to them as any city dweller jaded by the profusion of technology all around him.

Life in any community, no matter how isolated it seemed to be, was always linked to the outside world. Until the last months of the siege of Canudos in the late 1890s, with the full force of the Brazilian army racing in the hills surrounding the millenarian community, paths remained open, residents came and went, and letters were even delivered.[23] Still, old traditions lingered within communities. Often they clashed with new ways of doing things. In the vertical and segmentary clan structure inherited from the colonial era, where loyalties of family members were to one another and did not recognize authorities beyond clan leaders, most forms of exchange were informal. They were based on kinship, ritual kinship, mutual assistance, and clientage; they must have been jolted when local authorities unexpectedly announced the need for license fees before a countryman could sell his produce at the weekly market, or buy a horse, or bury his child. Informal exchange always was a key element in economic survival.

New actors entered the stage as time passed. Muleteers and peddlers arrived on the scene, demanding currency for their wares. Merchants set up shops, independent of local landowners. Slaves rented out by masters competed with free laborers for wages. Sometimes free laborers were hired on plantations that for the most part were worked by slaves.[24] Sometimes the opening of a butcher shop, where animals were slaughtered and then sold in pieces, represented the transition point between a truly rural place and an urban locus in a rural setting.[25] The export-based economy brought in imported goods as well, raising the quality of life for the affluent. Many lower-class households broke down as agriculture became more specialized and capitalized. Some successful merchants and employees of foreign companies married into Brazilian high society. The traditional clans still controlled the major sources of labor and credit, but their own borders became elastic.[26] As the dependence of clan leaders on the informal exchange system began to lessen and the old equilibriums began to crack, factiousness within the landed elite worsened, sometimes leading to violence, especially in the backlands. On the larger scale, juridical and institutional change moved society more toward class than caste or estate relationship. The decline in influence of the old artisan guilds by the 1840s, which had controlled access to these occupations, created a freer atmosphere, less tied to traditional patterns. The 1850 Land Law made it easier to aggregate large quantities of land, and the 1888 abolition decree forever ended the legality of slavery. Wealth, not status, now became the more controlling factor. Changes, nonetheless, were always incomplete as old institutions adapted to coexist with new ones. Informal relations continued to thrive amidst even the most modern innovations.

As small-plot farming became more inefficient and agro-industrial output took an increasingly large share of food production, sharecroppers, renters, and other rural tenants were displaced from the land and turned into day laborers, hired only when needed. In São Paulo, salaried day laborers were first used to harvest oranges in the Ribeirão Preto region, and later to cut sugar cane. By 1984, an estimated 3 million rural workers in São Paulo state were day workers, or *bóias-frias,* named for the cold lunches they packed to take with them to work. These *bóias-frias* lived miserable lives, waking up at 3:00 or 4:00 A.M., waiting at the hiring office, being loaded onto an open truck for a one- to two-hour ride to the fields, working a ten-to-twelve-hour day, and returning home at night to hope for work the following day. Paid for what he picks or cuts, the *bóia-fria* rarely earns the minimum wage, thus being condemned to poverty. Between 1979 and 1981 as many as 300,000 rural day laborers struck in the state of Pernambuco for higher wages, but they were simply replaced by others willing to work for virtually anything.[27]

The names used for lower-class rural people today reflect the impact of stereotype. From the Amazon to the coastal Northeast, they are called *caboclos,* describing their mixed-race origins. The Bahian term is *tabaréu;* in São Paulo they are called *jecas* or *caipiras* (rustics, or hicks). They stayed in rural areas except during period of insupportable drought or calamity. Until about 1950, in cities of any size, especially in the South, lower-class persons in manual trades (a "working class," in contrast to the much larger group of irregularly employed people), were immigrants, especially Italians. Things then began to change. The children of immigrants tended to rise to higher social levels, the first step being to the level of skilled craftsmen or white-collar retail employees, and their places as manual laborers and domestics came to be taken by Brazilians, migrants from the interior and especially from the Northeast. São Paulo's North train station, located in the midst of an enormous working-class Italian population, became the arrival point of *nordestinos,* stereotyped as rustics and ridiculed by coarse jokes but ultimately making up more than 10 percent of the population of the city's industrial districts.[28]

In rural areas, landowners, especially after the 1950s, began to rely less on traditional (and inefficient) sharecropping arrangements in response to the demands of the market-oriented agricultural economy. Instead, they hired more salaried workers. In addition, rural workers, aided by progressives (including many rural-based Roman Catholic priests) began to organize in their own behalf. Ironically, the greatest gains among rural trade unions occurred during the period of the military dictatorship, from 1964 to 1985. Not all the efforts to organize in the countryside were successful, but what did occur was impressive. More than 2,700 unions and 23 union federations emerged, representing almost 10 million men and women despite the trend throughout the Southern Cone of effective military repression of unions.[29]

The Urban Poor

Albert Camus expressed astonishment in 1949 at the contrast between the palatial apartment houses and modern buildings in the cities he visited, and people living in misery, black and white, sometimes at less than 100 meters distance. In Rio, he observed, women who have no running water have to stand for hours with buckets on their heads, lined up to draw water from a single tap, while in front of them pass "silent" modern automobiles manufactured in the United States and imported to Brazil. "I have never seen," he wrote, "luxury and misery so insolently mixed." He repeated what his host told him, however: "At least [the poor] enjoy themselves a good deal."[30]

Many other visitors have been shocked by the sheer size of the hundreds of individual favelas—of more than a thousand of them across Brazil—which cover nearly every hill and vacant urban space adjacent to more affluent residential neighborhoods. They see the squalor and imagine the *favelados* to be rootless, migrants without pasts, marginal to their surroundings. Still, favela dwellers actually have a deep sense of origin beneath the surface, as strong a coping mechanism as any practiced by less precarious urban residents. When their squatments are torn down, they build them up again. In a few cases, most notably the Brás de Pina favela in Rio de Janeiro, where one-third of the population live in shantytowns, favela families have stood up against demolition and collaborated with authorities to bring urban services to their community, although hundreds of thousands remained passive when removed in the 1970s to outlying urban housing projects too far from places of work to avoid hardship.

A characteristic of Brazil's urban life is that the poorest and most miserable of city inhabitants—*favelados* in Rio de Janeiro and São Paulo, *mocambeiros* in Recife, and so on—live precariously on the economic margin performing labor necessary for the functioning of city life. The first favela was constructed on the Morro da Providencia—the Hill of Providence—the site of a military observation post built in 1830. By the early 1900s, thousands of people, many of them soldiers released from the army after the Canudos campaign without being given their back pay, had constructed shantytown shacks on land overlooking the city. Favelas were the inevitable by-product of post-1930 industrialization without urban planning and of the gaping disparity in opportunities for work between the hinterland and the coast. Although popular wisdom among the affluent held that favela dwellers shunned work, urban sociologists know that nearly every able-bodied slum resident worked most of the time. Most women were maids or laundresses; men labored in construction, worked at low-level trade occupations such as workers in restaurant kitchens, or peddled cheap goods on the street. Few held stable jobs, however; favela residents were the first to be fired and the last to earn any job security. What sometimes helped was the location of the favela itself. *Carioca* (from Rio) *favelados* finding themselves in the Praia do Pinto and other favelas located adjacent to expensive housing inevitably worked as servants or doormen or as common laborers, whereas Brás de Pina residents, near Avenida Brasil, a major highway, often took advantage of this to start businesses of their own.[31]

Many poor Brazilians lack birth certificates, or register under the names of men who are not their real fathers. Some, unable to read their own papers, are confused about their names, or their dates of birth. Many birth certificates contain names that were misspelled when the child was born, or not comprehended. A high number of favela children have no birth certificates at all, because their births were not recorded, just as many poor children who die in rural areas and are buried by family members are not registered either, and therefore are never known to official society. The problem is a circular one: if you do not have a proper birth certificate, you cannot be buried legally without authorization from a judge. So many are buried illegally as well.

Brazilian cities remained rigidly segregated according to the economic station of their inhabitants, although refined and not-so-refined neighborhoods often had stood in close proximity. During colonial times, genteel families occupied the high ground, removed from the stench of sea-level standing water and dumped garbage, taking advantage of the breezes found at higher elevations. When they stood closer to tenements and other kinds of slums, the houses of the wealthy invariably were surrounded by high stone or wrought-iron fences. More recently, these fences have often been topped with jagged shards of glass. High-rise apartment complexes have been surrounded with walls topped by barbed wire, or protected by more sophisticated electronic surveillance systems. Private homes in recent decades have been equipped with card-operated garage-door openers; residences in the posher neighborhoods of São Paulo and Rio de Janeiro have been outfitted with concrete pillboxes for twenty-four-hour armed guards, although homeowners have complained that many of the men they hired to provide security were themselves untrustworthy, and occasionally stories would surface about robberies and kidnappings carried out by the guards or their accomplices.

Residential zones inhabited by members of the lower classes always were sited on undesirable land. In São Paulo, "suburban" neighborhoods (the word has a pejorative connotation in Brazilian Portuguese) took shape in remote, dirty low-lying areas, vulnerable to flooding; slums within the city proper were, like Brás in São Paulo, flooded often, and were cut off by the rivers that rose out of their banks regularly during the rainy season. Poor residents of Rio de Janeiro clustered in tenements carved out of decaying buildings in deteriorating sections of the city, such as São Cristóvão, or in low-grade housing erected by speculators and rented. Decent workers' housing existed only on the grounds of some factories, usually run by English factory managers who believed that healthy and happy workers performed better work. The practice of building workers' villages adjacent to industrial plants started during the 1870s, and continued sporadically but with no great enthusiasm throughout the following decades.

Working families able to afford even tenement housing were in the minority. Much more numerous were the vast numbers of underemployed and unskilled shantytown dwellers, usually migrants from the hinterland or from the Northeast, or demobilized soldiers cast off without so much as a pension. The explosion of squatter settlements resulted from the failure of state and national officials to provide low-cost urban housing in the face of the rapid urbanization which gripped Brazil after the return to prosperity that followed the Second World War. Before the urban boom, workers and their families lived in tenements or warehouses that had been subdivided into tiny living quarters. As time passed, it was impossible to squeeze all newcomers into such housing, especially given that many migrants had no income at all and tenement landlords charged rent. In addition, urban renewal projects, popular since the beginning of the century, saw many tenements torn down. An engineer in President Rodrigues Alves's employ published a report addressing the urban housing problem in 1906, but no serious government consideration was given to the problem until the 1930s, when migration to cities heightened in the wake of worsening agricultural crisis.

What was remarkable about the squatter settlements was how they were completed without benefit of civil engineers or architects. Shantytowns were precarious (they were prone to floods and fires and a host of other disasters), but they managed to house thousands and tens of thousands of residents, most in transit, some with a degree of permanence. Residents lined up to get water from public spigots; some wired their sheds illegally to utility company electric poles; others opened businesses right in the favela, some legitimate, some not. Some favelas grew to be miniature cities, although some were torn down by angry property owners. Others provided shelter over a number of years; still others became transformed into permanent working-class neighborhoods, with brick and cement block replacing tin and wood. Residents exited during the day to earn wages in the city as domestics, artisans, or taxi drivers; to work as prostitutes, or con men, or street vendors; or to carry out assaults and robberies.

Intermittently and without any lasting success, officials in cities scattered throughout Brazil attempted to provide public housing to counter the unchecked growth of squatter settlements. The first agency to plan public housing was Vargas's Institute for Retirement and Social Welfare (IAPI), one of three such agencies at the federal level at that time that were supposed to provide housing for the needy but that in fact did very little. The most famous project, completed in the mid-1940s in the industrial neighborhood of Realengo west of Rio de Janeiro, was the "Little Moscow," so named because many of its residents participated in or were sympathetic to the Brazilian Communist Party, especially between 1945 and 1947, the years in which the party was granted legal status.[32] This is not what IAPI's conservative social engineers wanted to see, of course, and the experiment further reinforced the predilections of some politicians to go even slower when planning public housing.

As long as the size of shantytown slums remained manageable, a variety of educational and charitable programs were established, some under the auspices of the Roman Catholic Church's Leão XIII Foundation, to urbanize the favelas by creating, on a limited basis, social centers, schools, and clinics. In succeeding decades, officials vacillated between plans to remove their inhabitants and return the land to its original owners, and alternate plans to improve conditions and permit the residents to stay.[33] Rising land prices, however, almost always prompted officials to level the favelas.

Estado Novo corporatism, borrowed from Oliveira Salazar's Portuguese fascist regime of the same name as well as from Mussolini's Italian fascism, in theory regulated the interests of all social groups, but in political practice it focused on workers' organizations and demands in order to control them. The Institute for Retirement and Social Welfare represented one of the institutional anchors for this policy, with the Labor Ministry and the regulatory Labor Code and its administrative apparatus. Each category of workers was assigned to an institute for regulation, financed by compulsory employee contributions consisting of from 3 to 8 percent of their union dues, and by an additional 2 percent from the state budget. Only workers approved for membership in the state-run unions, of course, received Institute benefits, a key part of the corporatist system of control. Competent labor officials, moreover, were rewarded for their loyalty to the state by being granted jobs in the bureaucracy. IAPI was the first institute to enact a housing program for its members, a response to the crushing urban housing shortage during the 1940s caused by deteriorating worker housing and increased pressures of migration as well as by the breakdown of the rental market owing to inflation. By providing cheap housing, the state could keep wages down and at the same time expand its political legitimacy among favored workers. IAPI tenants, much like Michigan Ford Motor Company workers in the 1930s, were expected not only to be loyal politically but also to be model workers and exemplary family members.

Realengo, the first large-scale government housing project, was not followed by many others. A half million workers paid union dues to IAPI, but the Institute eventually built only 100,000 housing units. Extensive media coverage gave the impression that far more workers were being benefited nationwide. Construction at Realengo took several years before the first 2,000 families could move in, by 1943. Most of the housing was three stories in height, with commercial shops and IAPI offices on the ground floor. Houses, some of which were semidetached, were painted white. Medical and other forms of social assistance were provided. Workers with exemplary job records and large numbers of children were given preference, although connections and other forms of patronage significantly influenced whether a family's application would be successful. One-parent and female-headed households were completely excluded. Workers came from several sectors in the industrial infrastructure of the area, especially textiles but also shoemaking, printing, dressmaking, and metalworking.

Once residents took possession of their units, many objected to regulations that were so detailed and restricted that tenants were not even allowed to put nails into their walls. IAPI accused complainers of ingratitude. The conflicts spiraled, reaching a peak during the late 1950s when IAPI withdrew, leaving tenants to their own devices. Residents then added rooms to their houses, clearing the trees that had been planted on the grounds to make space for the extensions. In 1964, the Institutes were abolished and replaced by the Banco Nacional de Habitação (BNH), a national housing agency that built and sold houses to workers in the pension system.

Brazil's construction of public housing, never even barely adequate, peaked in the late 1950s. Although sometimes projects were designed with flair by architects determined to avoid the prisonlike atmosphere most often associated with housing for the poor, they invariably degenerated into scarred urban jungles lacking essentials from working elevators to basic hygiene. Much more often, the urban poor occupied abandoned housing that had been subdivided into tenements, or lived in the acres of teeming favelas, neighborhoods of shacks usually built on precarious hillsides, that were deluged with water after rainstorms, that lacked sewers, and that usually lacked electricity except when it was stolen by rigged wiring tapped into utility company poles on the street. More recent arrivals to the cities, usually migrants from the rural hinterland, lived in shacks made of tin, boards, and other materials removed from construction sites or found in junkyards. While some of the older, more established favelas gradually acquired infrastructure—health posts, cement block or brick walls, electricity, water spigots—the raw, newer slums were little more than festering camps built out of garbage, perched under bridges or in vacant lots or alongside empty factory buildings.

Working-class families—those with one or more breadwinners earning wages, however inadequate—lived in austere houses made out of cement block or, more usually, in monstrous, concrete apartment houses located far from sites of employment, often hours away from work sites by crowded and not inexpensive public buses. Very infrequently, officials experimented with innovative kinds of housing for the urban poor. The Alliance for Progress of the administration of President John F. Kennedy (which gave more funds to Brazil than to any other Latin American nation, largely because in the early 1960s the rise of socialist-minded peasant leagues in the Brazilian Northeast had stirred fears that Brazil would become the next Cuba), gave millions of dollars in housing subsidies. Alliance housing programs, carried out under the direction of the U.S. Agency for International Development (USAID), built model neighborhoods providing individual families with their own little houses, built in neat rows, with opportunities for small garden plots, separate bedrooms for adult family members, and the expectation that schools would be built by thankful local authorities, and health posts, and factories. Vila Kennedy, constructed with USAID funds in a remote part of Rio de Janeiro's working-class North Zone, had a small replica of the Statue of Liberty in its tiny public square. Similar USAID villages, designed to give occupants the stability that comes with home ownership (they could obtain deeds to their properties through a subsidized mortgage plan), were erected in cities across Brazil.

The projects failed, to the delight of many Brazilians angry at what they considered to be USAID's heavy-handed meddling. Local politicians, instinctively figuring out how to profit from such social programs, dealt out construction contracts for kickbacks ranging from 15 to 40 percent. Surplus food (powdered milk, rice, butter, and other products) donated under the Alliance for Progress was stolen at the docks or otherwise ended up in local grocery stores. In Natal, Rio Grande do Norte, Governor Aluísio Alves extracted political mileage from the local Vila Aliança project, built entirely with U.S. government funds, and used his control of the social service apparatus to dole out houses on the basis of political patronage. Of even greater consequence was the failure almost without exception of state and local government to integrate these housing projects into the larger urban infrastructure. No jobs were provided; transportation to job sites took hours and consumed a large portion of the miserable daily wage. The model communities were regularly forsaken by their dwellers, who ended up in favelas nearer to their work after their own original favela dwellings had been bulldozed, the land turned over to private developers who erected luxury hotels and condominiums on the sites.

By the 1990s, for the first time in this century and possibly at any time in history, Brazilian children growing to adulthood by the age of thirty faced prospects of a lower standard of living than their parents. Among the urban lower classes, this took the form of deteriorated housing conditions, larger-than-ever squalid favelas, and makeshift shantytowns not stable enough to be called favelas; thousands had to shield themselves from the elements behind pieces of cardboard under bridges and highway overpasses. In April 1994, Rio de Janeiro issued an ordinance requiring garbage scavengers to register as "professionals" so that they would be eligible to receive shovels, cans, and uniforms. Fathers and mothers searching for food in garbage piles would now be able to place their children in day-care centers, so that the children would not have to spend their days with their parents amid the stench of rotting detritus.[34]

As recently as 1993, 52.9 percent of Brazilian workers earned substantially less than the poverty level in any western country. Many more, like the tragic and homeless street children who inhabit the streets of every Brazilian city, earn no legal income and therefore are not included in official statistics. Gradations in poverty, however, do exist in every sector of society, in Brazil from region to region, from city to city, and from neighborhood to neighborhood. Not only is there now a niche in the lower class where people live adequately in spite of their low incomes, but there has been for almost a century a certain percentage of the lower classes who are articulate and who express their opinions publicly. During the populist 1950s these people were cultivated by politicians and sometimes invited to make statements at political rallies; they were listened to when favors were dispensed. Between 1899 and 1935, the *Jornal do Brasil*, Rio de Janeiro's major newspaper, which then represented an opposition, monarchist position, printed a daily column, "As Queixas do Povo," the "People's Complaints." Inhibited from ever confronting officials directly even in the face of neglect or misdoing, men and women wrote letters to the newspaper asking for justice. About a third of the published letters addressed labor problems: low wages, unhealthy working conditions, and so on; the remaining two-thirds dealt with living conditions, from the need for security to the sanitary conditions of the streets. Not only were these letters courageous, but the fact that the column survived for years testifies to the emergence of a sense of citizenship, a belief that every person, regardless of income or status, had the right to be heard.

It was disclosed in the early 1990s that it was possible to hire a "slave" worker by long-distance telephone from São Paulo. This was merely a high-technology modern version of the ages-old practice of luring hapless rural workers to remote plantations and ranches, and then preventing them from leaving by various guises, one being debt servitude based on exorbitant charges for transportation to the site. In other cases, the threat of physical violence was used to keep people working just for food and shelter. In April 1993, a *paulista* rancher demonstrated how he could contract for workers who would be paid no salary, for work in Southern Pará clearing land or taking care of cattle. The contracting agent promised to deliver a set number of undocumented workers recruited from Goiás or the Northeast for $300 paid in U.S. dollars. The workers would be delivered in buses with the windows boarded up to prevent their being seen by highway police. The Pará arrangement turned out to be small in comparison with other slave labor operation, including a coal mine in Mato Grosso do Sul with 8,235 workers classified as slaves by a watchdog group, the Pastoral Land Commission (CPT), about half of the total number of slave laborers verified to be in servitude in nine states. Overseers admitted that they whipped the "peons" (as they called them) if they did not cooperate, and allegations were made that some slaves were forced to perform sexual acts and that others had been shot as examples.[35] Young girls were taken from debt-ridden families and auctioned as slaves to raucous prospectors, with virgins fetching the highest prices.[36]

Poor Brazilians know about these things. Canoe fishermen in southern Bahia say for public consumption that "there is only one people. We are all *gente* and *povo*. It is true that one may live in a better condition than another, but we are all equal."[37] Everyday speech makes sharp distinction between the terms. "Você é *gente*," one fisherman says to another in a show of camaraderie. The word connotes respect; *povo* is used for other people, more abstractly, with a sense of deprecation. Sometimes members of the *povo* share secrets. For years, historians have written that the reason that lower-class urban residents resisted health officials attempting to inoculate them against yellow fever at the turn of the century—leading to riots and police violence—was a Luddite fear of the instruments of modern life. Now we know that at least according to one source, the descendant of a spiritist priest *(pai de santo)*, the reason that resistance started was that city officials attempted to invade a sacred *macumba* site, in their ignorance of and contempt for the people's religion.

So few except for soccer players and a few entertainers have managed to achieve upward mobility in one generation that their stories make the news, as do examples of successes of persons born in the interior, even if not in poverty. When Lázaro de Melo Brandão in 1980 became president of a leading bank, newspaper accounts emphasized that he had been born in Itápolis (SP) and attended school in the city of Lins. He took his first job at fifteen and eventually rose to the position of inspector general, then vice president, and finally president. The press story noted with incredulity that Melo Brandão "neither attends parties nor appears in social columns" but that he preferred to spend his vacations at his farm in Itatiba riding horses.[38] "Once a *caipira*, always a *caipira*" was the message. The story noted that the new bank president arrived at work between 7:00 and 7:30 A.M. every day and only left twelve hours later. Bankers from more notable backgrounds presumably kept less strenuous hours.

The overwhelming number of lower-class Brazilians have moved only incrementally higher or lower on the mobility ladder from the rung on which they were born. The next chapter will consider persons who find themselves "outside" the system, and their own struggles to improve their lives.

Notes

1. See José Murilo de Carvalho, "Political Elites and State Building: The Case of Nineteenth-Century Brazil," in Daniel H. Levine, ed., *Constructing Culture and Power in Latin America* (Ann Arbor: University of Michigan Press, 1993), 403–28, especially 420.

2. T. Lynn Smith, *Brazil: People and Institutions,* 4th ed. (Baton Rouge: Louisiana State University Press, 1972), 203–4.

3. Archibald O. Haller, "Power: How Brazil Works," *Luso-Brazilian Review* 29:1 (Summer 1992), 115–20.

4. Charles Wagley, *Introduction to Brazil* (New York: Columbia University Press, 1963), 111–12.

5. Lopes Brandão, "Escolha Ocupacional e Origem Social de Ginasianos em São Paulo," *Educação e Ciências Sociais* 1 (1956), 43–62.

6. *Veja,* 31 March 1993, 80.

7. See Susan K. Besse, "Crimes of Passion: The Campaign against Wife Killing in Brazil, 1910–1940," *Journal of Social History* 22:4 (1989), 653–66.

8. Nathaniel C. Nash, *New York Times,* 16 February 1993, A4.

9. Helen I. Safa, "Women, Production and Reproduction in Industrial Capitalism: A Comparison of Brazilian and U.S. Factory Workers," ms., c. 1980, in Latin Tenure Center Library, University of Wisconsin, Madison.

10. Related to author by Ana Navarro, Coral Gables, 8 September 1993.

11. See Biorn Maybury-Lewis, *The Politics of the Possible: The Brazilian Rural Workers' Trade Union Movement, 1964–1985* (Philadelphia: Temple University Press, 1994), 3.

12. Charles H. Wood and Marianne Schmink, "Blaming the Victim: Small Farmer Production in an Amazon Colonization Project," 1982, clipping file, Land Tenure Center Library, University of Wisconsin, Madison, 84–85.

13. Josué de Castro, *As Condições de Vida das Classes Operárias no Recife* (Rio de Janeiro, 1935), 11; T. L. Smith, *Brazil: People and Institutions,* 207.

14. C. Wagley, *Introduction to Brazil,* 98–99.

15. Harry W. Hutchinson, *Village and Plantation Life in Northeastern Brazil* (Seattle: University of Washington Press, 1957), 180.

16. Stephen M. Soiffer and Gary N. Howe, "Patrons, Clients and the Articulation of Modes of Production: An Examination of the Penetration of Capitalism into Peripheral Agriculture in Northeastern Brazil," *Journal of Peasant Studies* 9:2 (January 1982), 176–206.

17. S. Soiffer and G. Howe, "Peripheral Agriculture," 181–201. See also the classic study of rural political and economic hegemony, Victor Nunes Leal's *Coronelism: The Municipality and the Vote* (Cambridge, 1977).

18. Unnamed interviewee, cited in S. Soiffer and G. Howe, "Peripheral Agriculture," 185.

19. S. Soiffer and G. Howe, "Peripheral Agriculture," 194.

20. Paraphrased from statement by anonymous interviewee, quoted by Violeta Refkalefsky Loureiro, *A Miséria da Ascensão Social: Capitalismo e Pequena Produção na Amazônia* (São Paulo, 1987), 85–86.

21. Gilberto Freyre, quoted in E.B. Burns, *Latin America,* 87.

22. Conrad P. Kottak, *Prime-Time Society* (Belmont, CA: Wadsworth, 1990), 122–23.

23. See the author's *Vale of Tears* (Berkeley: University of California Press, 1993), 121–52.

24. Stuart B. Schwartz, *Sugar Plantations in the Formation of Brazilian Society: Bahia: 1550–1835* (Cambridge: Cambridge University Press. 1985), 313–37.

25. For an analysis of a primitive town with a slaughterhouse, see Alfredo Dantas Landim, Robert Comfort, and Victor Valla, *'Soca-Braço,' um Bairro Popular do Município de Uriçuca* (Salvador: Centro de Pesquisas do Cacau, 1975), 5–19.

26. Elizabeth Anne Kuznesof, "From Eighteenth-Century 'Depression' to Nineteenth-Century Industrialization: Analyzing the Mysterious Modernization Process in São Paulo, Brazil," paper delivered to the American Historical Association, December 1991, Session 97, 10–19.

27. Maria Conceição d'Incão, *Qual É a Questão Bóia-Fria?* (São Paulo: Brasiliense, 1984), 7–10.

28. Francisco C. Weffort, "Nordestinos em São Paulo: Notas para un Estudo sobre Cultura Nacional e Cultura Popular," in Edênio Valle and José J. Queiróz, org., *A Cultura do Povo* (São Paulo: Editora da Universidade Católica de São Paulo, 1979), 13–23.

29. B. Maybury-Lewis, *The Politics of the Possible,* 11–12, 24–25.

30. Albert Camus, *Diário de Viagem* (São Paolo: Distribuidora Record, 1985), 75–76.

31. J.C. Pino, "Family and Favela," ms., 30.

32. Wilma Mangabeira, "Memories of 'Little Moscow' (1943–64): Study of a Public Housing Experiment for Industrial Workers in Rio de Janeiro, Brazil," *Social History* 17:2 (May 1992), 271–87.

33. Anthony Leeds and Elizabeth Leeds, *A Sociologia do Brasil Urbano* (Rio de Janeiro: Zahar Editores), 1978, 189–200.

34. *Jornal do Brasil* (Rio de Janeiro), 27 April 1994, 14.

35. *Folha de São Paulo,* 10 March 1993, 4; 4 April 1993, 4; *Veja,* 14 April 1993, 54–56; *Tempo e Presença* 15 (March–April 1993), 25–26.

36. *Boletim da Commissão Pastoral da Terra-CPT,* no. 108 (February 1993).

37. Francisco, a canoe fisherman in Camurim, Bahia, quoted by Antonius C.G.M. Robben, *Sons of the Sea Goddess: Economic Practice and Discursive Conflict in Brazil* (New York: Columbia University Press, 1989), 236–37.

38. *Folha de São Paulo,* 2 November 1980, 4.

3

Outsiders

Lisbon's colonial apparatus forbade foreigners to immigrate or settle although the Portuguese never enforced exclusionary laws to the extent that the Spanish did in their territory. Once resident in Brazil, however, individuals from places other than Portugal were subject to harsh repression if Crown authorities so willed. Gypsies, for example, who had been persecuted in Portugal before the sixteenth century and who sought refuge in Brazil, faced deportation and sentencing to the galley ships if they were convicted of vagrancy or other antisocial acts. Brazil's Roman Catholic Church maintained pressure on authorities to expel gypsies refusing to marry in the Church or to baptize their children. Gypsies who managed to escape deportation were stigmatized as pariahs, as were the Jews who emigrated to northeastern Brazil during the seventeenth-century Dutch occupation. When Dutch Brazil fell in 1654, the Jews were deported from the colony, seeking exile in Jamaica, the Dutch islands in the Caribbean, and ultimately New Amsterdam. In time, gypsies managed to carve out a social space amid the tensions of a society dominated by slaves, thereby winning a better situation in Brazil than their relatives had in Europe, where they were subject to constant ethnic oppression.

Broader-scale immigration to Brazil began in the early nineteenth century. Many French citizens, displaced by the Napoleonic wars, came, especially to Rio de Janeiro and São Paulo. A Swiss colony was founded in 1818 at Nova Friburgo, in the low mountains not far from Rio de Janeiro. Another Swiss settlement, São Leopoldo, was established in 1824. Imperial officials worked hard to attract European settlers, offering transportation subsidies and other incentives. After 1847, European colonies were founded at São Pedro de Alcântara in Paraná, Petrópolis in Rio de Janeiro (the summer residence of the monarchy), and Blumenau in Santa Catarina, which attracted Germans. The continued reliance on slavery, though, discouraged larger numbers of immigrants from coming, so that the total number of new arrivals before midcentury probably reached only a few tens of thousands.

Immigration spiraled after 1880. Italians, Portuguese, Spaniards, Germans, Lebanese, Poles, Japanese, Spaniards, and other nationalities flocked to Brazil, enticed in some cases by free ship passage and various colonization schemes which in reality amounted to little more than forced debt servitude in spite of promises of free or cheap land. Almost all the Brazilian provinces (called states after 1889) sought to attract Europeans, although most came to the South. Nearly 400,000 Spaniards came, not only to agricultural areas but to cities—Belém, Salvador, Recife, Rio de Janeiro, and São Paulo, where they started up retail shops and engaged in commerce. Despite the high proportion of unskilled agricultural laborers among them, Spaniards rose rapidly in social and economic status. Initially, they were the most endogamous group of immigrants, but intermarriage caused a rapid loss of ethnic identity and individuality by the 1930s.[1] Over 4,000 more came between 1931 and 1936, expatriates from the growing conflict in Republican Spain. Thousands of Latvians, many of them Baptists fleeing religious persecution, came to Brazil as early as the 1850s and as late as the 1920s. While editors, politicians, and officials of the period favored "whitening" the Brazilian racial stock through an infusion of Caucasian blood, preferably from northern Europe, most of the newcomers were from the lands of the Mediterranean. This disappointed eugenics-minded intellectuals, who preferred "Nordics," then "Alpine" peoples, and only then the swarthy-skinned peasants from southern Italy, the Algarve, Galicia, the Canary Islands, Madeira, and the territories of the Ottoman Empire and Japan, who arrived in steerage from across the seas.

Swiss and German colonists who arrived throughout the nineteenth century and settled mainly in the South tended to stay within their own communities, which were German-speaking until the late 1930s, when Getúlio Vargas imposed his dictatorship and closed foreign-language schools and newspapers. More than 140,000 Poles, as well as smaller numbers of Ukrainians, came to Paraná and Santa Catarina; they tended to stay close to the agricultural lands on which they settled. All the Central and East Europeans remained insular, regarding the Brazilians as their inferiors. So did the large number of Japanese, who also came to the South, until the postwar years. Italians, many of whom went back and forth to Italy as seasonal agricultural laborers, followed two different paths. Some remained in southern agricultural areas, while others migrated to the large cities. Life was not easy for those who sought to stay. The first Italian *colonos* in São Caetano do Sul in the province of São Paulo, for example, were settlers on bog-like land saturated with mosquitoes, considered pestilential even before the connection between insects and disease was known scientifically.

Those who remained in rural communities formed tightly knit self-interest groups, to protect the weakest among themselves and to benefit from shared expertise. Spaniards followed suit, although, as in the case of the Italians, a certain number settled in the cities, where they worked in industry and became Brazil's first factory workers (and syndicalists). Portuguese immigrants, mostly retail sellers, went to towns and cities. So did Syrio-Lebanese, and Sephardic and Eastern (Ashkenazic) Jews, who started out as peddlers and who later became merchants and retail entrepreneurs. Common to all the immigrant groups was the enormous success some of the immigrants (and their children) achieved financially: notably the Jafets, Simonsens, Klabins, Sterns, and the family of Count Francisco Matarazzo, the wealthiest man in Brazil. Wealthy immigrants rarely suffered discrimination. Some children of immigrants married into old traditional families and produced very Brazilian offspring with foreign-sounding names: Felinto Müller, Vargas's police chief; and Fernando Collor de Mello's grandfather, Lindolfo. Immigrants and the children of immigrants also did well in the professions, especially medicine and architecture, and the post-1970 generation saw a host of Brazilians with non-Portuguese ethnic backgrounds (Jaime Lerner, Paulo Maluf, Celso Lafer) succeed in the public arena. Still, three of Brazil's four billionaires during the early 1990s were from "traditional" families; the fourth, Edmundo Safra of the Republic Bank, a Sephardic Jew from Alleppo, made his fortune in the United States and in Europe, although he remained a Brazilian citizen.

The tendency, nonetheless, was to preserve the "outsider" label for even the most successful immigrants and their descendants. The exceptions occurred when unusually successful individuals married into the traditional Portuguese elite, especially when families needed an infusion of wealth. Brazil, lacking a tradition of public education, despite its emphasis since the 1960s on civic education, has never endorsed the melting-pot myth so significant in the United States after the First World War. Brazilian culture, more like that of Canada, preserves ethnic identity: a person even in the third or fourth generation is an Arab, a Japanese, a Jew, or a Portuguese; this identity is always in the open, and alluded to, even though immigrant-descended members of the "new" upper classes have not been barred from social clubs or from high-level employment, as they have been in many other Latin American countries. What is telling about Brazil's experiences with immigrants, however, is that for the most part immigrants have not followed the path taken elsewhere, especially in the United States, where individuals restricted by exclusionary barriers have formed interest groups to fight for acceptance and change. The explanation may be that outsiders in Brazil either have understood that the barriers were insurmountable or have been placated by the live-and-let-live sense of interpersonal relations. In any case, Brazil has never had a National Association for the Advancement of Colored People (NAACP) or an Anti-Defamation League (ADL). In addition, some outsiders sought to align themselves with persons and groups sharing the same extrinsic reference points used to discriminate against them.

Non-European immigrants have fared the poorest. West Indians, mostly from overcrowded Barbados, were brought to work on the Madeira-Mamoré Railroad on the Bolivian border, between 1907 and 1912, with tragic consequences for many of the laborers, who died of disease; the remainder settled in the jungle, or in Porto Velho in the present-day state of Rondônia. In recent times, new groups of immigrants, many of them illegal aliens, have come to Brazil to work. Thousands of Bolivians have taken up residence in the shabby old industrial zone of Pari, near the center of São Paulo, where they work in sweatshop-like clothing factories owned by Koreans, themselves immigrants sometimes as recently as three years earlier. The finished merchandise is sold in specialty shops and shopping centers throughout the city, at a very high markup. The Bolivians, for their work, receive an average of $100 per month for sixteen-hour days, the wages calculated on the basis of how many items they finish. Some Brazilians have worked in this industry as well, but like the Bolivians they have had no papers. As a result, they have had no protection, sharing the ages-old dilemma of the immigrant. To be sure, the newcomers have found ways to cope. Some of the Korean factory owners say that the Bolivians no longer want to work for them: that there is a "Bolivian Mafia" pressuring their countrymen to refuse jobs.

Beginning in 1990, the Rio de Janeiro branch of Caritas, the international Catholic relief agency funded by the United Nations Commission on Refugees, has been sponsoring the arrival of refugees from African nations. Seven hundred Angolans arrived during the first few months of 1993; they continue arriving at a rate of ten per day. Their first impressions were not good ones: they were forced into old hotels or into housing on unpleasant streets in seedy Lapa or near the Sambadrome's warehouse district. Suspected of having acquired immune deficiency syndrome (AIDS), the refugees have been regularly cursed at in public. Shots have been fired at them for conversing loudly in the street. Because these Africans have been unable to work and dependent on international charity, their bad reception has pointed out the harsh realities faced by unwanted immigrants in recession-stricken times.[2]

Outsiders from the Hinterland

The construction of the Transamazon Highway in the 1960s raised alarms throughout the world about the potential destruction of the rainforest. Denying that this could possibly occur, government officials poured resources into developing the vast frontier region, inviting in land developers, multinational agribusiness, and other interests; and upgrading the presence of armed forces personnel. Planners announced an impressive-sounding scheme for planned growth along the long highway, calling for three kinds of residential communities based on the concept of "rural urbanism." The smallest unit would be the *agrovila,* a small urban center inhabited by workers engaged in farming and ranching, designed to provide social integration of rural inhabitants and decent living conditions. *Agrovilas* were intended to have primary schools, kindergartens, and day nurseries; small administrative and medical-sanitary centers, gardens, playgrounds, and other recreational facilities; and churches (presumably Roman Catholic). The *agrovilas* would be scattered around the radius of a single *agrópolis,* a small urban agro-industrial, cultural, and administrative center, extending over an area of about six miles and serving from eight to ten agrovilas around it. Beyond this would be the *rurópolis,* the center of an area including *agrovilas* and more than one *agrópolis,* extending up to seventy-five miles depending on topographical, hydrographic, and other conditions. The *rurópolis* centers would provide at least 20,000 residents with full urban services.

Nothing came of the plans. Funds channeled for the construction of these communities were diverted or never appropriated in the first place. Rapid urban development along the frontier did occur, but in unplanned, helter-skelter fashion—rife with vice, corruption, intimidation of the weak by the strong, and general lawlessness. The isolation of small Brazilian towns and villages, even on the coast, was traditionally so complete in some ways that anthropologists found that residents had no way of knowing that they were living in poverty without traveling to the outside. In Santa Isabel, in Amazonas state, visitors in 1975 noticed that women would sometimes disappear for part of the day without explanation. It turned out that they were washing and drying their one item of clothing, and therefore had to wait inside their shacks so as not to be seen naked. In the coastal Bahian town of Arembepe, external social patterns, including class-based distinctions, did not penetrate before the 1960s. Residents who did leave to visit Salvador (for activities ranging from seeking jobs to visiting prostitutes to buying supplies), often remarked on the rudeness of city folk, because in the capital the village egalitarian ethic did not prevail. For the first time in their lives, the villagers found themselves looked down upon and mocked for their way of speaking, their coarse clothing, and their naivete. They had been unaware of Brazilian norms of behavior, and they were ridiculed for their ignorance. Rural folk tended to be superstitious. Their diet was limited by taboos against mixing kinds of food. Some of these taboos came from Portugal; others were practiced by indigenous tribes. Drinking water after eating watermelon caused fever, one taboo went; others prohibited drinking cold water when eating hot bread, or after eating spicy foods. Bathing retards digestion, it was commonly said; never wash after consuming a dish of *sarapatel* (an African dish made with tripe) or *mocotó,* people believed.

Radio penetrated the rural hinterland during the late 1930s, when government spokesmen, starting in 1934, addressed the nation nightly on the *Hora do Brasil.* The full impact of nationwide communications, however, did not come until the end of the 1960s. In 1967, a study of several rural municipalities in the state of Rio Grande do Sul found that about half the residents listened to the radio at least once per week, although almost no one listened to the radio every day. Very few houses had electricity, and most workers could not afford batteries even if they had portable sets. Not a single resident surveyed had ever read a newspaper—most were illiterate—and only about half ever received any mail.[3] By 1970, however, the year in which Brazil inaugurated its first nationwide television hookup by satellite in time for the World Cup championship—a poll in the tiny town of Lajedo, in Pernambuco's eastern *agreste* zone near Garanhuns, found that 100 percent of the residents listened to the radio, often up to six hours a day. Men watched little television—presumably they were working most of the day—but a high percentage of the young women surveyed watched *telenovelas,* musical shows, and variety programs, usually in someone else's house because very few families owned television sets. The same pattern characterized newspaper reading: far more females than males read, but few men asked women for their political opinions.

Women

According to the widespread pattern of the Brazilian patriarchal family, a woman was obliged to be submissive, was dominated by a powerful husband who was seemingly more interested sexually in his black slave mistresses than in his wife, and was relegated to the home and to raising her children. John Luccock, a visiting British merchant in 1808, described upper-class women as corpulent; ill-tempered; indolent; and, by age twenty-five or thirty, wrinkled and old.[4] A Portuguese proverb said that virtuous women of good families left their homes three times during their lives: when they were baptized, married, and buried. This was not true, but most women in the upper class did have to cope with very restrictive lives. The freest of women were widows, who often ran their family's businesses or plantations; other single women entered convents, where they had both privacy and freedom to engage in business activities.

Women when they married passed from their fathers' domination to their husbands'. Daughters needed parental permission to marry; sons who graduated from law or medical school did not. Women could not hold property in their own name. They rarely engaged in commerce; they had to be closely chaperoned. Even when their husbands died, widows did not have a male's legal rights over their estate. Girls received much less rigorous education than boys. When upper-class girls were able to go to good schools, they left early to marry, often at thirteen or fourteen. In 1827, a law permitted females to attend elementary school but not any higher level. The result was that women were almost twice as likely to be illiterate as men were. Only 11.5 percent of females in 1872, at the time of the first national census, were listed as being able to read and write, a lower proportion than for males. Out of a total population exceeding 10 million, only 46,246 girls were in school in 1873. The "best" families employed private tutors, but these were relatively rare. To be sure, as time passed women may have been more involved in social changes and economic opportunities than we know, because traditional histories overlooked them. Still, well into the twentieth century, women played mainly subordinate roles to men.

In the countryside, women always faced far more restrictions than men, but the rural code placing survival first sometimes permitted women, out of economic necessity or when no males were present, to perform tasks normally forbidden to them. So women herded cattle alongside their fathers, or worked as carpenters or bricklayers, when there were not enough brothers to go around. One sociologist found a greater incidence of indifference to socialized roles in the rural hinterland than the norm. The freedom to work, nonetheless, did not extend to other realms. Young single women still were heavily restricted in their social contacts; once married, women were subject to traditional restrictions, although they shared decision making with their husbands; as widows or as wives abandoned by their husbands, many of the limitations imposed on single women were resumed, forcing them to rely on their family networks to survive.[5]

Much of Brazil's early industrial labor force was made of women, weaving and spinning for manufacturers whose nineteenth-century small-scale operations resembled what one economic historian has termed "proto-in-dustrialization." After the decline of gold production in Minas Gerais, a market developed for cheap manufactured fabric, mostly cotton, to be used for sacking and to clothe slaves. Nearly 60 percent of all female members of the work force, free as well as, in some cases, slave, in the first third of the nineteenth century in Minas Gerais, as well as large numbers of women in Maranhão, Bahia, Sergipe, and even Mato Grosso, were employed weaving and spinning this kind of cloth, which undersold imported English goods because of high transportation costs. From 150,000 to 200,000 women worked in this trade. It created brisk interprovincial commerce in cotton goods, and, during the period of the American Civil War, led to substantial exports of the cloth. By the 1870s, however, this formerly energetic cottage industry had entered a steady decline. It simply could not compete with mechanized large-scale textile factories, Brazilian or foreign. The reliance on women workers in fact may explain the reluctance of the proprietors of these small mills to seek capital to expand their production. Cultural norms hindered the producers from visualizing a modern factory industry based on a female work force. Most of the merchants and entrepreneurs in the zone where this industry had taken root, moreover, were slave owners. Their reliance on docile women workers whom they mistrusted and never were able to see as autonomous, more productive workers (the way they envi-sioned immigrants to be), severely limited their vision and reinforced the preconditions for the disappearance of this once-thriving activity.[6]

Females of all social classes were held back by archaic laws imposed during the colonial era. Victims of sexual abuse were often blamed for their predicament. Misogyny was so widespread that it became taken for granted. During the nineteenth century, when monarchy reigned, women of the upper classes had played decorative roles; those in the lower classes had served. The exclusion of women was not required under the nineteenth-cen-tury political system, because society believed in family values and because those values, reinforced by the Roman Catholic Church, were never ques-tioned. Women were admitted to most legal rights of civil society, but well into the twentieth century married women could not have bank accounts of their own; nor could they travel with their children abroad without the written and notarized signatures of their husbands. Women were excluded from voting until the 1930s and even then were not taken seriously by politicians, who believed that their place was in the home. Physical abuse by husbands or other sexual partners was almost never punished by the judicial system.[7] Men who raped young girls were regularly condemned by court decree to marry the girls to protect their honor.

Women who were raped as virgins or minors could sue for damages only if their assailants refused to marry them. Thousands of women were murdered in unpunished "crimes of passion" by husbands, lovers, fiancés, fathers, or brothers who believed that the victim had committed adultery or other sexual improprieties. After 1940, the Vargas government, claiming to protect and elevate women, issued a large number of new laws and policies regulating marriage, family life, reproduction, and employment, all effectively subordinating women's individual interests to the collectivity.[8] Nevertheless, Brazilian women until the 1970s were not allowed to travel abroad without their husbands' written permission or to open bank accounts in their own names. Among the elite, most women did not pursue careers, although individual Brazilian women have achieved higher and more important high administrative positions than women in most countries in the world. Nor was the elite as intolerant as, say, the American upper class up to at least the Second World War. An example was Maria Carlota (Lota) Constellat de Macedo Soares, who was born in Paris and educated in convents, and who, as an adult, was the sexual partner of the American poet Elizabeth Bishop, among other women. Lota had indefatigable energy, and personally supervised the building of the splendid Rio de Janeiro's Flamengo landscaped highway bypass *(aterro)* for Governor Carlos Lacerda, a monumental undertaking in urban redesign.

Brazilian women—especially underprivileged women—remained outsiders within national culture. We do not know as much as we might about women in evolving Brazilian society because until recently few have studied Brazilian women's history. Anthropologists have studied the household-family unit for decades, but economists have not. Women form a vital part of extended-family groupings, sometimes working inside the home but more often than not working outside as well. Family work patterns in Brazil have long been influenced by the fact that most middle- and upper-class women in Brazil have always had maids. In recent years, then, given changing attitudes and economic conditions, this has made it easier for skilled females (their mistresses) to work in the formal economy. Women who migrate also have very different experiences from those of men, since they invariably have to take care of their families under difficult circumstances. Their daunting responsibilities in rearing and educating their children as well as contributing to family income, usually in unregulated (and therefore unprotected) ways, have caused hardships even greater than those faced by men who migrate in search of improved lives.

Traditionally, Brazil's strongest cultural identities have been those of men. *Gaúchos,* for example, like their counterparts in Uruguay and Argentina, have been aggrandized by a masculine folkloric identity: violent, equestrian, based on honor and on segregation from women on cattle ranches. Gender and culture are inseparable in traditional *gaúcho* life; male avoidance of women parallels romantic fantasies about female seduction of men. Women have lived in small settlements bordering ranches, devoting themselves to raising children, gardening, healing, and magic. Achieving any semblance of equality in this culture was virtually impossible, especially given the acceptance of the *gaúcho* identity as part of the national myth, especially in urban centers in Rio Grande do Sul and in other points south. Even so, there were a tiny number of exceptions to the conditions that wasted women's lives. One was Nísia Floresta Brasileira Augusta, from Rio Grande do Norte (b. 1809). She was forced by her father to marry when she was a girl, but she abandoned her husband; she journeyed to Olinda, in Pernambuco, where she took up with a lover. He died when she was twenty-four, and she found herself in the far South, in Porto Alegre, with two children and a mother to support. Like some later feminists and other Brazilian women, she became a schoolteacher, opening a school in Rio de Janeiro that survived seventeen years. In 1832, she translated Mary Wollstonecraft's *A Vindication of the Rights of Women* into Portuguese.

In conservative Minas Gerais after the turn of the twentieth century, the Roman Catholic hierarchy, seeking to establish its authority over the religious system and to accommodate local beliefs and traditions to orthodox Roman Catholic values, reached out to women, setting up lay associations under the strict guidance of a priest, to use the women as teachers of moral values. Women, otherwise ignored by the Church, were considered the Church's sole hope against the deterioration of family values. They were employed as catechism teachers, lay social workers, and religious role models.

Immigrant families by and large relegated their women to the same subservient roles as traditional families of Portuguese origin. Families, during the pioneer days of Italian *colono* families in Rio Grande do Sul before 1930, were likened by an anthropologist to "small islands in the forest, where the father reigned." Families lived in virtual isolation, and contacts with the outside, mostly through the market, were restricted to the male head of the family. Some farms were five or six kilometers from the nearest neighbors. The family served as the sole unit of production and consumption, using the labor of outsiders only in cases of unusual necessity. Women and children respected and obeyed the men without question. In return, men behaved with brutality toward the others, especially their wives, and especially when they expressed the desire to leave their farm to make contact with others.

Today, things have changed substantially in the region. The surge in population has reduced isolation; people are connected to the modern world, and the father's authority has shrunk. Men are still seen as symbolic heads of families, and women are still defined principally as mothers, but in almost every other way relations between men and women have become more equal. Life, however, remains very traditional. Control of land owner-ship and use is still exerted by men. Men and women spend their leisure time separately: among the Italo-Brazilians of the region, on Sundays, men visit sports clubs or bars, while women visit with family members and neighbors. Young women sew and embroider, adding items to their trous-seaus. Curiously, the only area in which men's roles have grown among these descendants of Italian agricultural immigrants is in local Catholicism, where during the 1980s men began to take a more active part in the reli-gious life of their parishes, which had been traditionally relegated to women.[9]

Women in the emerging urban middle class did have opportunities to become teachers. By the turn of the century, enrollment at normal schools for teacher training had become acceptable. For most, becoming a school-teacher meant living without sexual activity. Teachers who married had to leave their jobs and devote themselves to their families; unmarried teachers were kept under constant scrutiny. Women teachers' salaries were low, and always lower than men's. Teaching was considered socially acceptable, and it gave women a chance to leave the house and to work with others. Women also began to enter pharmaceutical careers (men preferred medicine) and nursing. Some gave piano or violin lessons, or did translations. A tiny number became lawyers and physicians. Some women found employment in telegraph offices by the late nineteenth century and as clerks by 1920. This was true mainly in the largest cities, not in the small cities of the coast and the interior. As a result, women seeking to enlarge their horizons set out for the cities of the South, as long as they had family members who could house them and therefore preserve their reputations.

Women lower on the socioeconomic scale did not make advances with-out great difficulty. Black women could hope only to be domestic servants or laundresses, jobs paying barely enough to survive, although black women over the decades were always more likely to be single heads of poor households than were white women.[10] All working-class women's lives were extremely hard. These women received even lower wages than men; they were subject to abuse from employers and overseers; and, if they were married and were permitted to continue working, when they returned home they had to take care of their households. Women during the nineteenth century worked as maids, laundresses, street sellers, cooks, wet nurses, and streetwalkers. Luiza Ferreira de Medeiros recalls starting to work at Rio's Bangu textile factory when she was seven, at the time of the First World War. Work started at 6:00 A.M. and continued to 5:00 P.M., with no set lunch time. The foreman decided whether the workers could eat, depending on how the work was going. Girls starting out were called "apprentices" and received no wages at all. Meals were taken next to the machines; mill hands dressed in clothes called "dried meat" because the fabric was made from cloth with dye stains and broken threads. One faucet over a slimy tub served as both drinking fountain and washbasin. The mill hands came from large families, with between five and sixteen children. The foreman would assign women who resisted his advances to broken machines, or would give them bad thread to hamper their work. They were expected to submit to him at any time in his office, but at the same time he forced them to cover themselves completely, to close their blouses at the neck and at the wrists, and to wear skirts scraping the floor in the name of morality.[11]

In 1945, a decade after women had been legally empowered to vote, nearly twenty women ran for Congress, but none won election. Women working full days at factory jobs still had to take complete care of their households when they returned home, although child care and other domestic tasks were sometimes done by their unemployed mothers, in-laws, or other relatives. Working-class families facing hard economic burdens (having to pay for schoolbooks and uniforms, for example, or for cram courses to prepare for college entrance examinations) often gave preference to male children. As a result, fewer women obtained training in skills leading to higher-paying jobs, so that the women became mired in low-skilled employment at the lowest wages. Studies of wages paid to male and female workers show a continued persistence of the practice of paying women substantially less for the same jobs, even in advanced cities like Rio de Janeiro and São Paulo.[12]

Rural women who left home to find work as domestics received wretched wages but were given room, board, and (often used) clothing. If they were considered sexually attractive, they were at the mercy of males in their patrons' families. Young women from the interior often were sent for to work as maids by men who wanted to give them to their sons to deflower. When pregnancy occurred, the women were usually dismissed and abandoned; not only were they left without support for their children, but they were ostracized if they attempted to return to their homes. Black women continued to work at the same menial activities as had their slave ancestors. They rarely had the opportunity to learn to read and write. Women of all races toiled in factories, sweatshops, and laundries, as well as at home, doing piecework. Seamstresses worked sixteen-hour days, sewing lingerie, slippers, gloves, and dresses. Women in the countryside were completely segregated from men, even at social events. They could not sell goods in markets or stores, or dance, or wear stylish clothing. Unmarried women were continually accompanied, lest their moral standing be compromised. Even urban women lived in virtual seclusion into the twentieth century.[13] Over the generations, the lack of employment opportunities for women, especially those unprotected by their families, pushed many young women into domestic service, where they worked their entire lives as almost slaves, or into prostitution, where they sold the use of their bodies.

Recent decades have seen a small increase in resistance. In the midst of rising labor activity among middle- and lower-class workers, representatives met in 1961 in Rio de Janeiro to form a national association of domestics, the first step toward gaining legal recognition as a trade union. The founders issued a statement *(Manifesto às Patroas),* in which they "stated their rights and duties, as they, the domestics, intended them to be understood." They asked to be considered with "love, respect and understanding within the houses in which we work, being considered members of the family." In return, they pledged "to guard the secrets of the families of which we are considered members."[14]

Meanwhile, however, old patterns of social behavior have not only survived but kept pace with the times. Since the 1960s, every Brazilian city of any size has seen the growth of ornately decorated motels, constructed at highway exits usually on the outskirts of town—places where not only men seeking prostitutes but also couples, married or otherwise, can spend a few hours on heart-shaped beds in rooms with whirlpool baths, mirrors, and television sets equipped with VCRs. These "love motels" are listed (and rated for comfort) in the Guia *Quatro Rodas,* Brazil's equivalent of the Automobile Association of America or Mobil travel guidebooks. They are so popular that on Saturday nights numbers are handed out to those waiting for rooms. Brothels for working-class men, located in cities large and small, charge as little as a dollar for the use of a prostitute for a few minutes. In frontier regions and in the interior, prostitution networks involving teenage girls victimized by pimps and virtually enslaved are the rule. *O Estado de São Paulo* journalist Gilberto Dimenstein spent six months during 1991 following the flow of traffic in girls starting in Belém along the Brasília-Belém highway through the Center-West, visiting Maranhão, the near-empty state of Tocantins, newly created out of political cupidity, and Mato Grosso, ending up in the town of Cuiú-Cuiú on the Amazonian frontier with Peru. He spent his trip interviewing and photographing dozens of girls, most in their early teens, some pregnant or already mothers, many infected with human immunodeficiency virus (HIV) or other diseases. Girls who resist are beaten savagely with belts or electrical cords, gashed with knives, sometimes killed; a popular method is to shoot them in the vagina. In the end Dimenstein observed the liberation of some thirty of these child prostitutes imprisoned in nightclubs in Cuiú-Cuiú, only to admit that most of them, taken by airplane in Belém, had no other way to survive than to sell their bodies again. "Here is a women to be peeled *(ralada),*" shouted one of several prostitutes displaying themselves to potential customers from an open truck cruising through town.[15] Brazil's frontier regions have been heavily populated with migrants from other regions, in recent years including large numbers of single women. For these women, historical social mores have not changed very much. Just as in the early twentieth century, women living in the hinterland were watched closely for behavior considered immoral (that is, personal independence), in contrast to São Paulo, and Rio de Janeiro, and other large cities where a broad range of sexual behavior is tolerated, in places like Rondônia today women who display too much independence, or who are identified as being lesbians, are met with reactions of fear, discomfort, and withdrawal. In other ways, however, life on the frontier, keyed almost exclusively to building, succeeding, and making money, is more forgiving than in places where traditional social patterns endure.[16]

A 1990 study based on data furnished by the federal police concluded that 500,000 girls under the age of eighteen (and as young as ten), or 1 out of every 300 people in the population, worked in Brazil as prostitutes. More and more, prostitution is linked to drug use and addiction, so the number of addicts is spiraling upward as well. Girls enter prostitution in many ways. In northeastern Ceará, for example, girls from interior towns are sent by family members to work as maids in larger cities, where they earn far less than a dollar a day. Many, according to the report prepared by CBIA (the Brazilian Center for Childhood and Adolescence), are brought from the interior for the purpose of serving as the first sexual partner of a son of the head of the family. In the Amazon and the Center-West, girls are taken to truck stops by their parents and sold to truck drivers as "trip companions." Some, dubbed "ants," are used to carry drugs on such trips. When the girls are caught, it is they who are punished by the legal system, not those who sent them. In larger urban centers, girls leave their families in the far-flung, impoverished suburbs and travel to residential neighborhoods or downtown areas of cities, where they get set up in small apartments run by pimps.[17]

All major groups in Brazilian society made absolute gains between 1960 and 1980 in education and wages, but the economic rewards of these gains were not distributed equally. Women continued to suffer relative disadvantage.[18] Women made the most gains in cities. Institutionally, their greatest advances were within the lay structure of the Roman Catholic Church. Women who achieved important positions often were widows, no longer encumbered with the tasks of managing a household. A sociologist found this true for the women taking active roles in Church community associations or in Pentecostal sects, and within the Catholic base communities, neighborhood social action groups founded by progressive clergy influenced by the "liberation theology" movement of the 1960s and 1970s. With the transformation of everyday survival problems into political problems, women have been drawn into positions of leadership. Interestingly, Pentecostalism strongly encourages men to be more present in family life, whereas the Catholic base community groups, made up of three-quarters women, make women more active in the public sphere of politics.

Children

As early as 1838, Rio's police chief announced his intention to take off the streets "the great number of boys who, barely past their infancy, wander the streets acquiring the bad habits of idleness, gambling, etc., preparing themselves for a youth that, far from being advantageous for the state, will on the contrary be harmful, due to the crimes they will probably engage in." His solution was to arrest them and house them in a special space in the House of Correction where they would be taught a trade under prison supervision. The problem was considered so pressing during the First Republic that special police details were sent to deal with it.[19] Abandoned children today come from among the families of the 40 million people who moved from rural to urban areas between 1960 and 1980: usually they are runaways who have been abused, or simply driven from their families. Half of Brazil's 60 million children survive on less than $1 a day, a contingent of children equal to the entire population of Argentina or Colombia.

Legions of children have been deserted by families or by individual women unable to care for them. The estimated numbers of abandoned children on the streets today are so high that they defy belief: 7 million in one case.[20] Until the end of the nineteenth century, some charitable institutions had wooden mechanical devices—called foundling wheels—built into a doorway so that infants could be placed on a seat, which was then swiveled on ball bearings to the inside, thus deposited there anonymously. Today, street children beg for scraps of food and money, defecate on the sidewalks, sniff glue, and fend for themselves.

José, age eighteen, from São Paulo, typifies the plight of the homeless children.[21] His mother left him at Fundação Estadual do Bem Estar do Menor (FEBEM), the state institution for children, when he was small. No one knew his surname; one was given to him. At age ten, he was put to work by FEBEM officials at a cement products factory. When he was first sent to the plant he complained angrily, but after he was accepted by the other boys he resigned himself to work. Like most other children forced to do manual labor, he was expected to give well over forty hours a week and receive only a portion of the minimum wage.[22] He ran away at age fourteen. FEBEM made no apparent effort to find him. He joined the legions of adolescents and preadolescents on the street. José survived not by thievery but by working as a *biscateiro,* doing temporary jobs, usually of a few day's duration. He was hired to sell hot dogs from a cart at stadiums, for example; sometimes he worked as a mechanic's helper. He desperately tried to attend school, although he was much older than most of the other pupils. It was unclear how much longer he could continue to do this, and whether even if he finished school he would be able to get a full-time job because of his stigma as a homeless product of a state institution. In 1991, officials in the Federal District of Brasília announced a plan to remove from the streets the estimated 68,000 homeless children living there, a portion of the 400,000 children living in desperate conditions in Brazil's capital. Many of them had AIDS, the spokesman for the government said, obtained from using contaminated needles to inject narcotics. Official statistics admitted that some of the street children were younger than seven.[23]

Some girls have been shunted into prostitution, sometimes as early as the age of nine. Many northeastern girls were found who had been recruited from rural families with the promise of jobs as cooks or maids in other cities; they were transported to remote areas, particularly in the mining regions of the Amazon. They were trapped into paying for room and board at the nightclubs and bars where they were put to work, and they were forced to pay off their debt through sex. To pay for their freedom girls had to ante up five grams of gold, the currency of the gold mine frontier.

Many other children simply live in the street of their own volition. In Goiânia, police in 1992 reported that more than half of the city's permanent population of homeless teenagers were runaways, some from the city, others from the hinterland and even from other states.[24] Unless they are caught committing a crime, street children are usually ignored. Attitudes have hardened: questioned after the murder of some street children in Rio de Janeiro in 1992, the president of a leading retail store owners' association was quoted as saying: "When you kill a street brat, you're doing society a favor."[25]

In his "pained preface" *(prefácio doloroso)* to Yara Dulce Bandeira de Ataíde's book based on 121 oral histories of Salvador's street children, José Carlos Sebe Bom Meihy links the suffering of the homeless boys and girls to nationwide collective apathy. Brazilians, he observes, sidestep the reality of misery either by declaring it an insolvable problem or treating it as a question of "folklore."[26] Anthropologist Ataíde found that her subjects fell into four groups: children who lived in the street but maintained permanent contact with their families; those with sporadic contact; runaways from broken families; and those permanently abandoned. Children in the first group suffered from the stress of having to support their families economically by not going to school, by skipping their childhoods. The second group consisted of children from families brutalized by alcoholism, drugs, or violence. These children had been rejected by their families, although the children, often more resilient than their parents, strive to maintain contact in spite of being rejected. The third group demonstrated the most severe pathologies: psychoses, addiction, mental retardation, and criminality. The fourth group, hardened delinquents, usually ended up "protected" by older criminals, who used them to commit armed robberies and murders because children under eighteen cannot be prosecuted for criminal acts.

"My father told me," an eleven-year-old boy nicknamed Joca told his informant, "that people who steal deserve to die." He added, "But here [in the street], they say that if you don't steal you will die anyway."[27] Street children, then, are brutalized by a system that expects that they will conform to social stereotypes and commit crimes, even though the children reveal themselves to be sensitive and insightful, not at all the hardened criminals they are painted to be. Some of the street children display an almost moralistic outlook: "All politicians steal," thirteen-year-old Almir observed, "although I like [Governor] Antonio Carlos Magalhães better than Fernando Collor, because Collor runs with thugs, who kill people."[28] Jucélia, about ten years old, remembered how her mentally ill father savagely beat her and her mother, but said, now that she lives on the street alone, she is ashamed of her mother, because although she is homeless and takes care of an infant and another child, she drinks all day. Then she curses, does bad things, and fights with everyone. "I'm ashamed of her, but I still like her," Jucélia concluded, "I only don't like her when she is drunk." Twelve-year-old Zeli claimed, "I hate my stepmother. She is vile, a pestilence, and if I could I'd kill her and cut her into tiny pieces.[29]

It is remarkable that such children, forced to fend for themselves in a heartless system that blames them for their condition, still exhibit feelings of decency and compassion. Eleven-year-old Bolo-fofo, who began to live on the street when he was six, complained that policemen steal from the street children, and said that his friends watch out for one another in solidarity against those trying to take advantage of them. "Love is a beautiful thing," remarked twelve-year-old Gera, one of ten children. "My mother gave it to me, but not my father, who was a *crente* [Fundamentalist Protestant] who beat me until I ran away." Others fantasize: "I want to be a policeman," noted ten-year-old Miro, "because [a policeman] can kill without being jailed." A thirteen-year-old black child named Tito, one of fourteen brothers and sisters, boasts that he "knows that the police will kill me, so I want to kill a thousand first."[30]

A human rights organization blamed police death squads for 57 percent of the murders of children in the city of Salvador. A total of 4,611 children were reported murdered between 1988 and 1990, a form, in the words of a cynic, of "vigilante euthanasia." The National Movement in Behalf of Street Children reported an average of two killings a day in 1993; police in Rio de Janeiro listed 320 children murdered during the first half of the year, part of the 4,000 homicides of all kinds predicted for the year. Hundreds of bodies of street children have been discarded in ditches in Nova Jerusalem, on the outskirts of the city.[31] In Rio in July 1993, gunmen in military police uniforms, members of a self-styled "extermination squad," killed eight homeless boys and wounded two others by cruising through downtown streets in a taxi and private car, spraying a group of forty-five sleeping children in front of the gold-encrusted Candelária Church with machine gun pistols and also killing two more boys sleeping in the gardens of the Museum of Modern Art. The violence was allegedly related to the arrest a few days earlier of a youth for sniffing shoemaker's glue, a narcotic. When his friends stoned a military police car, injuring one policeman, the vigilante squad moved into action.

Protests do little good. Typically, whenever public opinion has responded to one or another outrage of vigilantism, police have reverted to quieter methods, kidnapping street boys, sometimes torturing them, and them dumping their bodies in remote locations. A few citizens' groups (the Center for the Representation of Marginalized Peoples, and Rio's São Martinho Society, a Roman Catholic group) work with street children, but otherwise the system waits until a child is arrested or sequestered or killed before doing anything.[32] Most Brazilians know about these things—vigilantes want their acts to be known, and frequently inform newspaper editors of their deeds—but there has been little sustained outcry. In 1981, plans for a documentary film on this subject were blocked by a legal degree of prohibition; in response, the Argentine film director Hector Babenco bought the rights to a published novel, José Lourenço's *Infância dos Mortos,* using it as the basis for *Pixote,* a fictionalized tale of a ten-year-old boy thrown into an overcrowded reformatory and hardened into a criminal forced to steal, run cocaine, and kill in order to survive. The film's star, Fernando Ramos da Silva, was an angel-faced cherub born in a favela. Babenco himself called the character Pixote "marked," destined for an unhappy life. At the end of the film, a message states that no one will ever be able to save Pixote.[33]

On the outside, life imitated art. Fernando Ramos da Silva, the boy actor, earned worldwide acclaim but then quickly returned to a life of impoverishment. He had a second chance in films and television, but ended up being killed by the police. Officially he was shot while participating in a robbery, although Caco Barcellos, an investigative reporter whose allegations of police brutality and lawlessness forced him to flee Brazil, claims in his book on the elite São Paulo Rota 66 police vigilante squad that Fernando, resented for the fame he had achieved, was dragged out from under a bed; after he cried "For the love of God, don't kill me; I have a child to raise," they shot him seven or eight times. They then fired their guns into the walls to make it look like there had been a gunfight.[34]

Homosexuals

Openly homosexual men and women have been outsiders in most societies. In Brazil, homosexuals have fared badly in formal society, although urban elites, especially in the late twentieth century, have demonstrated a degree of toleration not only for homosexual but also for bisexual behavior, not unlike that shown in Western Europe. Gays have played major roles in the evolution of *macumba* spiritism and, especially, in Brazilian Carnival. Persecution of transvestites, however, during the military regime and to some extent after, has led thousands of gays and transvestites to flee to Europe. French officials, claiming that 10,000 Brazilian transvestites had taken up residence in Paris, obliged Brazilians to have a visa to enter France, the only member of the European Community to require this.

Within Brazil, attitudes toward homosexuality have changed in recent decades, although mostly among the well-educated. There is less tolerance for homosexuals who display their sexuality publicly, especially in attention-catching ways, than for those who live quietly. Brazilian gays claim that their country has the largest number of public transvestites in the world, and that, as a result of permissiveness about extralegal violence, one homosexual has been murdered every five days, for a total of as many as 2,400 killings since 1980, with only 10 percent of the cases leading to arrests.[35] In late 1993, a São Paulo grand jury was called to hear the case against former police officer Cirineu Carlos Laetang da Silva, not because of charges that he had murdered at least eight transvestites but because he had been involved in a savage police massacre at the Carandiru penitentiary earlier.

Movements in defense of gay and lesbian rights have emerged in Brazil, but on the whole cautiously. Efforts by gay students to protest have led on occasion to violence, as occurred in Rio de Janeiro in November 1993 when a group of fifty youths between the ages of fifteen and seventeen physically attacked a march by gay students protesting their expulsion from a pre-vestibular course in Tijuca, and burned the marchers' banners. On the whole, mainstream Brazilian youth have continued to reject the timid demands of gay groups for recognition, just as most educated Brazilians have remained hostile to feminist discourse and demands for women's rights. Urban gangs and skinheads have made gays special targets, often without public criticism. Some journalists reporting on gang activity have seemed to be as much amused by clever gang names (VASP, for example, the acronym of a Brazilian airline but also "Vagabundos Anónimos Sustentados pelo País," and FF "Fugitivos da FEBEM") as moved to condemn their excesses—in this case, violent gang invasions of public schools in impoverished neighborhoods in Belém, the capital of the state of Pará.[36] Gays claimed that more than 2,400 homosexuals were known to have been murdered in Brazil since the early 1980s. Intellectuals have tended to be sympathetic to complaints from gay spokesmen, but an attitude of stark intolerance has pervaded most of the rest of Brazilian society.

The Native Population

Brazil's indigenous inhabitants have suffered more than any other ethnic or racial group. At first, the native population—hunters and gatherers, not farmers like the Incas or Aztecs—peacefully traded red dyewood and foodstuffs to the Portuguese in exchange for trinkets. Soon, however, the Portuguese began to enslave them, and the Indians responded by attacking and burning Portuguese settlements. Decimated by Old World diseases, the surviving Indians were driven into the interior. The trauma eventually reduced the Indian population as drastically as the reduction that had occurred in the Caribbean islands.[37] During the twentieth century, Indians were betrayed and mistreated by the federal agency—the Indian Protection Service—that was created to shield them. In spite of patronizing efforts by intellectuals during the nineteenth and early twentieth centuries to idealize them as noble savages, Indians were rejected by mainstream Brazilian culture. The Brazilian equivalent for the expression "a waste of time" is "an Indian thing." In Brazil as everywhere else in the Western Hemisphere, most of the aboriginal population has died out, with the remnants living on shrinking government reservations. Their best lands have been deforested or taken from them, and they are scourged by epidemic disease, poverty, and psychological depression.

Mistreatment has often taken the form of murder. One such incident occurred in mid-1993, when renegade *garimpeiros* (prospectors) from Hoximú, Roraima, guided by mercenary Yanomamo trackers, killed dozens of Yanomamos in the remote Venezuelan village of Hashimo-teri, across the border; their heinous acts included the decapitations of Indian children with machete blows. This was the worst documented massacre in the region since 1910. Adults were killed by machine-gun fire after they were tricked by the miners with promises of food. Local officials prevaricated, although in October a Brazilian federal police inspector announced that twenty-three Brazilians would be tried for the massacre. Leading local opposition to any prosecution has been the Roman Catholic Salesian missionary order. Their presence goes back to 1915, when the Brazilian government granted them extensive secular authorities. A visiting anthropologist in 1993 claimed that the Salesians lure Indians to their missions, which have a death rate from disease four times the rate found in remote villages. Striving to subdue media attention, the Salesians reportedly have squelched news of *garimpeiro* atrocities lest their privileged position be threatened.[38]

The National Indian Foundation (FUNAI), a government agency, estimates that in all Amazônia at least 40 percent of the indigenous population are chronic alcoholics. Nearly three-quarters suffer from anemia. Mothers, when their children come down with dysentery, tuberculosis, or any of the many other ailments endemic to the reservation, become listless, sometimes failing to seek medical treatment at the Presbyterian-run hospital.[39] As far as the Kaiowá are concerned, in 1990 it was reported in the national press that conditions of psychological depression among the Kaiowá were driving a disproportionately high number of tribe members, particularly young men, to suicide by hanging. At least eighty-eight suicides occurred on the reservation between 1986 and 1993, among a total of 247 Guarani-Kaiowá families living in the Jarara indigenous area. Alcohol, technically prohibited from being sold in the Indian village, was widely used, and FUNAI officials did nothing either to intervene in the liquor sales or to investigate the mental health of the residents.[40]

Marcos Veron's story embodies the Kaiowá's misfortune. Veron is the owner of a small plot of land that he shares with his two married sons; the land is insufficient even for subsistence cultivation. There are only three tractors to be shared with the entire community. Veron and his sons have had to work at part-time jobs on soybean and sugar cane plantations in the region, even though such employers always pay lower wages to Indians. The Kaiowá have lost their ancient arts of constructing houses of *sapé*; instead, they live in sordid shacks made of wood. A neighbor, Laurentino Rodrigues, age thirty-eight, born and raised on the reservation, blames the tribal chiefs for failing to help solve the problems of chronic alcoholism.[41]

Ireno Isnard, one of the elders of the tribe at almost ninety-three years of age, a man of calm and lucidity, gave his life story to a team headed by José Carlos Sebe Bom Meihy:

I am the son of the oldest family among our people. . . . I have always
lived here on the reservation, with our people and other peoples: the Guarani,
and the Jaguapiru. . . . Our people suffered much in the Paraguayan War. . . .
With the arrival of the first farmers, the Indians began to develop tastes for
new things: salt, coffee, meat, soap; good things, no? There were only a few
farmers, and we got along well with them. . . . They gave us things we
needed. . . . But the whites also brought with them many problems . . . not
only good things. . . . General Rondón told us that we needed to learn the
white man's language to be able to defend ourselves. . . . He told me not to
let the whites take our land. . . . What happened was that the land became
subdivided again and again; children inherited less and less. Before, we loved
life . . . we told stories, sang, joked, danced. . . . We thank God for giving us
the land. . . . Now there are too many whites here . . . even in the Indian
village . . . too many whites . . . we are surrounded by them . . . they don't
respect us, and are always cursing us. . . . I have two living sons and two who
died, one from disease before the Mission was established. The other was
knifed to death. . . . We do not fear death . . . there is a place for us to go, a
path selected for us by God. . . . As long as the world does not end, people
die here but they do not go to the next world. . . . The next world is a good
one, and we are waiting for it to come. . . . [42]

Outsiders' Fate

Brazil's entrenched and resilient social structure and its seeming im-
penetrability despite modernizing change in virtually every phase of everyday life have produced gross inequities. Fifty-five percent of the inhabitants
of the vast Northeast lived below Brazil's poverty line, $110 a month, in
1993. Fifteen percent of the entire country lives in acute misery. In November 1992, a United Nations report placed Brazil in the same category as Sri
Lanka, Zambia, Mali, and Kenya as places where rural poverty had grown
over the last twenty years. Brazil, with 73 percent of its rural population in
poverty, ranked behind only Peru and Bolivia in Latin America. Urban
poverty is worst along the Rio de Janeiro–São Paulo axis, the most prosperous industrial zone in Brazil. Half of Brazil's adolescents live in poverty;
the homes of 56 percent of children and adolescents lack toilets, 38 percent
have no electricity, and only 34 percent have running water.

Perverse "solutions" have sprouted out of circumstantial realities. The
majority of the 150,000 residents of the favelas of Lixão, Vila Ideal, and
Vila Cruz in Rio de Janeiro's Baixada Fluminense live on the refuse
dumped here from Rio de Janeiro supermarkets. The Lixão favela ("Moun-
tain of Garbage") has for some time attempted to change its name to Vila
Nova, but the stench as well as the tradition of the unofficial name has
stuck. Shacks in the favela, holding an average of eight or nine people, are
usually constructed of plastered cement block subdivided with cardboard.

An open sewage canal flows through the favela exactly where children play.[43]

In spite of the diversity of Brazil's population, then, and in spite of a national self-image that acknowledges the continual role played by outsiders in its history, insiders have always controlled, and for the most part still do control, access to influence and privilege. Chapter 4 examines politics and the spoils system, the vehicle through which institutional control has been maintained for decades. Chapter 6 examines some of the aggressive ways in which some groups have attempted to free themselves from despair; one of them is suicide, which is almost endemic on Indian reservations.

In spite of Brazil's historical insularity, its elite has always shown less rigidity than, say, its peers among its Spanish-speaking neighbors. That a José Maria Whitaker (who did not know a word of English) could rise to the post of finance minister during the 1930s, or a Juscelino Kubitschek could become president in the late 1950s, demonstrates that mobility into the elite has always been possible. Brazilians have fewer disparaging words in their vocabulary for blacks than Americans do (although words for blackness are sometimes used as insults), and none at all for Jews. The term *turco* for Arab was never explicitly pejorative, and was applied rather indiscriminately to Greeks and Sephardic Jews as well as to Christian and Muslim Arabs. Racial discrimination, then, is not ingrained in Brazilian culture the way it is in Europe and North America. Outsiders are outsiders in Brazil, but the live-and-let-live atmosphere gives them access to the mainstream.

Notes

1. Herbert S. Klein, "La Integración Social y Económica de los Inmigrantes Españoles en Brasil," *Revista de História Económica* 7:2 (1989), 438–57.

2. *Veja Rio* 26:18 (5 May 1993), 16–17.

3. Laudelino T. Medeiros, *O Peão de Estância: Um Tipo de Trabalhador Rural* (Pôrto Alegre: Estudos e Trabalhos Mimeografados No. 8, 1967), 27–29.

4. John Luccock, *Notes on Rio de Janeiro and the Southern Parts of Brazil Taken During a Residence of Ten Years . . . 1808–1818* (London: S. Leigh, 1820), 112–13, cited by June E. Hahner, *Emancipating the Female Sex: The Struggle for Women's Rights in Brazil, 1850–1940* (Durham: Duke University Press, 1990), 1, 3.

5. Lia Freitas Garcia Fukui, *Sertão e Bairro Rural* (São Paulo: Editora Ática, 1979), 230–31.

6. Douglas Libby, "Proto-Industrialization and Nineteenth-Century Economic Development in Minas Gerais: Why Didn't It Work?" Paper presented to the Brazilian Studies Committee, American Historical Association, Washington, DC, 27 December 1992.

7. See Marlise Vinagre Silva, *Violência contra a Mulher: Quem Mete a Colher?* (São Paulo: Cortez Editora, 1992).

8. See Susan K. Besse, "Crimes of Passion," *Journal of Social History* 22:4 (Summer 1989), 653–65.

9. Ineke van Halsema, *Housewives in the Field: Power, Culture and Gender in a South-Brazilian Village* (Amsterdam: CEDLA, 1991), 47, 66, 103–05.

10. L.E. Oliveira et al., *O Lugar do Negro na Força do Trabalho* (Rio de Janeiro: Instituto Brasileiro de Geografia e Estatística, 1985).

11. Luiza Ferreira de Medeiros, interview, 1970, cited by J.E. Hahner, *Emancipating the Female Sex,* 220–21. On labor legislation concerning mothers, see Eliane Moura da Silva, "Trabalhadora Normalizada: Mãe, Esposa e Dona-de-Casa Reguladas," *História* 5–6 (1986–87), 35–46.

12. Helen I. Safa, "Women, Production and Reproduction in Industrial Capitalism: A Comparison of Brazilian and U.S. Factory Workers," ms., University of Florida Institute for Latin American Studies, Gainesville: c. 1980, 8–18; Leticia Borges Costa, "Mulher e Trabalho: Considerações e Perguntas Suscitadas pela Comparação dos Resultados dos Dois Últimos Censos," ms., Ford Foundation, Rio de Janeiro. Both sources in Land Tenure Center Library, University of Wisconsin.

13. J.E. Hahner, *Emancipating the Female Sex,* 82–84.

14. Sandra Lauderdale Graham, *House and Street: The Domestic World of Servants and Masters in Nineteenth-Century Rio de Janeiro,* paperback edition (Austin: University of Texas Press, 1992), 137, citing *O Estado de São Paulo* and *Correio da Manhã,* both 4 February 1961.

15. Gilberto Dimenstein, *Meninas da Noite,* 5th ed. (São Paulo: Ed. Ática, 1992).

16. Nana Mendonça, "International Lesbianism," in *Feminist Review* 34 (Spring 1990), 8–11.

17. Gilberto Dimenstein, "Brasil Tem 500 Mil Menores Prostitutas," *Folha de São Paulo,* 25 October 1990, C1.

18. Peggy A. Lovell, "Race, Gender, and Development in Brazil," *Latin American Research Review* 29:3 (1994), 7–36, esp. 30.

19. Thomas H. Holloway, *Policing Rio de Janeiro: Repression and Resistance in a 19th-Century City* (Stanford: Stanford University Press, 1993), 133–34. See also Luiz Roberto Netto, "Por Debaixo dos Panos: A Máquina Policial e o Problema da Infância Desvalida na Cidade de São Paulo, 1910–1930," *Revista Brasileira de História* 9:17 (1989), 129–41.

20. Margaret Keck, "Equity and Justice Issues in Contemporary Brazil," *Inter-American Dialogue: Brazil in a New World* (Washington, DC: Aspen Institute, June 1993), 28–34, 31.

21. Cláudia Pereira Vianna and Dirce Spedo Rodrigues, eds., *Eu, Ex-Menor Abandonado* (São Paulo: Edicões Loyola, 1989).

22. See Fundação Centro Brasileiro, *Perfil de Crianças e dos Adolescentes na Cidade de São Paulo* (São Paulo: Fundação Centro Brasileiro, 1993).

23. See, for example, *Miséria Urbana: Uma Radiografia da Região Metropolitana do Recife* (Recife: ETAPAS, 1991), 103.

24. Grácia M. Fenelon, et al., *Meninas de Rua: Uma Vida em Movimento* (Goiânia: Universidade Federal de Golás, 1992), 45–49.

25. Sam Dillon, "Suffer the Children," *Miami Herald Tropic,* 5 January 1992, 12.

26. José Carlos Sebe Bom Meihy, Preface to Yara Dulce Bandeira de Ataíde, *Decifra-me ou Devoro-te: História Oral da Vida dos Meninos de Rua de Salvador* (São Paulo: Edições Loyola, 1993), 11.

27. Y. Bandeira de Ataíde, *Decifra-me,* 36.

28. Ibid., 47.

29. Ibid., 133.

30. Ibid., 52, 55, 71, 87, 115.

31. John Krich, *Why Is This Country Dancing?* (New York: Simon and Schuster, 1993), 96; Gilberto Dimenstein, *Brazil: War on Children* (London: Latin American Bureau, 1991), 71; Alma Guillermoprieto, "Obsessed in Rio," *New Yorker,* 16 August 1993, 44.

32. *New York Times,* 24 July 1993, 3.

33. See George Csicsery, "Individual Solutions: An Interview with Hector Babenco," *Film Quarterly,* 36:1 (Fall 1982), 7–8.

34. Caco Barcellos, *Rota 66: A História da Polícia que Mata* (São Paulo: Globo, 1992), 238–41.

35. Luiz Mott of the Gay Group of Bahia, quoted in *New York Times,* 12 August 1993, A4.

36. Abnor Gondim, "Cem Gangues se Enfrentam," *Folha de São Paulo,* 27 October 1993, 4. VASP was one of Brazil's leading airlines in the 1980s, although it fell on hard times thereafter.

37. Richard Boulind, in *The Cambridge Encyclopedia of Latin America and the Caribbean,* 2nd ed. (Cambridge: Cambridge University Press, 1992), 195–96.

38. *New York Times,* 23 October 1993, A13; 21 August 1993, 3.

39. Altair Thury, "Caiuá Luta pela Sobrevivência," *Jornal do Brasil,* 19 January 1992, 1, 15; Anastácio F. Morgado, "Epidemia de Suicídio entre os Guaraní-Kaiwá" [*sic*], in *Cadernos de Saúde Público: Saúde de Populações Indígenas,* 7:4 (October–December 1991), 585–98.

40. See *Istoé Senhor,* 24 October 1990, 1 September 1991, 43; Rainforest Action Network, information: www.wideopen.igc.org, 25 October 1996.

41. Altair Thury, in *Jornal do Brasil,* 19 January 1992, 1, 15.

42. José Carlos Sebe Bom Meihy, *Canto de Morte Kaiowá* (São Paulo: Edições Loyola, 1991), paraphrased from transcript on pp. 39–49.

43. *Folha de São Paulo,* 4 May 1993, n.p. (*Folha de São Paulo* clipping file).

4

The Brazilian Way

During most of the twentieth century, Brazil's political culture diminished the status of citizens. Part of the problem stemmed from the swollen bureaucracy at all levels of government. Everyday life in Brazil necessitated constant interaction with bureaucratic regulations, government officials, public agencies, and other representatives of authority. The system treated individuals differently according to who they were. The poorest Brazilians often were excluded entirely from the system and the social benefits it provided because, as marginals living below the thin safety net provided for salaried workers, they lacked proper papers. This problem was severest during the military dictatorship, when police frequently stopped people randomly and arrested them or beat them if they were found to be without papers. "Without identity documents," a large billboard in downtown Rio near the bus station proclaimed in 1969, "you do not exist." In the interior of the country, patronage politics maintained almost complete control of social and economic exchange.[1]

Ordinary Brazilians living documented lives spent untold time entangled in the bureaucratic labyrinth. Some cases of hopeless dealings stretched out for years. For those who could afford it or who possessed political influence, however, an antidote soon emerged in the person of the *despachante,* a professional facilitator able to cut through red tape. Sometimes bribery was involved, or small favors, but usually *despachantes* simply got things done (for a fee) faster and without hassle because they knew the right people on the inside. Some veteran *despachantes* seemed to have magical powers. Passports for which mere mortals had to wait on line for hours, then return to wait a second, third, or fourth time at the Federal Police headquarters, were

issued in minutes. Documents not available at all by legal means materialized the same way.

Most people had no access to these agile geniuses, but they used other
devices to beat the system. M., a maid working in an affluent condominium
complex in São Paulo, at age twenty-four married a seventeen-year-old
young man and had a child. When her mother-in-law told her that she
couldn't care for the baby all the time, M. sent for an eleven-year-old girl
from the interior, telling people that she was "adopting" her. The girl, who
presumably attended school a few hours each day, otherwise worked without papers (or wages) for M. as her servant.

What M. did is as much a part of the informal economy as a legal ruse
since she did not have to obtain permission from any civil authorities to
bring the girl to her home. In cases where regulations have to be confronted,
Brazilians pride themselves on being especially creative in their array and
variety of gambits suitable for bending rules. Most of these ploys work best,
of course, for those with connections, even as low-level as a friend of a
relative who works in a certain office or department. The system also bends
for those who can throw their weight around. Thus, facing down a policeman trying to write a ticket on an illegally parked car is easy for someone
who is wearing a Rolex and has been educated in an elite private school,
because the weaker party to the action knows full well that society expects
him to back away.

One element in the political culture that is available to almost everyone
possessing a modicum of poise and self-respect is the *jeito*. The *jeito* (di-
minutive, *jeitinho*), is the "way" to grease the wheels of government or the
bureaucracy, so as to obtain a favor or to bypass rules or regulations. *Jeitos*
fall halfway between legitimate favors and out-and-out corruption, but at
least in popular understanding they lean in the direction of the extralegal.
Favors, in addition, imply a measure of reciprocity, a courtesy to be returned. One never pays for a favor, however; but a *jeito,* which is often
granted by someone who is not a personal acquaintance, must be accompanied by a tip or even a larger payoff.

Peter Kellemen's 1963 tongue-in-cheek *Brazil for Beginners* offers an
example of how the system worked even within the bureaucracy. A recent
graduate of a European medical school was applying at the Brazilian Con-
sulate in Paris for a visa to emigrate to Brazil. When he appeared, the
Brazilian consul changed the applicant's profession from physician to
agronomist. When the candidate protested, saying that he did not want to
sign a false statement, the consul told him: "In that way I can issue you a
visa immediately. You know how these things are? Professional quotas,
confidential instructions from the department of immigration. Utter non-

sense! . . . In any event, this way will make it perfectly legal."[2] The consul explained that he was helping the applicant by employing the *jeito*. After the physician took up residence in Brazil, he understood: he had immigrated to a country, law professor Keith S. Rosenn notes, "where laws and regulations are enacted upon the assumption that a substantial percentage will be disobeyed," and where, quoting Kelleman, "civil servants, be they small or powerful, create their own law. Although this law does not happen to correspond with the original law, it meets with general approbation, provided that it is dictated by common sense."[3]

Several kinds of behavior are associated with the *jeito*. Officials fail to perform a legal duty (e.g., they issue contracts to the highest briber); persons employ subterfuges to circumvent a legal obligation that is proper (they may underinvoice import shipments, or receive part of a purchase price abroad in foreign currency to evade currency control and taxes on part of their profits); speedy completion of paperwork is available only in exchange for a bribe or because the official knows the applicant; officials skirt an unreasonable or economically prejudicial legal obligation (for example, laws requiring compensating bank balances or deposits at low interest); they fail to enforce rules or laws because they think the law is unjust or unrealistic (as in the above example of the visa applicant). The first three cases are corrupt, but the last two fall into a gray area where public purposes are arguably served by evading legal obligations.[4] Some applications of the *jeito,* of course, involve mixed kinds of motives, combining payoffs or favoritism with a sense that the outcome will be reasonable and even legitimate.

Jeitos affect everyone. Once I was traveling to the interior of Rio Grande do Norte, a desolate backlands region with few signs of life. The van in which I was riding broke down outside a tiny, dusty town. The passengers and driver walked to the town to attempt to find parts to fix the motor; while we were sitting in a café, waiting, a man came in and identified himself as the police chief. He wore no uniform and showed no badge, but everyone in the café showed him deference and we assumed that he was some kind of official. He then asked to see our documents. The Brazilians had their federal identity cards; I had my passport. The official demanded that each of the Brazilians pay the equivalent of $6 for being given "refuge" in his town, and he "fined" the driver of the van a slightly lower amount for having obstructed the roadway. Then he turned to me. He asked me what a foreigner was doing in his town. I told him. He then asked to see my passport, taking it and thumbing through the papers one by one. "Why had I gone to Mexico?" he asked me, seeing a visa stamp issued in Mérida. "Venezuela?" "France?" Was I working for the "U.S. Intelligence Service"?

I assured him that I was carrying out historical research. "Why are you carrying equipment?" he asked. I showed him my camera and lenses, and my notebook. He then grabbed my camera bag and my passport and stalked out the door.

More than two hours later, well after midnight, he returned. The van had been fixed and was sitting with its motor running because the driver was impatient to leave. By then I had visions of being stuck in this town or even being put in jail. Then the man returned. With a broad grin, he handed me my camera case and my passport. On one of the blank visa pages, he had painstakingly entered a "visa" for me to enter his town. It was handwritten, with various misspellings, and it had a cut-out printed paragraph from what probably was the state *Diário Oficial* pasted in—a regulation covering one rule or another that did not seem even closely pertinent to this case. He then demanded $140 for the "processing fee." At this point, my Brazilian host interceded, pulling him aside in conversation. He then hustled me and the others out to the van, and we drove off. He told me later that he had given the man about $2 and told him that he "should be honored to have a university professor passing through his jurisdiction."

Lívia Barbosa, a Brazilian social anthropologist, has argued that obtaining *jeitos* does not depend, at least directly, on elements that make up a person's social identity, such as wealth, status, family name, religion, and color. Someone who does not hold a privileged position in society is as capable of obtaining a *jeito* as someone who does, as long as he/she knows how to ask, is a good talker, and is pleasant and charming.[5] This is so only to a certain extent. Such an assertion ignores the realities of Brazilian life and insults the poor, unless what is meant as a *jeito* in the case of a poor person is something as meaningless as a free *cafezinho*. Even if it is true that hapless peoples can benefit from *jeitos,* there must be an enormous difference in scale in comparison to the kind of arrangement or special favor a poised, educated, well-connected member of the affluent classes can manage.

Senator Roberto de Oliveira Campos, an economist, ambassador, and politician who seems to have obtained more than his share of *jeitos* during his public career, defined the *jeito* as a "paralegal" action, neither legal nor illegal, and understandable in the light of Brazil's historical (Latin, not Anglo-Saxon) and religious history (in Roman Catholic countries, he writes, dogma is rigid and intolerant, so ways have to be found around things). By granting the *jeito* legally neutral status, of course, Campos seems to be justifying it as a forgivable transgression. Without it, he suggests, Brazilian society would find itself either paralyzed by compliance or exploded over incompatibilities among laws, customs, and facts of life.[6] For

João Camilo de Oliveira Tôrres, another old-school critic, *jeitos* are a way of being "particularly Brazilian."[7] Clóvis de Abreu, examining the results of an interview survey of twenty people at various bureaucratic levels carried out by a group of researchers in Rio de Janeiro during the early 1980s, came to some very specific conclusions about the *jeito,* calling it, in the end, a "recourse to power." Some of that study's conclusions included the following points: that the *jeito* system arises as a response to unbending bureaucracies; that *jeitinhos* occur anywhere people have to deal with hierarchies; that *jeitinhos* confirm the duality of a system that distinguishes between haves and have-nots.

Jeitos, in the end, say more about the system that rationalizes their value than about the theories spun about them. How far does the system stretch to accommodate sweet talkers, people who need personal favors or exceptions or exemptions? Anthropologist Barbosa asserts that according to Brazilian popular wisdom, women are more effective in obtaining *jeitos* because their personalities make them better able to twirl people around their fingers. They know how to charm. They are spontaneous. The need for *jeitos,* after all, arises unexpectedly; one cannot plan for them.[8]

Rationalizing the *jeito* as a flexible tool to expedite action from an obdurate system implies acceptance of the unfair advantages given to those who know how to bypass the system or to gain speedy treatment, especially when payoffs are involved. *Jeitos* that facilitate the evasion of taxes or regulations drive up prices (since the price of corruption is passed on to the consumer), and hurt workers for whose benefit the bypassed regulations have been enacted. The economist Gunnar Myrdal adds: "Corruption introduces an element of irrationality in plan fulfillment by influencing the actual course of development in a way that is contrary to the plan or, if such influence is foreseen, by limiting the horizon of the plan."[9]

Rewards of Incumbency

In Brazil, an underlying thread running from colony to republic in various guises has been the historical aversion to developing autonomous political participation. Political decisions have always been made by the elite stratum of professional government administrators drawn from the *classe conservadora*—the "conservative class." As early as 1885, the abolitionist Joaquim Nabuco complained that complacency had preserved a rotten system by which the state "sucked up all resources and redistributed them to its clients."[10] For generations, politicians regardless of ideology saw themselves as members of a "political class," entitled to obtain patronage and resources for themselves, their families, and their clients. It was never important whether individual members considered themselves "liberal" or "conservative." Such distinctions in Latin America usually referred to views on religion, or on federalism versus centralism; but on most matters, opposing political views simply represented squabbling within the same family.

Members of this class were traditionally referred to as the *gente decente,* "the decent people." They offered little sympathy for the principle of citizens' rights because their privilege shielded them. The system presupposed the wisdom of hierarchy and rationalized its power as a paternalistic duty. Top-level administrators and civil servants rewarded supporters by bestowing favors—special investment incentives for a group of industrialists, for example, or the construction of a road or water storage facility for an important landowner. Business groups received exemptions from import duties. To the growing urban middle class and to the controlled labor unions, the system gave patronage benefits in exchange for acquiescence.

The political elite diversified after 1930, extending membership to industrialists, businessmen, and technocrats as well as large agrobusiness interests. It expanded again still later to take in representatives of multinational firms, retired career military officers in the private sector, and financiers. Politicians had always taken for granted that holding an appointed or an elected office carried with it the right to generous patronage. With the advent of federalism (and the establishment of states as more autonomous units), opportunities for patronage multiplied. What all these versions shared was a closed, hierarchical, and elitist outlook dominated by insiders jealously guarding their prerogative to profit from their control of power. The political process permitted the ancien régime to survive, even if in new clothing; holders of political power, as always, agreed to make "concessions to new power contenders" only if they could hold onto their original privileges and benefits.[11]

Weak central institutions early in Brazil's history led to the development of informal systems of local rule as well to informal (and extralegal) forms of enforcement. Conflicting interests and suspicion of a strong central state in deference to federalist demands hampered the development of a fair formal legal system. Land law tended to promote conflict, not resolution, because it set the terms through which usurpation of land was legalized. The extraordinary ability of illegal institutions to survive in symbiosis with the political and legal system—the *jogo de bicho,* for example, the century-old numbers game intricately tied in with police corruption, protection for racketeers, and political spoils—undermined efforts to reform the system.

For a country with a tradition of political stability, Brazil has experienced remarkably few open and direct elections in its history. Authoritarianism has had a long and unshakable tradition. During the transition from colony to Empire, in the early nineteenth century, voting rights were limited to literate adult males from "traditional families" of European background, whose annual income from property or employment exceeded 100 *mil réis,* or about £10 in 1830.[12] During the course of the Empire, these income requirements were made even more stringent, and prospective officeholders had to show even more substantial wealth, although at the same time participation in the voting process became more widespread. In 1846, illiterates were allowed to vote, a concession to the rising power of rural *coronéis,* who manipulated vote totals and sent mostly fraudulent results to their provincial capitals, contributing, in turn, to rural overrepresentation within most provinces. Voting rights for illiterates, however, were stripped away during later decades, and out of 8 million Brazilians in 1870, only 20,000 held the right to vote. The 1881 Saraiva Law, which implemented direct legislative elections and was supposedly an electoral reform, retained the income requirement for voting, although it expanded suffrage rather than contracting it.

There were many reasons for this reluctance to enlarge the power of voters. During the nineteenth century, slavery still flourished in Brazil, and elites kept a cautious eye on free people of color. The Brazilian Empire had been buffeted during 1848 and 1849 by separatist movements in the North and Northeast relatively analogous to the rebellions sweeping Europe from France to Hungary during 1848–51. Mountaineers in the Barousse, in Hautes-Pyrénées, destroyed government registers as well as schoolbooks in a protest against outsiders. Brazil saw efforts to launch a "Confederation of the Equator" in 1848 and a socialist-led insurrection in Recife, the *Praieira,* in 1848–49. In all cases, the uprisings were suppressed. They never touched the hearts of the ordinary population, unaware of the larger world.

Down to the present century, political power descended from family to family, anchored by powerful clans. The Albuquerques traced their lineage back to Jerônimo de Albuquerque and his brother-in-law Duarto Coelho, first proprietor of Pernambuco. Other powerful clans included the Cavalcantis in the North and the Prados, the Lemes, and the Buenos in the South, who were even more powerful when their dynasties merged, as in the case of the Albuquerque Cavalcantis. Secondary clans, no less powerful, rose to power at the provincial level during the nineteenth century: the Maltas (Alagoas), the Nerys (Amazonas), the Aciolis (Ceará), the Leites (Maranhão), the Lemos (Pará), the Rosa e Silvas (Pernambuco), the Garcias (Sergipe), the Pessoas (Paraíba), and so on. Political and economic leadership remained over the long term unusually close, at least down to the eve of World War II. In the Northeast and, especially, in São Paulo, political power continued to be concentrated in the hands of owners of vast properties, producing a powerful elite class always looking out for its own interests.[13]

One reason for the power of family clans was the lack of alternative sources of power outside the landed oligarchy. Brazil had few effective voluntary associations or political clubs (as France did after the mid-nineteenth century), and the absence of comprehensive universities delayed the rise of a meritocracy. Access to positions in public life had to be obtained through direct dealings with the oligarchies and their agents. Newspapers reflected entirely the outlook of their owners, who invariably were prominent citizens with interests to protect. Freemasonry did exist across Brazil, but mostly in ceremonial fashion; unlike European masons, Brazilian masons rarely entertained revolutionary notions or proposals about democracy or fraternity. There is little evidence that Brazilian masons were interested in politics. Auguste Comte's doctrine of positivism was grandly influential in Brazil among power brokers, who used the philosophy as an excuse to hold off democratic reforms and to concentrate on material progress and the importation of foreign ideas. Republicanism, when it was organized in opposition to the monarchy in 1870, always remained a movement for the rich, although republican clubs superficially looked like their European counterparts. Republican proselytism reached virtually no one in the general population, unlike France, where towns and small cities were the centers of the movement and most republicans petty bourgeois or artisans. Nor were Brazilian republicans in favor of democracy. They abhorred the idea of reform, preferring to preserve class distinctions; in Argentina and Chile, in contrast, positivists demanded improved educational resources to elevate the population at large.

In the late nineteenth century, citizens who had enough money to buy newspapers could choose from a broad spectrum. In small cities there often were three or four newspapers from which to choose and in larger cities as many as twenty. The leading newspapers campaigned furiously for their political allies, and paid minute attention to the ins and outs of political fortunes. Every time a banquet was held honoring a landowner or a notable civic figure—and banquets were *de rigueur* in the years before the First World War—newspapers published photographs of the guests sitting down to eat, next to an outline key identifying each person sitting around the table or tables. By looking to see who was seated where and in proximity to whom at the banquet, readers could chart status and shifting political fortunes, just as Kremlinologists in later decades charted the rise and fall of Soviet political influence by analyzing photographs of the order in which officials stood on their balcony reviewing patriotic parades in Red Square.

When republicanism surfaced in earnest in 1870, its partisans did not advocate democracy. Rather, they endorsed long-standing notions about the inherent backwardness of the population and tended to ignore social problems in favor of economic development. After the fall of the monarchy in 1889 and the Republic's first elections a half-dozen years later, although income requirements were removed, fewer than 2 percent of the adult population voted in presidential elections. The 1891 Constitution gave the vote to literate males over twenty-one years of age who were employed or possessed certifiable sources of income. Through 1929, the median level of electoral participation remained at 3 percent. Fewer than 5 percent of the adult population voted in the hotly contested 1930 presidential election, when in any case the results were thrown out by the coup which placed in power the bloc that had officially lost the election, blighted by imposing fraud on both sides. From 1872 to 1930, the country's urban population had grown by more than 450 percent, but the electorate had remained static. The climate had grown more confrontational: some workers, especially stevedores as well as printers and textile operators, had become organized into unions, but after a wave of strikes in 1919 and 1920 in large cities that were repressed, labor activity dwindled.

Even after the fall of the First Republic in 1930, dominated chiefly by rural landed interests, sparsely populated rural areas remained overrepresented, whereas flourishing urban districts were underrepresented. At all levels of government, voting was manipulated; many officially certified results were plainly fraudulent. Getúlio Vargas's electoral reforms during the 1930s gave the vote to women and expanded the overall size of the electorate to 1.5 million of the total population of 39 million. However, between 1931 and 1945 the expanded electorate was permitted to participate in national elections only twice: to elect representatives to the Constituent Assembly in 1933 and to vote for one of two generals to replace the ousted Vargas in 1945. Women voted in 1945, but not illiterates or men in military service. The 1945 election saw the Communist Party candidate, Yeddo Fiuza, win 10 percent of the vote and carry the northeastern state of Pernambuco. Luís Carlos Prestes, the Communist leader imprisoned since 1935, was elected to the Senate. Still, the two major postwar political parties, the Social Democrats and the National Democratic Union, each headed by a general, prevailed, and in 1947 President Dutra decreed the Communist Party back into illegality.

Under the corporatist Estado Novo from 1937 to 1945, Getúlio Vargas decreed hundreds of laws and regulations, extending government protection and benefits to individuals and groups willing to work within the nationalistic framework of controlled, state-sanctioned agencies. One possible reason for the great attraction of Rio de Janeiro as a pole of internal migration was that rural people heard about Vargas's social security system, which was not extended to rural areas. Not only did the federal government make cities a mecca for bureaucrats and employment seekers, but it also instructed Brazilians how to act. Sambas were composed extolling civic virtues as well as punctuality, moral living, and honest work. The Estado Novo's 1942 Consolidation of Brazilian Labor Law maintained the decade-old practice of granting legal status only to unions authorized by the Labor Ministry, which collected an annual membership fee, the equivalent of one day's work per worker, to be used by the unions and their national and regional federations and by the state. These funds could be frozen if regulations were broken. The labor minister could remove union officials at will and close down unions entirely. If more than one group attempted to organize in a given sector, the Labor Ministry could choose one from among them; the others would have to disband or operate as outlaw unions. The Estado Novo forged a multiclass alliance shaped by an emerging populist pact based on acceptance of state corporatism.

The 1946 Constitution enhanced the forms if not the substance of democracy. It legalized the right to association and implemented a multiparty system on the national level. This probably was the inevitable result of the shift of the population from a rural to an urban majority, but electoral power remained disproportionately weighted in favor of rural areas dominated by large landowners and their patrons. By 1945, the electorate had grown to nearly 7.5 million. By 1950, when Getúlio Vargas, ousted by the military as president in 1945, ran and was elected to the presidency, the electorate had reached 11.5 million, about 20 percent of the population, in a system where voting was now obligatory for those who met the qualifications. In 1960, 15.5 million Brazilians voted, about a fourth of the total number of Brazilian citizens. By 1970, 30.6 percent of the population was registered to vote, although by then the military dictatorship rendered voting rights meaningless. The military also suppressed efforts at independent union organization, intervening in unions no fewer than 536 times during the 1970s and the early 1980s. Democracy was being restored nominally, but only under tightly controlled circumstances. A massive metalworkers' strike in the industrial region of São Paulo (dubbed the ABC region because it was centered in Santo André, São Bernardo, and São Caetano), was ruled legal by the labor court, but under military pressure the decision was reversed. More than 200,000 workers struck despite the ruling, and in retaliation the government ordered the union closed and arrested 1,600 union activists, including Lula, the union's president. Strikers returned to work after forty-one days without winning any of their demands. The regime was not ready to make any concessions to challenges to its hegemony.

Corruption became more open than ever. City government took on the shape of a top-down pyramid dispensing favors in exchange for votes, other forms of allegiance, and acquiescence. The classic example was São Paulo governor Adhemar de Barros, who maintained widespread popularity despite popular cynicism about his personal corruption ("Rouba mas faz," the slogan went: "He steals but he gets things done"), a darker version of Chicago boss Mayor Richard Daley's making sure that garbage was collected regularly and that his constituents always knew whom on his staff to approach for favors. Popular wisdom accepted avarice on the part of officeholders; it seemed simply to go with the system. Some political figures (for one, Getúlio Vargas), led austere lives, profiting little from their offices, but many went to the other extreme, flaunting their illicit gains.

At the same time, the growing size of the electorate indicated even more sweeping changes in the lives of Brazilians. In many ways, the turning point came in 1958. Vargas's death had rocked the system and threatened to return it to Old Republic levels of instability, but the inauguration as president in 1958 of Belo Horizonte's Juscelino Kubitschek, a populist politician skilled in cultivating relations with the mass of voting Brazilians, ushered in considerable change built on the foundation of Vargas's record. Kubitschek relied on patronage to buy political support, and counted on his massive public works projects to provide jobs. External factors contributed to make 1958 a fateful year as well. The drought of that year was the worst in decades: when President Kubitschek traveled to the Northeast to survey the calamity—the first sitting chief of state ever to have done so—he publicly cried about what he saw. The same year saw the inauguration of the construction of Brasília, not only a nationalistic symbol and a pork-barrel project of monumental proportions, but the impetus for streams of migrants from all parts of Brazil to flow to the vacant central part of the country. Brasília was a new pole of attraction that rivaled the gold rush to Minas Gerais in the eighteenth century.

The late 1950s also saw the massive influx of foreign investment capital, invited by Kubitschek as part of the rhythm of national development, and the acquisition by foreign multinational corporations of a share of domestic industrial production. Reformist Catholic clergy, drawing from what soon would be called "liberation theology," began to organize in favor of massive redistribution of agricultural land. *Sputnik* went up in 1958, highlighting Brazil's need to catch up in its scientific and technological capacity. Brazil's internationalization took other forms as well. President Kubitschek's daughter made her social debut in France, at Versailles. Brazil's first supermarkets opened in 1958, as did the first shopping mall, Iguatemi in São Paulo. Cultural patterns changed overnight. Men stopped wearing dour black suits with thin black ties—or, in more traditional places, suits of white linen with black ties—and began wearing fashions imported directly or copied from Italy and France. Teenagers in the 1960s began to wear jeans *(Calças Lee)* and sneakers, to go crazy over foreign music and films, and to chew gum. Hollywood always had been influential, but now a more generic, internationalized kind of popular culture soared in popularity, couched in the ambiguity of captivating affluent urban Brazilian youth wholly while at the same time spawning trendy anti-Americanism, attacking the United States for what was derided as its superficial culture and for its imperialist politics and economy. Millions watched the Miss Brazil and Miss Universe contests—before 1958 always lily-white and usually blond in the selection of its contestants chosen to represent Brazil abroad, lest foreigners get the wrong idea, and in later decades almost always white or light-skinned *mulata*. Television made a major impact in the late 1950s, giving greater power to skillful manipulation by handlers of telegenic candidates and ending the hallowed tradition of the *comicio,* the public campaign rallies at which it was not only candidates who orated; common people could come up out of the audience and challenge speakers. Carolina Maria de Jesus did this often, and was known to the mayor and the governor of São Paulo even before her diary was published. Television and growing reliance on political advertising after 1958 made the *comicio* obsolete.

The abrupt resignation from the presidency of reformist Jânio Quadros in 1961 elevated João Goulart, his vice president, to office. The *getulismo* of the 1950s, based on the personal popularity of Vargas, elected president in 1950 after five years of domestic exile, had given rise to two distinct but parallel political movements, the middle-class Social Democrats whose mantle had been assumed by Juscelino Kubitschek, and labor movement *trabalhalismo,* headed by João Goulart, one of Vargas's protégés. Under his presidency, labor unionism grew in strength, reaching even the remote interior. The left, consistent with its past record, throughout the 1960s crippled itself by splitting into warring ideological factions. There were the Maoists, the Stalinists, a socialist Leninist group, and a radical Catholic movement that would ally itself with the Maoists. The official line of the Communist Party was, in the words of Emir Sader, "formally wedded to Goulart's government."[14] The left's tiresome exercise in self-destruction alienated any potential followers among affluent groups except for militant students and academics, and the country slid into military dictatorship after the 1964 coup.

Brazilians were just learning how to deal with open elections in a multiparty structure when the door slammed shut. Military rule, especially after the term of Humberto Castelo Branco, who (unlike those who followed him) showed a human face to the generals, hardened. Left-wing militants led by Carlos Marighella, who had quit the Communist Party in disgust, launched guerrilla resistance to the regime, a tactic that resulted not only in its being crushed but in repression for thousands of moderates and liberals not connected in any way to the radical left. Under Chief of State General Emílio Garrastazú Médici, every branch of the armed forces perfected its own kidnapping and torture apparatus. A later military president, the ill-tempered General João Figueiredo, admitted that he preferred the smell of horses to the stink of the *povo,* and an equestrian photograph of him on horseback jumping over a prone subordinate was distributed widely. A few courageous individuals spoke out against the regime, including Cardinal Paulo Evaristo Arns of São Paulo, a soft-spoken Franciscan who went to army bases and prisons and demanded information about prisoners, and Heraclito Sobral Pinto, a civil rights lawyer who defended persons charged with subversion. Most opposition was stifled by the blanket of authoritarian rule. Despite promises for democratization as early as the mid-1970s, the first direct election for the presidency since 1960 did not take place until November 15, 1989.

The bleak military years saw dramatic economic growth at the cost of human rights and meaningful civil participation in government, especially between 1969 and 1984. Strikes were suppressed and labor unions kept under surveillance or completely disbanded. Businessmen and industrialists welcomed the government's role and referred to Brazil's "economic miracle." Opponents called it the triumph of "savage capitalism," the victory of technocrats who combined countercyclical investment policies with exchange controls, subsidies, negative rates of interest, and the deliberate creation of monetary disequilibrium to achieve a forced transition from backwardness to modernity. The results benefited the wealthy and the powerful to the detriment of other Brazilians. Income concentration increased substantially during the period.[15]

After 1985, when civilians readied themselves to return to power, domestic interests generally prevailed over military preferences, although the military continued to exercise decisive influence over governmental decision making. During the transitory period of "decompression," as it was called, during the late 1970s and the early 1980s, when civilians began to be reintegrated into political leadership, the old forms of political behavior resurfaced. Despite some talk on the part of individual high armed forces officers that Brazil should not return to its old political ways, clientelism survived, especially at the local level. This arrangement, by which office-holders and others in power distributed favors in direct exchange for political support, had dominated the political arena from the 1930s through 1964. Clientelism was especially dominant in the rural interior and in slum districts in the cities. The military's seizure of power, however, bent the rules of the game if it did not change them entirely, adapting clientelism to a political arena inhabited by powerful new players, most notably the television screen and, on the political left, the Workers' Party (PT). Lower-class Brazilians, however, rather than flocking to the PT's banners, responded to the advertising blitz and defeated the candidate who spoke for them.

More than anything else, the new atmosphere reflected new resistance to the authoritarian regime. Professional middle-class groups raised their voices, as did some members of the hierarchy of the Catholic Church, especially in São Paulo. New neighborhood associations, no longer tools of incumbent machines, began to organize and to join in statewide federations. The PT, which was founded in 1979, was led by intellectuals but emphasized a grassroots membership base. That political style proved very resilient, and it has survived well into the 1990s. Illustrating this is the example of Vila Brasil, a favela an hour's bus ride west of downtown Rio de Janeiro. Vila Brasil, founded in 1946, now was crowded, with many houses gaining new second stories because of lack of space to expand laterally. It was small for a mature favela, with 524 residences housing a total population of about 2,700. Although poverty-stricken, especially at its center, by 1986 it boasted running water, electricity, and paved roads and alleyways. Vila Brasil achieved this, Robert Gay asserts, through successful clientelistic negotiations on the part of the new president and directorate of the dweller association, first elected in 1979. Clientelism, in other words, may leave a bad taste in the mouth for purists, but for Vila Brasil's residents it was a valuable resource, a vehicle through which the favela's needs could be realized.[16]

The arrangement worked through the alliance forged between the favela association and a local politician, for whom Vila Brasil's president worked as a political organizer *(cabo eleitoral)*. The politician, Jorge Leite, spent most of his time cultivating a "network of personal relationships that [were] sustained through the trafficking of favors and the promise of favors."[17] It paid off in 1982 for both sides, on the occasion of the first election for federal legislators permitted under the military regime. Leite received Vila Brasil's support and in turn saw that the favela's roads and alleyways were paved in the eight days leading up the November 15 elections. Leite also sent lorry loads of sand and cement to assist in the reconstruction of the association building. He won his election with more than 170,000 votes, by far the most voted-for candidate in his party. Not only did he come out ahead, but the association president's own influence increased enormously. He was credited personally for improving the lives of "his" *favelados,* in ways "that had seemed beyond the realm of possibility before he took office." Because the system had not worked for the *favelados* in the past, the president's success with it made it seem all the more a case of personal skill and effectiveness. Basking in his success, he was quoted as saying that politicians were "all thieves," but that he was "a much better thief than any of them." They are unconcerned with anything but personal power, he said; they manipulate the poor as a source of cheap votes. He expressed no allegiance to any political party or group: he simply extracted the best deal he could for his community. He expressed absolutely no loyalty to Leite, whom he had supported off and on for nearly five years.

When Leite decided to run for mayor in 1985, he promised Vila Brasil's president cash and patronage jobs for his children if elected. He lost, however, receiving only 8.6 percent of the vote. The favela's leadership was now open to offers from other candidates. In the gubernatorial election of 1986, Vila Brasil's president, receiving at least one call a day from candidates seeking to purchase the community's vote, finally made a deal with five of them, telling each one that the first to help complete the second story of the association building would receive his support. The asking price, however, was too high, and all of the candidates balked. Vila Brasil finally settled for the construction of two bathrooms in the building. Ten days before the election, the candidate showed up with a check for the agreed amount. He was immediately endorsed as the "president's candidate" and taken from door to door to greet his new followers.

The new practice of *favelados* using votes as leverage to gain favors was only a small part of the system. Favela associations, in fact, not only had to deal with elected and appointed officials, but with other latter-day *coronéis,* most notably numbers bosses and drug dealers (estimated to number 6,500 in Rio de Janeiro alone) using the favelas as sanctuaries or as institutional sources of power. Among the broader urban population, another category of *coronéis,* the *cartolas,* have held commanding influence for decades. *Cartolas* ("top hats," the men who control soccer clubs, federations, and their resources) amassed tremendous power when professional soccer emerged in the 1930s as Brazil's national passion. Indirectly (or directly) tapped into the patronage system, these men often commanded empires of fans, benefactors, players, and the media, holding more lasting power in local settings than more transitory elected officials.

Political alliances continued to operate through the networking system of the *panelinha.* Unlike the United States, where political ties are usually to a home district or locality, or to certain interest groups (the defense industry, or agriculture, or inner city residents), connections in Brazil usually follow personal business interests or other private agendas based on friendship or allegiances with inside people. Orestes Quércia, a veteran São Paulo politician and later governor, used his claimed lack of establishment *panelinha* ties to defend himself as an outsider discriminated against by the "insiders."

He was implicated in a corruption scandal when he was candidate for governor in 1986. Quércia, formerly a small-time local politician, declared, "What is being flung against me," he said, "is prejudice: I'm a businessman, I come from the interior, and I'm not connected to the university. Elitism is what is being used against me." Quércia, Maluf, and scores of other self-described "outsider" politicians thrived through the use of alliances bought with patronage and donations. As governor, Maluf personally sent ambulances to every *município* in the state of São Paulo, with the implicit message that more such plums would come in exchange for support. Clientelism remained alive and well despite the political changes that emerged in the 1980s. Vila Brasil's voting-age residents, nearly 60 percent of whom had not completed the first grade, put their trust in their association president to make the best deal. By 1986, he had become skilled enough to win gifts from more than one candidate (one sent two sets of soccer shirts to the favela, although in the end he was not supported). Vila Brasil's president, through pragmatism, good negotiating skills, and a single-minded determination to get things for his constituency, emerged as a kind of modern-day *coronel,* a power broker of sorts lacking any power or influence himself except for the value of the votes of his fellow *favelados.* The truth is, however, that he did not win jobs or schools, and except for the soccer shirts and bathrooms for its association building, Vila Brasil gained nothing through him but the paved roads that the municipality should have provided in the first place.

For the country as a whole, the slow pace of the restoration of democracy during the mid-1980s had brought widespread disillusionment. This was felt most keenly in the 1984 Direitas Já campaign seeking the direct election of the president. Under pressure form the military, Congress refused, despite overwhelming public support. Popular pressure for change then led to the election, by indirect vote, of Tancredo Neves, a civilian who had mildly opposed the military regime. His victory generated even higher levels of euphoria, but he died on the eve of his inauguration after being stricken unexpectedly. His death ushered in the opportunistic government of José Sarney, a Maranhão-based hardliner who had firmly backed the military government previously.

Sarney's five-year term (1985–90) not only dampened the hopes of electors who had hoped for a sharp break with the civilian hardliners who had supported the military dictatorship, but saw Sarney, as president, use gross political bartering and payoffs to retain power, as a result crippling the federal government and fanning inflationary fires. The 1988 Constitution removed the literacy requirement and empowered sixteen-year-olds to vote. More than half of the population were now registered voters. Government at all levels had become bloated and unstable. Cabinet ministers in such key posts as Finance often lasted less than several months, resigning or being forced out as the result of political in-fighting. Government-owned agencies—PETROBRAS, for example, the petroleum monopoly—employed thousands of managers and other employees who treated their jobs like government sinecures. State and local governments controlled ten times the number of patronage jobs as in the United States. Cracks began to appear in the facade. In some states, wretchedly paid public school teachers went without any pay at all for months because state treasuries ran out. In São Paulo, Brazil's most prosperous state, medical doctors employed by some state hospitals in March 1992 earned $440 a month for a twenty-hour workweek.

The cynical acquiescence of Congress in carving out new, sparsely populated states acceded to the subdividing of large but underpopulated rural states (Mato Grosso and Goiás) and to the elevation of obscure federal territories (Acre, Amapá, Rondônia, Roraima) to statehood—shams to create new patronage apparatuses and to bolster the power of conservative rural interests against underrepresented urban areas—was evidence that the traditional system of manipulation in the name of reform still thrived. It took 10,750 voters to elect a congressman in the state of Roraima, compared with 330,000 in the state of São Paulo. A vote cast in Roraima, with eight federal deputies and 0.08 percent of Brazil's population, carries the same weight as a *paulista*'s vote, from a state with 23 percent of the population and only sixty federal deputies. The state-creating ploy cynically created a boom in political patronage, further reduced the proportional disadvantage of the most populous states, and elevated political cynicism and arrogance to new heights.

The transition from manipulated local elections to mass campaigns in which voters freely cast their ballots was not easy. A documentary film produced in 1986 showed Francisco (Chico) Mendes, then a candidate for state deputy in Amazonas, walking down the main street in his hometown of Xapuri. As he greeted friends and acquaintances, people came up to him and asked how much he would pay for their votes. When he replied that he had no money to give, they walked away; he lost the election. Mendes, born in 1944 into a humble rubber tapper's family in Xapuri in the then-territory of Acre, had gone to work tapping trees at the age of nine. He never attended school, but learned to read and write from an activist who came to Xapuri after fleeing Bolivia, where he had worked with local tribes before being expelled. Few listened to him locally, although Mendes attained international fame as a crusader for the rights of Amazonian forest workers against rubber producers and cattle ranchers. Chico Mendes was gunned down in 1988. When the two assassins hired to kill him were caught, skeptics responded that they would never remain in prison. Killed three days before Christmas, 1988, Mendes had claimed to the world that no fewer than 1,684 rubber gatherers had been murdered. The gunmen who shot him were sentenced in December 1990 to terms of nineteen years. A year later, however, they were absolved of the crime on appeal, although they remained in jail in Francisco de Oliveira Conde prison in Rio Branco, in the state of Acre, for other crimes they had committed. One year later, they boldly escaped, under suspicious circumstances. The convicts had held parties in jail; their cells were always unlocked; and they had become friends of the guards and prison officials. One of them had bragged that he regularly walked to the bank to cash checks. Chico Mendes was considered a nuisance in the Amazon region, and officials responded accordingly. Finally, they simply walked out of their jail cell and disappeared without a trace. Security remained so lax in the prison that within the next two months, 112 more inmates escaped—a third of the prison population. The Justice Minister, Maurício Corrêa, vowed to capture them—as it turned out, an empty promise.

The Brazilian Congress's decision to continue to obligate voting while removing all educational requirements in a country still largely functionally illiterate was an unprecedented boon to the media, especially television. During the 1960s and 1970s, telecasting, notably in the form of the three hour-long prime-time *novelas* devoured by virtually the entire population, substituted for absent opportunities for Brazilians to interact through political mobilization. Networks used separate programs appealing to segmented audiences aimed at a single goal: the creation of an image of a populace moving toward modernity; glamour; and a comfortable, materially enriched, upwardly mobile lifestyle. The results were startling. Local and regional programming abruptly ended. Network television, dominated by TV Globo, with its 80 percent market share and its owners' strongly conservative political agenda, hawked optimism and erased almost overnight the fragmentation of communications into isolated regional forms of expression.

Progressive spokesmen issued warnings about the fragility of the political environment. In an interview with *Veja,* the leading newsmagazine, Senator Fernando Henrique Cardoso offered the following observation:

> Up to a certain point, trading posts and favors is a normal fact of any political system. What has become abnormal in our current political situation is that favor is traded for favor, post for post. In other words, there is no more politics, no more political debate. . . . The result is that we are witnessing a restoration of oligarchical power, the same type of power that was utilized in 1964 to contain popular pressure.[18]

Equally powerful during the electoral campaign was media coverage, especially television. Political mobilization rose to temporarily high levels, but its impact was overshadowed by massive advertising, brilliantly orchestrated, and especially influential among the 50–70 percent of the electorate who, according to political analysts, were insufficiently informed to make "rational voting decisions."[19]

The result was the election of thirty-nine-year-old Fernando Collor de Mello. Collor came to the national arena lacking an identifiable political constituency. As a youth in Maceió, he had been a playboy, and his brother Paulo later alleged that he had used cocaine, a charge Collor's adversaries were quick to use against him.[20] Fernando overcame great odds in rising to the top of the political heap despite help from his powerful family and their allies. He had a dubious reputation and his policies were unknown except for grandstanding when he was governor of Alagoas. His election was the result of two principal factors: lavishly financed television advertising and the nature of the electorate. The polo-playing karate champion posed as a white knight, although his campaign was filled with dirty tricks, including sabotage of the public transport systems in poor sections of several major cities on voting day.[21] The slickness of the media campaign overshadowed its political substance. Taking advantage of the pent-up anger over Sarney's presidency, the relatively unknown Alagoan ran as a miracle worker, promising to return government to the people, to sweep away political dishonesty and privilege. Collor was swept into power on the strength of his media skills and the lofty promise of his message.

Collor directed his electoral campaign at the country's majority of poor but enfranchised voters, to whom he pandered through manipulative television advertisements, and to businessmen and industrialists who feared the other two leading candidates, Luis Inácio da Silva (Lula), the leader of the trade unionist Workers' Party, and Leonel Brizola, the erratic former governor of the State of Rio de Janeiro (and João Goulart's brother-in-law). Collor failed to win an outright majority, so he focused his runoff campaign with Lula on promises to end corruption. He tried to paint Lula as a dangerous leftist, and used smear tactics to embarrass his opponent, including a paid political advertisement featuring Lula's ex-wife accusing him of having pressured her to abort their child. He won with a majority of 52 percent although he outspent Lula considerably in the campaign, one filled with contradictions. Collor, who campaigned against privilege, was the grandson of Lindolfo Collor, one of the post powerful members of Getúlio Vargas's Liberal Alliance clique in the early 1930s, and a cabinet official. His father, Arnon de Mello, was a powerful deputy and senator who had used his close ties to the military and his family fortune to launch his son's career in politics by having him appointed by the military regime mayor of Maceió. Arnon, politically powerful because of his strong support for the military, had shot to death a fellow senator on the floor of Congress and gone unpunished. The murder was ruled an accident; in a sense, it was, because Arnon had intended to shoot someone else over a matter of honor. Fernando's mother, Leda Collor de Mello, an astute businesswoman and the forceful head of the family, exerted powerful influence until her son Pedro, whom she labeled a "stool pigeon," made public his allegations against Fernando in a sensational newsmagazine interview. Leda suffered three consecutive cardiac arrests, and remained in a coma. Fernando's twenty-eight-year-old second wife, Rosane Malta Collor, from the old Malta clan that "ruled over the most backward part of backward Alagoas," also was involved in accusations, when it was disclosed that the Legião Brasileira de Assistência, the national charity that she was named to head, while she was not on lavish shopping sprees in Paris, may have been siphoning off money to the Malta clan. It was alleged that the charity had swindled impoverished northeasterners out of emergency food supplies, and had falsely billed the government for fictitious equipment, for truckloads of water earmarked for drought-stricken areas, and even for children's coffins.

Once elected, Collor enacted legislation to open markets to free trade, gaining him the temporary support of manufacturers and the international community. His government, however, soon began to founder when, lacking a party base in the powerful Congress, he began to broker deals, many of which were improper. The business climate soon soured. The regime's corruption directly touched every aspect of political life: demanding cash payments equivalent in value to more than 20 percent of the amount of public contracts, helping to unblock frozen bank accounts, granting contracts without bidding, appointing and removing thousands of officials at every level on the basis of patronage. The president's defenders, including his business agent and treasurer, Paulo César Farias (widely called "P.C."), accused detractors of hypocrisy, claiming that everyone in politics did the same. Bystanders flinched when the garrulous Farias, a failed Alagoan businessman, netted millions by masterminding an influence-peddling ring while being Collor's right-hand man, blandly demanding "seventy percent for the boss; thirty percent for me." He evaded an arrest warrant, when it finally came in July 1993 after thirteen months of an official investigation.[22] The standard kickback for release of funds under public contracts rose steadily as Collor's administration progressed.

Farias was under investigation almost continuously. Hours before an arrest warrant was issued on June 30, he escaped, assisted by two military policemen who worked off-duty as his bodyguards. "The dream of every

Brazilian is to see this man in prison, and now he has disappeared," Justice Minister Maurício Corrêa was quoted as saying. "It's very frustrating."[23] Finally, in late November, Farias was spotted by a Brazilian tourist in a luxury hotel in Bangkok and turned over to authorities, who arrested him because his visa had expired. He returned to Brazil denying all allegations against him.

It was revealed that Cubans, who had sought to sell medical vaccines to Brazil, had been forced to pay bribes to obtain import licenses for the vaccines and were cheated a second time on the transaction when the delivered goods were never fully paid for. Many politicians were caught up in the public outcry against dishonesty that accompanied Collor's slide from power, but not a single accused politician was either tried or punished. Newsmagazines claimed that Antônio Ermírio raised the unprecedented sum of $100 million for his run for the governorship of São Paulo in 1986, with only a third of the money accounted for afterward. Leonel Brizola was accused of diverting a $300,000 campaign donation from a German source in 1989 to his wife Leda's charity. Even leftist candidates did not escape allegations: Roberto Freire, a presidential candidate in 1989 and a former communist, received under-the-table help from his right-wing friend José Lourenço and from landowners in Mato Grosso. Itamar Franco's justice minister, Maurício Corrêa, stepped down after the *Jornal do Brasil* published documents claiming that the then-candidate for the Senate personally received $500,000 from the "Palestinian community in Brasília." Investigative reporters accused Inocêncio Oliveira, the political boss of Serra Talhada, Pernambuco, of holding up the distribution of thirty tons of black beans sent to his district to feed the hungry, in a move calculated to embarrass his political opponents. The same deputy was also accused of using state money to have wells dug on nearly 3,000 private properties, including those of two senators from Pernambuco and the father of another. Nothing, of course, came of the accusations. One state deputy, Messias Góis, defended his having received a state-dug well by saying that "if it had been done with private money, it would have been much more expensive."[24]

In November 1993, Paulo Maluf, who was, according to Carlos Eduardo Lins da Silva, the heir to Adhemar de Barros and (in da Silva's words) "known during the military regime as the most extreme example of corruption in power," bested Eduardo Matarrazo Suplicy, one of the politicians in Brazil best known for his personal ethics. Even after being exposed to evidence of Collor's gross culpability, many remained prepared to look the other way. Collor and Farias had overstepped the traditional limits of extortion for preferential treatment, benefits, and red-tape cutting, asking for direct payments in the form of checks that left a paper trail documenting the stench of what everyone knew. Collor's own brother, Pedro, turned in the president, claiming in an extraordinary interview in the newsmagazine *Veja* that the bribes demanded were so high that the family's own enterprises would be driven to the brink of ruin. The ensuing campaign against the president, inevitably dubbed "Collorgate" by the emboldened press, reached unprecedented proportions. Collor did not even manage to serve half of his elected term. Mounting evidence of fraud crippled his ability to govern and fed the pressures for impeachment. Farias blithely flew on his private jet plane from Recife to Spain seeking medical correction of a snoring problem, but Collor refused to budge, waiting until the day of the impeachment vote to make his move. Farias had been unemployed since May but he stayed at Barcelona's most expensive hotel, at a cost of $940 a day. Collor resigned twenty-two minutes after the start of the Senate's impeachment trial. By a vote of 73 to 8, the senators agreed to continue the trial despite his resignation.

A new 7:00 P.M. TV Globo soap opera began on television late in 1992. Entitled *God Help Us,* it depicted Brazil as drowning in a sea of mud. Most observers agreed that if even one link in the fortuitous series of circumstances that led to Collor's impeachment vote had been broken, he most certainly would have escaped with his political skin. At the end, only the fact that the final impeachment vote was televised forced deputies to cast their vote against Collor, as they had publicly pledged to do. Collor, moreover, faced the future with a short penalty (for a forty-two-year-old), an eight-year ban until the year 2001 from seeking public office again. Few were sure that Collor wouldn't still be able to resurrect himself and save his political career, however venal it had been.

That Collor fell from power was made possible by unsettled institutional rivalries between Congress and the presidency that crystallized in the passage from military to civilian rule in the 1980s and 1990s. Since 1974, Congress had been the driving force behind the redemocratization process, whereby after 1982, direct gubernatorial elections aligned the armed forces command and oppositionist governors against one another, and set the stage for the massive 1984 Direitas Já civic movement, which raised expectations but did little else. Collor's outcome troubled Brazilians who saw in his dilemma the fact that neither the president nor the Congress would be able to govern effectively under the new double-ballot plebiscitary system, which was designed to grant officeholders undisputed legitimacy. The events also frightened Brazilians who had seen him as a reform candidate. Industrialists, after all, had considered him an heir to Jânio Quadros, also a conservative populist, also young (forty-three years of age), and also elected on an anticorruption platform after a meteoric political rise. Quadros resigned mysteriously in 1961, after only seven months in office, although he was never accused of corruption; his resignation was likely a miscalculated effort on his part to be granted greater executive power by the Congress.

After being charged with personally receiving $6.5 million in bribes solicited in his name in exchange for government influence and favors, Collor resigned on December 29, 1992. His departure would not have occurred without the courageous work of opposition investigative journalists, the refusal of the courts to waver, and the ubiquitous presence of television cameras at the session during which impeachment was voted. Nor would Collor have been forced to resign if public anger had not driven millions into the street in protest. Brazil's ability to achieve a peaceful transition from Collor to Franco was a remarkable sign that its democratic institutions were strong and able to rise to the occasion when necessary. The country has become a "kleptocracy," declared the normally staid weekly *Istoé*. Brazil's fortunes are in hands of a "predatory state," pronounced its rival, *Veja*.[25] As the impeachment process inched toward conclusion, Collor loyalists in Brasília offered bribes to legislators right up the final vote. Daniel Tourinho, the head of Collor's political party, offered several congressmen "one million lettuce leaves" (U.S. dollars) each; others were offered cash or massive public works projects for their districts in exchange for their support. Collor resigned only after impeachment was assured, protesting his innocence and retreating to his residence (and its private *candomblé* altar on which the president supposedly conducted black magic, ritually using animal sacrifices to gain revenge against his enemies).[26]

The events leading up to the impeachment vote shook the public and cast a pall over national morale. Nonetheless, observers saw a silver lining in the process, a sign of the vitality of Brazilian democratic institutions even in the face of terrible strain. The military, after all, stood on the sidelines and permitted constitutional procedures to play out. The charges against Collor and his associates were published by newspapers and magazines in an atmosphere of press freedom; when Collor personally sued Otávio Frias Filho, the editor of *Folha de São Paulo,* because of stories denouncing Collor, the courts backed the editor. Congressmen, generally viewed as "a bunch of thieves" (in the words of journalist Carlos Eduardo Lins da Silva), chose to be (under the eye of television cameras) more receptive to public opinion than to open bribes in the form of public works largess offered by the president. The judiciary maintained its independence. Political parties, though they were typically undisciplined, on this occasion demonstrated internal coherence and acted responsibly.

Collor, for his part, stubbornly clung to his story that he was a victim of "political persecution by coup-mongers." Taking refuge in his home state of Alagoas, where he was met at the airport by the governor and 5,000 cheering supporters, he agreed to speak only with the foreign press and instructed his lawyers to appeal to the supreme court for the annulment of the Senate's impeachment verdict.[27] Months after his downfall he began to appear frequently on the beach in Maceió, behaving like the playboy of old, smilingly denying all accusations of corruption leveled against him. Eight-six percent of persons interviewed in February 1993 by a leading polling agency said that influential lawbreakers would likely never be punished; 80 percent said that the justice system punishes the poor and protects the rich. Not a single person involved in any major scandal involving millions of dollars in purloined funds over more than a decade, *Veja* added, ever had been punished.

When Collor and Paulo César Farias were indicted on corruption charges, the Supreme Justice Tribunal accepted only part of the prosecutor's indictment, dismissing the charges that accused Collor and Farias of having formed a "team" devoted to corruption. This fed cynicism in Brazil that Collor and P.C. would escape all punishments, since virtually no one believed that their corruption was anything less than flat-out and aggressive. Sociologist Renato Lessa expressed this widespread feeling of disgust when he coined the term "Camorra" for Collor's administration. A "Camorra," he wrote, was a "criminal association controlled by a few people and characterized by an internal ethic of secrecy, which means that nobody gives anybody away."[28] Collor's disgrace did little to dent the enormous infrastructure of privilege and special favors made available to politicians at every level. In the midst of a financial crisis so severe that Labor Minister Walter Barelli on May Day was forced to state that the government would not be able to raise the minimum wage of under $100 a month, Congress offered $90,000 a month in lodging subsidies to legislators who did not own a house or an apartment in Brasília. No accounting was required to document how these funds were actually spent. "It is left to the conscience of each member to use the money honestly or not," a parliamentary official was quoted as having explained.[29]

On the level of national politics, the atmosphere seemed to approach the boiling point. Early in 1993, no fewer than thirty-three federal congressmen, in spite of their parliamentary immunity from prosecution, faced legal charges against them: twenty-one for slander, the rest for alleged crimes ranging from electoral fraud to extortion to homicide. These charges were scattered, but in October, a sensational case brought before Congress itself nearly brought the Franco regime to a standstill. José Carlos Alves dos Santos, ex-director of the federal budget, publicly charged twenty-seven congressmen, six cabinet ministers, and three state governors with scheming to steal millions of dollars from public funds. Not only was the accusation unprecedented in its magnitude, but it came from one of the country's most respected bureaucrats. The way the allegations were made was also extraordinary. Earlier in the month, Alves was arrested for police as a suspect in the disappearance of his wife, who was presumed dead. A search of his house discovered $800,000 in dollars under a mattress and another $300,000 in a safe deposit box. Police also claimed to find traces of cocaine in his private airplane and "gaping holes in his version of his wife's disappearance." Charged with drug trafficking and tax evasion, Alves claimed innocence and accused the police of torturing him to extract a confession. In testimony to Congress, Alves promised to provide evidence to substantiate his claims. Newspapers estimated that he had moved at least $32 million in bribes through Congress during the Collor administration. Asked about his great personal wealth on a bureaucrat's salary, he claimed that he had won the lottery 24,000 times, and that God had helped him obtain the money. Immune from prosecution along with all other elected legislators, he was not accused of any crime, although he faced removal from office and loss of that immunity.

In the middle of the Alves scandal, Ronaldo Cunha Lima, the incumbent governor of Paraíba, walked into an elegant seaside restaurant in the state capital, took out a pistol, and shot ex-governor Tarciso Burity, his political rival, three times in the face. Burity had claimed publicly that the governor's son Cássio, the head of the federal regional development agency for the Northeast, SUDENE, had approved private construction projects to benefit congressional allies. The governor then walked out of the restaurant and drove off in an official state car, although some hours later he was detained by federal police and held for five hours in a handsomely equipped cell prepared especially for him. He was then released when his lawyers successfully argued that as an elected official he was immune from prosecution. His spokesman told the press that after a week of "rest," the governor would be back at his desk. The president of the Brazilian senate, Humberto Lucena, was quoted in Rio de Janeiro's leading daily newspaper, the *Jornal do Brasil,* as commending Cunha Lima's "honorable attitude" in attacking his enemy himself instead of hiring someone to do it.[30]

The range of the continued allegations of corruption through 1994 and the electrified political atmosphere dismayed nearly everyone, especially members of the generation of Brazilians that had come to maturity unfamiliar with democratic elections and disillusioned by the failure of the successive civilian governments after 1984 to pull things together. A court annulled the October 1994 legislative elections in Rio de Janeiro State, citing "gigantic" fraud. On the other hand, all the other elections across Brazil were considered honest, and the nation looked forward to the new administration, which it hoped would be able to stem traditional corrupt practices.

Crime without Punishment

James Brooke recalls the Brazilian fable about a sixteenth-century Portuguese bishop who wanted to encourage skeptical peasants to settle in far-off Brazil. Addressing his devout flock, the cleric decreed, "No sin exists south of the equator." Five centuries later, Brooke adds, modern Brazil at times seems to have incorporated this motto as its moral cornerstone.[31] More than any other attribute, impunity, guaranteed by differential justice—as it were, crime without punishment—has plagued Brazil's legal system.

Impunity and preferential treatment for privileged lawbreakers, together with frequent police complicity in disdaining the law, have compounded the dilemma. According to the Comissão Pastoral da Terra, a religious group working in behalf of the rubber workers, of 1,684 recorded murders in the region over the previous three decades, only 29 were ever brought to trial. In the wake of the 1992 massacre of 111 prisoners in São Paulo's Carandiru prison, depositions filled 10,800 pages of official record, but not a single step was taken against any of the accused policemen who precipitated the deadly riot. Prisoners ruled within the walls of penal institutions. Rio de Janeiro's Bangu Penitentiary, constructed to hold the most dangerous criminals in the country, was said to be ruled by three inside gangs, the Comando Vermelho, the Terceiro Comando, and the Falange Jacaré. In Porto Velho, Rondônia, at the other end of the country, the army had to be called in to guard prisoners because penitentiary guards simply walked off the job in demand of higher wages. Within the prison, chaos reigned, with inmates taking out private revenge on other inmates with impunity.

Brazil employs 7,000 judges for its 150 million citizens; Germany, with 80 million, has 120,000. Brazil's Supreme Tribunal of Justice (STJ), with thirty-three judges, faces a backlog of 34,000 cases. The police are equally burdened: each police official in São Paulo averages a caseload of 2,000 unsolved crimes to investigate. According to investigative journalists, judges known to have sold favorable verdicts to persons charged with crimes, including narcotics trafficking, are not punished. One judge charged $10,000 just to agree to meet with a lawyer seeking a writ of habeas corpus for his client, the director of a multinational firm. The writ was signed before the lawyer's airplane touched down at São Paulo's Garulhos airport.[32] At the other end of the system, 95 percent of incarcerated prisoners have no money to hire their own lawyer. The class differences between everyday criminals and influential men accused of abusing public trust are so enormous that the system remains paralyzed. So quickly did people give up any hope that Farias and Collor would be brought to justice that P.C., who blithely continued to expand his business empire as the revelations of his venality piled up, became a kind of perverse folk hero, a Brazilian D.B. Cooper, who according to barroom legend jumped from an airplane carrying the loot from a bank robbery and made good his escape. During the 1993 Carnival, two Rio samba schools and one in São Paulo depicted Farias in their Carnival floats—floats the size of those in Macy's Thanksgiving Day Parade. Outrageous humor seemed to pervade the Carnival: another float, by the Caprichosos de Pilares group, depicted a larger-than-life armed holdup of a camera-toting tourist by a *carioca* mugger.

The impunity of the system extends to lower-class criminals as well. The United States, with 250 million people, had 1.1 million in jail in 1993; Brazil, with 150 million, had 126,000 in jail, in cells built for a total of 52,000. For an estimated 1 million major crimes committed annually on Brazilian territory, there were 345,000 outstanding arrest warrants in 1993. Hardened criminals evade detention with seeming immunity. At the other end of the scale, the wealthy and powerful benefited from laws unique to Brazil. Criminal suspects with no previous arrests remained exempt from pretrial detention. The 2 percent of those arrested and charged with crime who were able to afford lawyers were rarely convicted. College graduates received individual cells and special treatment. "The only penalty for the rich," said Edmundo Oliveira, the head of a Justice Ministry commission to survey the system's results, "is to have to pay dearly for a good lawyer."[33] Brazil lacks a death penalty, but thousands of "criminal suspects" have been killed yearly by military police and other police vigilantes. With courts hopelessly backlogged, vigilantism has been increasingly supported by public opinion, to the point where in 1993 it verged on respectability among many.

The tide, however, seemed to be turning as public opinion began to demand reform. The military policeman charged with the murder of eight homeless children on the grounds of Rio's Candelária Church in 1993 was sentenced to a total of 309 years in prison in May 1996. This was a symbolic sentence, since no one can serve more than 30 years in Brazil, but the press lauded the sentence and noted that the officials had brought one of the key witnesses back from Switzerland to testify against the perpetrators, after which time he was placed in a witness protection program. He had fled to Europe after receiving death threats.[34]

Still, the resilience of impunity kept the "system" in place decade after decade, no matter what was the ideology or outlook of the national government or its inner circle. Impunity characterized the attitude of officials during the Empire, the various republics, the Vargas-era dictatorship, the populist governments of the 1950s and early 1960s, the military dictatorship, and after *abertura*. That arrogance and privilege not only survived after Collor's reformist campaign but flourished at an unprecedented level has caused untold anguish, and may have been the cause for the unleashing of the mass media against what it now called the "rotten system of government." In January 1994, Justice Minister Maurício Corrêa disclosed that, when a congressional scandal broke four months earlier, alleging that $200 million in federal grants to charities had been stolen by dozens of legislators, a coalition of São Paulo businessmen and middle-level military officials had discussed a Fujimori-style coup, proposing to President Franco that he close Congress and the courts and rule by decree. Franco demurred, but voices grew louder to remove the "vampires" continuing to hover over the system. "Beware the anger of the legions," warned General Benedito Onofre Bezerra Leonel, the army chief of staff.[35]

Virtually no measures existed for oversight. After the exposure in 1991 of a colossal illegal scheme whereby judges, federal employees, and lawyers had been siphoning off millions of dollars in pensions destined for nonexistent retirees, news stories revealed that the businessmen arrested for the scam lived under detention with maid service, exercise classes, books, free access to their cellular telephones and their lawyers, and visits from friendly judges apparently hoping to curry favor with the prisoners by demonstrating their sympathy. In November 1993 the governor of Paraíba audaciously took out a pistol and shot his former rival in the state capital's most elegant restaurant. He walked out the door untouched by police, and by the time he was arrested by federal authorities, a lavishly equipped luxury jail cell had already been prepared for him, complete with telephones, fax machines, and the comforts of home. Nor are guidelines for policy implementation subject to independent scrutiny. Systemic corruption extends to the national level, where the powerlessness of Congress is seen in the fact that it controls well less than 10 percent of the revenue of the federal government. The three public figures voted the "most corrupt" in Brazil— Orestes Quércia, the president of the national PMDB party; Paulo César Farias; and ex-Minister Antonio Rogério Magri—remained free.

In Italy, *Veja* pointed out, twelve months after a Collor–P.C. type scandal in 1992, more than 1,000 high public functionaries, businessmen, and politicians were jailed at least for one night, and 300 were indicted on criminal charges.[36] But in December 1994, the Supreme Court cleared Collor of all charges after first deciding to exclude detailed evidence of his fraud because it had not been obtained properly and because there was no documented proof that Collor had performed favors in return for the tens of millions he received, the court said. Before leaving for a skiing trip in Snowmass, Colorado, the forty-five-year-old Collor sent telegraphs to sixty world leaders announcing his intention to return to politics, proclaiming "my world is alongside the masses."[37] Farias was absolved of all charges except one and received a ridiculous penalty: a minuscule fine and the requirement that he sleep in a luxury jail cell during a seven-year period while being completely free during the day. He was released after two years. Eighty-eight percent of Brazilians polled on the subject said they were furious at the system. In mid-1996, the story ended. Farias, age fifty, was found shot to death in a Maceió beach house alongside his twenty-eight-year-old mistress. Like Collor, he was planning a political comeback.[38]

Democratic systems give reformers ammunition to fight corruption by providing an independent judicial system and an unrestrained forum in the media to air charges and to inform citizens. But democracies are not exempt from corruption. Elections increase the need for politicians to raise large sums of money, tempting many to accept donations and bribes from special interests. A well-organized dictatorship, Norman Gall reminds us, allows for a "one-stop-shopping" form of corruption, in which everyone in the game knows the rules and where venality is protected by the closed nature of the system. When such a society opens up, new problems arise. A free press reduces public tolerance for corruption but often focuses attention at the national level, giving greater opportunities at the local level for corruption. Decentralization often makes reform more difficult, and without institutional guarantees, watchdog agencies are helpless. Gall points to Brazil's Tribunal of Public Accounts as an example, "employing several thousand political hacks as parasites at the federal and state levels while abdicating their supervisory functions."[39]

Ordinary Brazilians have paid the price of the historical impertinence of Brazilian political institutions. How Brazilians have attempted to cope with the stubborn legacy of the system is the subject of the next three chapters, the first on tools of survival and the second on the more aggressive measures taken beyond coping. The third considers ways of coping that have been successful.

Notes

1. See David Maybury-Lewis, *The Savage and the Innocent* (Cleveland: World Publishing Company, 1965), 161.

2. The Portuguese title of Peter Kelleman's book was *Brasil para Principiantes,* 8th ed. (Rio de Janeiro: Civilização Brasileira, 1964), n.p.; cited (on p. 2) by Keith S. Rosenn, "Brazil's Legal Culture: The Jeito Revisited," *Florida International Law Journal* 1:1 (Fall 1984), 2 (2–43).

3. P. Kelleman, *Brasil para Principiantes,* 11–12; K.S. Rosenn, "Brazil's Legal Culture," 2.

4. K.S. Rosenn, "Brazil's Legal Culture," 3–4.

5. Lívia Barbosa, *O Jeitinho Brasileiro* (Rio de Janeiro: Editora Campus, 1992), 41.

6. Robert de Oliveira Campos, "A Sociologia do *Jeito*," in *A Técnica e o Risco* (Rio de Janeiro: Edições Apec, 1966); cited by L. Barbosa, *O Jeitinho Brasileiro*, 15.

7. João Camilo de Oliveira Tôrres, *Interpretação da Realidade Brasileira* (Rio de Janeiro: José Olympio Editora, 1973); cited by L. Barbosa, *O Jeitinho Brasileiro*, 18.

8. Clóvis de Abreu et al., "O *Jeitinho* Brasileiro como um Recurso de Poder," *Revista de Administração Pública* (Rio de Janeiro: Fundação Getúlio Vargas, 1982); cited by L. Barbosa, *O Jeitinho Brasileiro*, 26–27.

9. Gunnar Myrdal, *Asian Drama: An Inquiry into the Poverty of Nations* (New York: Pantheon, 1968), 952; cited by K. Rosenn, "Brazil's Legal Culture," 38.

10. Kenneth Paul Erickson, *The Brazilian Corporative State*, 6–7, citing Joaquim Nabuco, *O Abolicionismo* (São Paulo: Ed. Progresso, 1949), 158.

11. Philippe Schmitter, *Interest Conflict and Political Change in Brazil* (Stanford: Stanford University Press, 1971), 369; Antônio Carlos de Medeiros, *Politics and Intergovernmental Relations in Brazil, 1964–1982* (New York: Garland Publishing, 1986), 32–33.

12. Maria D'Alva Gil Kinzo, *Representação Política e Sistema Eleitoral no Brasil* (São Paulo: Edições Símbolo, 1980), 53.

13. See Joseph L. Love Jr. and Bert J. Barickman, "Rulers and Owners: A Brazilian Case Study in Comparative Perspective," *Hispanic American Historical Review* 66:4 (1986), 743–65.

14. Emir Sader and Ken Silverstein, *Without Fear of Being Happy: Lula, the Workers' Party, and Brazil* (New York: Verso, 1991), 12–13.

15. R.C. de Andrade, "Brazil: The Economics of Savage Capitalism," in M. Bienfeld and M. Godfrey, eds., *The Struggle for Development* (London: John Wiley and Sons, 1982); Paul Cammack, "Brazil: The Triumph of Savage Capitalism," *Bulletin of Latin American Research* 4 (1984), 117–30.

16. Robert Gay, "Community Organization and Clientelist Politics in Contemporary Brazil: A Case Study from Suburban Rio de Janeiro," *International Journal of Urban and Regional Research* 14:4 (December 1990), 650 (648–66).

17. Gay, "Community Organization," 654.

18. Fernando Henrique Cardoso, *Veja* (São Paulo), 29 June 1988, quoted by Frances Hagopian, *Traditional Politics and Regime Change in Brazil* (Boulder, CO: Westview Press, 1996), xxi.

19. See Kurt von Mettenheim, *The Brazilian Voter: Mass Politics in Democratic Transition, 1974–1986* (Pittsburgh: University of Pittsburgh Press, 1995).

20. His alleged use of cocaine was the basis for the title of one ferocious journalistic attack: Gilberto Felisberto Vasconcelos's *Collor: A Cocaína dos Pobres* (São Paulo: Icone Editora, 1989).

21. John Krich, *Why Is This Country Dancing?* (New York: Simon and Schuster, 1993), 58.

22. For an overview of the Collor scandal, see Gustavo Krieger, Luiz Antonio Novaes, and Tales Faria, *Todos os Sócios do Presidente*, 3rd ed. (São Paulo: Atualidade, 1992).

23. *New York Times*, 4 July 1993, A8; 24 July 1993, A3.

24. *Jornal do Brasil*, 11 July 1993, 1; *Istoé*, no. 1242, 21 July 1993, 28–29; *Veja*, 21 April 1993, 16–18.

25. *Istoé*, no. 1239, 30 June 1993, 28–31; *Veja*, 31 March 1993, 81.

26. The allegations were made by Claudio Humberto Rosa e Silva, writing from self-exile in Portugal. *New York Times*, 14 April 1993, A4.

27. *Latin American Regional Reports–Brazil*, RB-93–02, 11 February 1993, 7.

28. Renato Lessa, in *Ciência Hoje*, cited in *Latin American Weekly Report*, WR-93-18 (13 May 1993), 214.

29. *Latin American Weekly Report,* WR-91–18 (13 May 1993), 214.

30. *Miami Herald,* 13 November 1993, A30.

31. James Brooke, in *New York Times,* 29 August 1993, E6.

32. *Veja,* 26:12 (24 March 1993), 18.

33. Cited by James Brooke, *New York Times,* 29 August 1993, E6.

34. *Latin American Regional Reports,* 16 May 996, 215; 6 June 1996, 8.

35. James Brooke, *New York Times,* 4 January 1994, 1; 9 January 1994, 4–2.

36. *Veja,* 26:12 (24 March 1993), 17.

37. *New York Times,* 30 December 1994, A4.

38. *O Globo* (Rio de Janeiro), 13 December, 1994, 1; *New York Times,* 24 June 1996, A5, 28 June 1996, A3.

39. Norman Gall, "Corruption and Democracy," *Braudel Papers* (São Paulo), 13 (1996), 6.

Carnival celebrants waiting for transportation, Rio de Janeiro, 1941

Street performers, Praça XV, Rio de Janeiro, 1941

All photographs by Genevieve Naylor (1915–1989). © by The Reznikoff Artistic Partnership. Courtesy of Peter Reznikoff.

Society matrons at Jockey Club, Rio de Janeiro, 1940

Working-class restaurant, Rio de Janeiro, 1941

Agricultural day laborers, location unknown, c. 1941

Laborers pushing a riverboat from a sand bar, São Francisco River, 1941

Audience at rally, probably Rio de Janeiro, 1941

Men and women outside café, Congonhas, Minas Gerais, 1941

Boy cobbler at his bench in violation of labor laws, location unknown, 1941

Rural water carriers, location unknown, 1941

Waiting room, town hall, São João del Rei, Minas Gerais, 1941

Musicians at Carnival, Rio de Janeiro, 1941

Religious penitents, Congonhas, Minas Gerais, 1941

Father and daughter aboard riverboat on São Francisco River, 1941

5

Tools for Survival

Everyday life masks the struggles of millions of Brazilians to earn enough to make ends meet. The coping strategies that the poor use are creative and diverse, but they do not always work. They include economic tactics to create and stretch income; political strategies (organizing, voting as a bloc, negotiating with politicians); economic strategies (exploiting the irregularity of work patterns, for example), and cultural strategies (adopting beliefs, symbols, and attitudes that govern behavior). Language can be a tool to sustain morale and to fight back: Afro-Brazilian cultists involved in *xangô* spiritism use vocabulary from their African heritage not only as a source of self-pride but to exclude nonpractitioners from their inner world. Humor also enters the picture, along with entrepreneurship. Within days of the revelations about Collor's corruption, artisans were selling on the street little birdcages holding tiny dolls representing Collor and his henchman, P.C. Farias. White-garbed *mães de santo* in Salvador sold Brazilian flags draped with black ribbons for waving during the pro-impeachment parades.

The poorest Brazilians do not have the luxury of devising long-range strategies because they have to scratch to provide enough food to assuage hunger. Homeless people and shantytown residents in Brazilian cities eat the foods left on the ground in *macumba* offerings. A destitute woman sitting with her child in the street watching a tourist toss grains of rice from a bag for the pigeons was observed picking up the rice grains, one by one, after the bird feeder left. Beggars and scavengers are often forced to employ exhaustive means to conserve resources. For instance, children board city buses and hand out to each passenger a message ("I am an orphan; I support eight brothers and sisters," for example) reproduced on photocopied paper and cut into rectangles a few inches in size; they collect alms from the passengers, then painstakingly return to each passenger to retrieve the printed message for use again and again—just as beggars do in the New York City subways or in American airport waiting lounges.

When people are hungry, or when behaving aggressively or according to socially unacceptable norms promises to yield more benefits than allowable behavior, more desperate behavior often ensues, even among people considered docile. Over the centuries, around the world, those in dire need have turned to begging. Brazil has been no exception. Brazilian elites were so worried that large numbers of ex-slaves would become mendicants that, following emancipation, virtually every state and locality issued laws and regulations enlarging legal definitions of vagrancy. Beggars permitted to sit in public could not be from another place; they had to be licensed, regulated, and controlled. Nonetheless, for generations beggars have thronged the streets of Brazilian cities, many of them deformed or displaying diseased limbs or vile rashes, others scooting legless down the sidewalks on crude wheeled boards, and still others holding infants screaming from hunger. Many have sat in the same place—at the foot of bridges, or in front of important buildings—for years. Blind beggars have had children with them as guides.

During the 1960s, Rio de Janeiro's governor, Carlos Lacerda, was believed to have ordered the police to clear the street of beggars, gathering them up in trucks and dumping them in sacks into the river; similar stories were believed in Recife and in many other cities in the Northeast. The effect of these "street cleanings" lasted only a few weeks, however, as swarms of new beggars from the interior took the place of the ones displaced. Affluent Brazilians learned to avoid beggars, just as Americans avoid homeless people in the streets. "They never get to keep what one gives them," one explanation went; others swore that mendicants earned too much from begging, or that they spent what they got on alcohol, which may have been true in some cases.

Beggars suffer continual abuse, including such taunts as "vagabond," "*malandro*" (good-for-nothing), "crazy," "burro's ass," "dirty," "garbage," and "dog." A 1977 study showed that many were children; many others more than forty-five years of age, and therefore considered unemployable. Beggars tended to come from smaller cities but with family origins in the rural lower class. The majority, as one would expect, were illiterate, unmarried, and veterans of more than five years of begging for a living. Virtually none of the beggars interviewed had other sources of income; they lived on the alms they received. Contrary to the prevailing wisdom about beggars as aggressive and shameless, almost all the beggars said that they suffered from embarrassment when they asked for handouts.

They made it clear that they would prefer to hold jobs. "When you work," a forty-nine-year-old man said, "you are not humiliated, you have a place for yourself; you are respected." A younger man said that he was forced to beg because he had been robbed and his documents stolen. A second man gave the same reason: he was taken ill, lost his job, and then was mugged and lost his papers. They admitted their weaknesses. A woman claimed that she asked for rum because when she entered a bar and asked for bread, they turned her down, but they always gave her a drink. She had become an alcoholic this way, she said. Another claimed that he drank because the liquor gave him courage to beg, an act he found terrifying. "It's preferable to beg than to steal, right?" another asked. In February 1993, a reporter counted 450 beggars living in São Paulo's Plantão da Sé, at the heart of the city's center, begging. Many were migrants who had left their families in the interior, hoping to find jobs before bringing them. To avoid humiliation, many of them wrote to their wives that things were good. Three hundred beggars, mostly teenage boys, slept under the protective overhang of a large department store.[1]

Coping Strategies

The poor contend with the hardships of their lives by using techniques that include not only innocent and ingenious ways to add income but also psychological devices and ruses to deal with individuals and institutions from the world from which the poor are excluded. There is likely little difference between strategies to endure and to overcome hardship. Forced by the system to endure patronizing behavior and required by employment to hide their emotions behind a servile demeanor, members of the lower class whose work brings them into close contact with the affluent often engage in role playing, assuming postures of deference and docility in the workplace and casting off these masks on returning to their own world. Sometimes this has brutal consequences: the built-up stress of servile behavior day after day can lead to excessive drinking, or to the abuse of women and children at home, especially when men frustrated by forced demeanors of servitude take their feelings out on those psychologically subservient to them.[2]

An example of one of the remarkable things Brazilians do to deal with hardship is the common practice of raising the children of others as a family's own. Legal adoption, requiring immense red tape, involves only a small percentage of the cases of children being cared for by others. Society has traditionally recognized "natural" children, fathered by the master of the household or one of his sons and borne illegitimately by slaves or servants. Large Brazilian families have typically been nonchalant about the small mulatto children underfoot. These children eventually would grow up and leave the house, sometimes with quiet financial help from their father, sometimes not. Being known as a "natural" child of an influential parent was an advantage and brought a certain degree of status.

Unlike the United States, where cross-racial adoptions are controversial and frowned on by many, in Brazil compassion about familyless children tends to be color-blind. In April 1996 I visited E., born in a São Paulo favela, now married and living with her family in a working-class suburb on the periphery of the city's industrial South zone. E. lives with her husband, a metalworker, four children, and seven dogs (all former strays). E. is a teacher in a middle school in which classrooms hold forty-two students and for which she is paid $2 per class. Her empathy for others has moved her to take in one of her brother's children, because he cannot provide for her, and in 1995 a woman "gave" her a three-month-old infant boy, whom she is raising. That the child is Caucasian and E. a *mulata* meant nothing. The child needed a home.

Ordinary Brazilians have always helped one another cope by extending heartwarming compassion in times of distress. Albert Camus saw this when during a tour of São Paulo in 1949 he was taken to a radio station where people in need of assistance were telling their stories on the air. During the program, a heavy, poorly dressed black man came to the microphone holding a five-month-old girl in his arms. He explained that his wife had left him and that he could not take care of the child. While he spoke, another participant in the program, a former pilot who had served in the Second World War and who now was looking for a job as a mechanic, held the baby and fed her a bottle. Then the telephones began to ring. Within a short time, an older black man entered the studio, dressed in pajamas. He had been sleeping, Camus wrote, but his wife had awakened him, telling him to go the radio station and "get the child." The infant girl was taken home with the man, to a new life.[3]

Alternative Economies

Brazilians have long turned to the informal, or alternate, economy to supplement their income. Studies show that it is virtually impossible for families to live on two minimum wages, the criterion on which the official definition of poverty is set. The main available options for such families are either extralegal, off-the-books employment or the holding of more than one full-time job by family members. Boys stand at intersections wiping windshields, "watch" parked cars, or carry shopping bags for tips that rarely bring in more than the equivalent of 50 cents a day. Men, women, and children sell things on the street—bags of nuts, combs, clothespins, Lifesavers *(drops),* blank audiotapes, watches, tools, bags of onions—whatever they can get from middlemen; some of the merchandise is stolen. When this does not produce enough to buy food, the itinerant salesmen resort to begging or stealing. Children wash cars parked on the street or "guard" them (these boys are called *flanelinhas;* if the motorist does not pay them, they might smash his windshield). Adults perform work in exchange for goods or services. Ironically, recent action by Rio's city government to regulate "car guard" charges on public streets (at $1 per car) has meant that the former extortionists now earn more in a weekend than some full-time workers receive for a month's labor.[4]

Some Brazilians estimate that more than half of *all* economic activity in the country is part of the parallel economy. Since the early 1980s, "indirect" wages, as economists call them, have increased steadily as a proportion of total income.[5] This is not readily apparent when examining official unemployment rates, because these rates are calculated as a percentage of the economically active population who have been looking for a job during a given thirty-day period. Since millions do not go through regular channels to find employment, Brazil's claimed rate of well under 10 percent unemployment cannot be taken seriously. On the other hand, in 1993, 42.2 percent of the 15.9 million economically active residents of the metropolitan areas of the largest cities (São Paulo, Rio de Janeiro, Belo Horizonte, Porto Alegre, Recife, and Salvador) were acknowledged by government statistics to be working off the books, a gain of five percentage points from three years earlier. In 1991, the United Nations' International Labor Organization (ILO) asserted that of the estimated 300 million people worldwide living off the informal economy, 32 million, or 11 percent of the world total, were Brazilians.[6]

The informal sector has all the known disadvantages of income variability due to lack of regular work. Still, it also has advantages. Off-the-books workers do not need to present educational credentials. They can have flexible working hours. The parallel economy allows for multiple job holding (working simultaneously in the formal and informal market), and permits participants to work as hard as they want to earn more. In the 1950s and 1960s, when imported goods were both costly and highly sought after, affluent Brazilians often traveled to the United States or Europe and returned with luggage filled with nylon stockings, cosmetics, or jeans. Selling them to their relatives and neighbors was an accepted way to raise cash: even Juscelino Kubitschek's wife, Sara, was reputed to have done this when she returned from Paris with dozens of large suitcases. More recently, the lower relative cost of air fares (able to be paid off in installments), has made reselling imported goods a middle-class business. Many housewives, moreover, sell to friends clothing and accessories that they purchase on credit from wholesalers or that they receive from relatives in the interior, where labor costs virtually nothing. Some students use their parents' home computers to publish newsletters or to produce spreadsheet printouts. For some, the decision to enter the underground economy pays lucrative dividends. "Six years ago I quit my job with the state," said Gisela Souza, age thirty-two, a *carioca,* because her off-the-books business selling handmade clothing to stores and in private homes brought in three times her old income, and she paid no taxes on her profits.[7] Middle-class parents sometimes buy automobiles on credit for their sons or daughters when they marry, as wedding gifts to be outfitted as taxis and rented out to gypsy cab drivers.

Even in colonial times and during the nineteenth century, rural areas supported a widespread alternative agrarian economy of the free poor and, later, immigrant producers. Ultimately the parallel economy accounted for a quarter of all coffee production in the South. *Colonos* (indebted land settlers) managed to sell vegetables and eggs and other produce from their garden plots and to use their income to buy small farms. Not only did they supply cheap raw materials to other sectors of the economy, but they came to constitute a domestic market for manufactures, thus spurring factory production in the region.[8] Child labor also fed the system. In 1990, more than 2.5 million Brazilian children under the age of seventeen worked in agriculture, each earning well under $30 a month. Children from ten to fourteen years old working on the land composed half of the total number, and their wages were even lower than those of the older children. Salaries in the Northeast were usually a third lower than in the more prosperous South. Children put to work by their parents, of course, received no wages at all.[9]

In towns and cities, private economic activity has often taken the form of small workshops and irregular factories, sometimes in garages or upper-floor apartments or garrets. Some of these activities are legitimate, run by industrial subcontractors taking advantage of accessible space in empty buildings and a willing work force. Others are semilegitimate; many others are completely "off the books," illegal, or even hidden. The gamut runs from piecework at home to criminal activity. Women are commonly hired for labor under unsanitary working conditions, including poor lighting, inadequate ventilation, and no safety measures at all. Wages are very low. Contracts between workers and employers, if they exist on paper at all, are not enforced; benefits are neither expected nor paid. Some workers, however, mostly those who are highly skilled, prefer their informal status, since it provides more independence. Unregistered factories in earlier decades produced handmade goods from lace to shawls; today workers are also engaged in such work as the illegal duplication of videotapes for rental shops, and putting together computers from imported parts. Clandestine factories manufacture bogus perfumes and scotch whiskey; cut and polish realistic-looking ersatz gems; and, of course, manufacture, cut, and package crack cocaine and a myriad of other illicit drugs.

Underground and illicit economic activity often yields higher profit than the formal economy. Since the 1970s, narcotics trafficking has altered the economic landscape of much of Brazil. In the early 1990s, northeastern Pernambuco became the world's largest producer of marijuana, producing $350 billion cruzeiros, employing 100,000 rural workers, and exporting more than 432,000 tons of the final product. Planter Francisco de Assís Bezerra of Sítio Vertentes, Mirandiba, in the central part of the state, admitted that the sale of one harvest of marijuana leaves brought in more profit than he would make in forty-one years of harvesting black beans, the usual crop in the region. One acre of marijuana—requiring relatively little labor, water, or fertilizer—yielded the same income as 26 acres of bananas, 59 acres of corn, or 104 acres of beans.[10] Illicit marijuana plantations in Pernambuco alone totaled one-quarter of the total amount of cultivated land in the state. Marijuana is grown in the arid hills, on Indian reservations, in the worker *agrovilas* constructed by hydroelectric power monopoly for its workers, on ranches, in parks, and on unused state and federal land. Marijuana wholly supported the economies of nineteen municipalities in Pernambuco, according to estimates cited in the national press.[11]

In the more prosperous agricultural regions of the South, family labor is supplemented by voluntary exchanges of work among neighbors. In the Northeast, this practice is called the *mutirão,* although in recent decades it has fallen somewhat into disuse. It survives as the *puxerão* in the far South, where large groups of neighbors assemble on one farm on a Saturday to bring in the harvest. After the work is completed, the host offers the workers a *churrasco* (barbecue), wine, and *cachaça* in thanks. Some complain that people come mostly for the food and drink, and that the work done is halfhearted. More frequent is the arrangement called *trocar dias,* exchanged labor done according to an agreed-upon number of days on each farm. This occurs also in urban areas, but the underground economy there offers more opportunities. These include the numbers game *(jogo de bicho);* drug trafficking; prostitution involving females, males, and male *travestis* (transvestites); sales by itinerant street vendors *(camelôs);* the work of off-the-books day laborers, domestics, and other employees; financial deals by money exchangers, con artists, predated check operators, and businesses and persons with bank accounts abroad; and all other parts of the economy and areas of government where bribes are involved. In working-class neighborhoods, houses bear handwritten notices offering manicures and pedicures, hairdressing, and small repairs. Streets are crowded with stands and carts selling plastic combs, hairdryers, cassette tapes (pirated, stolen, or both), cigarettes, candy, and prepared foods. When a bus breaks down, within minutes people come pouring out of their residences with trays of cakes or other homemade goods to sell to the stranded passengers. To counter the wave of tens of thousands of Bolivians who have arrived illegally in the cities of the South, especially São Paulo, Brazilian hustlers with travel papers journey by bus to Paraguay to buy cheap clothing for resale across the border.

For some, economic progress has reduced opportunities for making a living in the alternative economy. Many slum dwellers for decades have been able to survive by scavenging—walking the streets with sacks on their heads, collecting paper, tin, and other refuse to be sold by the pound. Carolina Maria de Jesus, the woman from Canindé favela in São Paulo whose published diary entries in 1960 electrified the world, was a professional scavenger who, in the pattern of such things, had established a regular route among customers who she knew would buy from her. Encroaching municipal services, including the hiring of garbagemen and the extension of collection services to poor districts, gave employment to some as sanitation workers but drove the marginalized garbage pickers out of business.

It is known that powerful people are linked to profits which originate in the parallel sector. The numbers racket kingpins, the *bicheiros*—like mafiosos in the United States—have diversified, and in many cases no longer are directly involved in the numbers game. Some have been involved in politics, paying off mayors and even governors; many have become involved in drug selling. Others have cultivated status as civic leaders, rising to the presidencies of important Carnival associations and sports clubs. Some have become engaged in smuggling and in rackets. There has long been national admiration for the *malandro,* the wise guy who beats the system using quick wits.

Being a little bit of a *malandro* is considered a positive trait. Millions have translated their dreams for better lives into betting on the outcome of soccer matches, laying down a sizable share of their tiny disposable incomes for lottery tickets. Numbers games, when they were introduced during the nineteenth century to Rio de Janeiro, immediately gained enormous popularity, and eventually authorities got into the act by formalizing lotteries and soccer pools. Stories about destitute families rescued from dire straits by the magic of a winning lottery ticket fill the tabloid press, although the odds of anyone's winning such a windfall remain astronomically high. Men and women also go to remarkable lengths to achieve personal gain: in São Paulo a "kissing marathon," offering a grand prize of a new automobile, went on for two months before all but one exhausted couple separated their lips.

A system flexible enough to permit entrepreneurship at all levels within an active alternative economy has its healthy side. I have long admired the figures made of clay and painted bright colors, popularized by the master Vitelino at the market in Caruraru, Pernambuco. For decades, he and his sons turned out tiny cowboys, backlands women, bandits, dentists pulling teeth, saints, and other replicas of characteristic regional figures. During the 1980s, northeastern migrants to the South began to sell the same kinds of clay objects at the handcraft fair held on Sundays at the Praça da República in São Paulo. On one visit, I remarked to my friend José Carlos Sebe Bom Meihy that it would be interesting to ask one of the artisans to make a chess set depicting backlands characters, perhaps even figures from the story of Canudos, which I was writing about. On his next visit to Miami, he surprised me with a gift: exactly such a set of chess pieces an inch or two high, with *bumba-meu-bois* (northeastern decorated bulls) for knights, black-cassocked backlands priests as the bishops, and cowhands as the pawns. Within a couple of years, moreover, the idea had spread to other northeastern artisans at the fair, and now everyone was making not only chess sets but children's games depicting folkloric themes. One day I saw such a set advertised in the Sunday paper. The sets were now being made in such numbers that they could be sold at the retail level, and priced accordingly. Sets which are the exact replicas of the one commissioned by José Carlos are now sold in every major tourist souvenir shop in the country, including the pricey gift shops in the international departure lounges of the airports in São Paulo and Rio. An entire mini-industry had been started from an off-hand observation. Only in an economy so open and flexible as the one described could this have happened so quickly. My hope is that the artisans who thought the idea was a good one are profiting from it, and that they have not yet been overwhelmed by the commercialization of their art.

Ritual Relations and Popular Culture

Public festivities, and especially the exuberant annual pre-Lenten festival of Carnival, permit the temporary suspension of status and the flight of passions in percussive rhythm, movement, and revelry. These activities, however, often deteriorate into *brigas* (violent brawls) in which drunken men beat their women, robbers prey on bystanders, and street brawlers fight and stab one another with knives. Most Carnival participants channel whatever aggression they may have through mimicry, in their costumes and in musical forms of stylized belligerence. Carnival tolerates aggression by labeling it play and by ignoring the year's harvest of Carnival injuries and murders in clubs, bars, and the street. An encounter involving mimicry requires agreement from both parties, and when this agreement breaks down, violence may result. Carnival affords opportunities to *desabafar,* to get things off one's chest, to expel the year's accumulated frustration and anger. When it ends in bloodshed, it is a sign that the system has broken down.

Individual encounters in a system in which wages earned by the majority of the population do not suffice can be harrowing. Brazilian interpersonal relations involve intimate social exchanges requiring physical presence and interaction. Touching, embraces, smiles, verbal play, and the emotive use of the voice all play a far greater role in Brazilian society than, for example, in Western Europe or Protestant North America. Physical contact has two facets: not only amity but enmity. Meetings between strangers or between persons from different cultures (say, the coast and the hinterland) are fraught with danger, because the circumstances bring out hostility and the need to defend one's moral ground.[12]

Insofar as aggressive behavior and *brigas* are ritualistic, conforming to unwritten but widely understood rules, they are also cultural performances. For the participants, they represent ways of coping with the hierarchy and their lack of privilege. In a way, the rules protect them, because they know how to back away at the last minute to save face and avoid violence. One of the most perilous aspects of the spreading influence of hard drugs in Brazilian life during and after the 1970s has been that persons under the influence of cocaine or heroin—much more so than *pinga,* Brazil's traditional inebriating substance—abandon the rules, and thus jeopardize themselves and their antagonists.

It has long been presumed that the Brazilian people's intense relationship with music, folk art, spirituality, and other forms of cultural expression function as a natural safety valve for pent-up frustrations. This is likely too simplistic an explanation to be valid, and it does not explain how there can be a phenomenal attraction to austere, reactionary evangelical religious cults in the midst of a culture as open and as tolerant to what outsiders see as libidinous sensuality. Brazil, Caetano Veloso once sang, may be "a little absurd," but it has "perfect pitch."[13] The national love affair with popular culture, after all, and particularly the ubiquitous love of music, amounts to a collective form of coping.[14]

Many cultural occurrences empower their participants psychologically. Runaway slaves (maroons) of Nigerian origin established a colony at Paracatu in Minas Gerais, in which they practiced *acotunda,* an eighteenth-century version of Nigerian spiritism that survived in the region long after the runaways were captured.[15] *Candomblé* flowered in the coastal planta-tion region at the same time that in the cattle ranches of the northeastern backlands from Maranhão to Bahia, a stylized musical folk drama, *bumba-meu-boi,* created by slaves during the second half of the eighteenth century, represented a sly form of cultural resistance to Brazil's European culture. The performance, often lasting through the night, was held during the days around São João and was accompanied by the sounds of native instruments, including *matracas,* blocks of wood that produce urgent sandpapery sounds when rubbed together. The pageant narrates the tale of a ranch master, a symbol of income and power in the region, who is outwitted by clever blacks, *caboclos,* and Indians; it includes masked figures dressed as clowns, bullies, and cowboys, all in a riot of color. The performances, or *boizinhas,* as they were sometimes called, which were rooted in the African tradition permitting insults when they were sung, were figured out by white elites, who banned them starting in the early nineteenth century. They began to be toler-ated again in some places during the 1860s, and for another century provided a fairly harmless outlet for locals who wanted to laugh at whites.

Religious movements offer extensive opportunities for coping, offering believers the motivation to fight back, or to endure hardship. Even the conservatism of such folk religious leaders as Padre Cícero Romão Batista, whose community in the backlands of Ceará attracted tens of thousands of devout settlers for several decades after 1889—masked elements of popular resistance. Even today, Padre Cícero symbolizes the defiant expression of independence in the present-day interior, as illustrated by the fact that virtu-ally every household from Maranhão to Bahia has a statue or medal of the turn-of-the-century backlands prelate in his black robes, although he was excommunicated by the Church a century earlier.

Long called by the Vatican the world's largest Roman Catholic country, Brazil nonetheless has presented nettlesome challenges to Catholic ortho-doxy. Only during the Babylonian Captivity between 1580 and 1640, when the zealous Spanish Crown acquired tutelage over Portugal under the tem-porary dynastic merger that saw Spanish monarchs rule over Portugal jointly for sixty years, did the Church in Brazil act aggressively to curb unorthodox religious practices among its flock. Men and women imported from Africa as slaves brought their own spiritist religions with them, al-though most were nominally converted to Catholicism. By 1818, the over-whelming presence in the population of black slaves meant not only that African spiritist ritual and cosmology imbued everyday Catholicism with its own particular flavor, but that in many cases (not only among slaves but among the free poor) the resulting blended forms of religious expression were more African and indigenous than Roman Catholic. Usually, officials left blacks to their own practices, but occasionally they cracked down, as in 1785 when the Calandu cult in Bahia's Recôncavo was ruthlessly suppressed. Ironically for the Vatican, the strong structural parallels between Catholicism and West African religious culture, as well as the lack of clerical authority at the parish level, due in part to understaffing, made it easier for people to drift from Catholicism to religious practices of African origin.

Brazil, of course, is steeped in five centuries of Catholicism, starting when the discoverer Pedro Álvares Cabral implanted a cross in Brazilian soil in 1500. Half of Brazil's sixteen national holidays are Catholic. Ten percent of all Brazilian cities and towns are named for saints. Crucifixes are displayed in state hospitals, classrooms, and public offices despite formal separation of Church and state in 1891. Yet, if the Brazilian state has been characterized by abrupt changes in orientation and direction over the centuries, the same may be said for the Brazilian Catholic Church. Institutionally, it was not nearly as wealthy as its Spanish-American counterparts during the colonial era. Until relatively late in the colonial period, Brazil was a backwater in the Portuguese overseas empire, and in any case much less missionary zeal emanated from Lisbon than from Madrid. The Jesuits made an impact in rural frontier areas, but they were expelled in 1759. During the nineteenth century the Church remained understaffed and underfinanced. With the exception of one seminary, in Fortaleza, Ceará, where new priests were instilled with a good dose of orthodoxy, Church practices (and the personal morality of priests) tended to be lax. European-born missionaries from such regular orders as the Franciscans, Salesians, and Dominicans arriving in the nineteenth century from France, Italy, Germany, and other Western European countries were often scandalized by the living habits of native-born priests and by what they considered to be the frightfully primitive nature of the religious expression of the *povo*.

It did not help that Emperor Pedro II, who considered himself enlightened, was a thirty-third-degree Mason—heresy for the titular head of the national Catholic Church. After midcentury, with the popularity of the monarchy waning, both republicanism and anticlerical positivism grew steadily in influence. Church fathers dueled with the government and lost; the 1891 republican Constitution disestablished Catholicism as the state religion and separated Church and state, nominally at least—a striking act for a country steeped exclusively in Catholic tradition. Responding to Vatican pressures to enforce orthodoxy in sacramental practices but lacking the manpower to instruct the population, the Church lost more and more souls to *candomblé* and other forms of spiritism. Protestantism also made inroads among elites seeking to modernize Brazil and equating Protestantism with progress. Presbyterian, Methodist, Baptist, and other North American–based ministries established private schools around the turn of the century, and for decades, at least some Brazilians of note attended them, including the ethnohistorian Gilberto Freyre and the nonsmoking, nondrinking soccer star Almir Albuquerque, "O Pernambuquinho." This Protestantism differed greatly from the fundamentalist Pentecostal sects that would make inroads fifty years later, with a much more lower-class appeal.

For generations, *candomblé* was suppressed by officials angered at the religion's use of Catholic saints to hide the African deities. In time, however, attitudes began to relax. The role of *oguns* (deacons), honorary positions which conferred rights and privileges at the cult centers, began to be taken by upper-class whites. These *oguns* acted as agents representing the *candomblé* practitioners, exchanging protection for votes. The religion, then, although entirely a product of African culture, came to depend on negotiated links to the elite world of whites. This was the first step in the transformation of *candomblé* into a practice gradually accepted by the general population, by tourist officials, and even by intellectuals and the Catholic Church.[16]

After all, in the small towns and villages of the vast hinterland, all but nominal Church influence was meager. Many outlying parishes were visited by priests, traveling in the manner of circuit judges, once every several years. The landless population of the interior, especially in the Northeast, believed that life yielded suffering and other acts of misfortune brought upon by divine retribution for failure of individuals to accept their circumstances. During a period of excessive rainfall that caused farmers to lose their crops of beans in one community, most of the local residents attributed the calamity to the fact that a neighbor had earlier cursed God for neglecting to send rain. Backlanders viewed individual saints as protectors or patrons. They stressed the fatherly nature of God: dispensing protection and benevolence but also stern punishment, just as did the traditional landowner or patron. At the same time, saints were feared. Misfortunes—disease, ill luck, even devastating weather—were blamed on individuals' misdeeds. Saints were thought to punish sinners, in the tradition of the Golden Legend *(Legenda Áurea)* dating back to twelfth-century France and Italy. As a result, the backlands were filled with shrines to which devout souls came, often under hardship and sometimes crawling on bloodied knees, to make *promessas,* or penitential vows, sometimes to thank a saint for a favorable personal intervention, more often to plead for help or to beg for forgiveness. The tradition helped shape the singular nature of Catholicism as practiced by the rural poor. Promises were made directly to Jesus or to a saint on a *quid pro quo* basis for a specific desire on the part of the votary. As a result, the faith of humble backlanders was often tinged with fear: without much hope of hierarchical aid, for priests rarely were available in rural communities, they had to negotiate not only with the world but the devil, whose presence was always felt, and with the supernatural.

After the 1880s the intrusion of the outside world increased. People-to-people relationships remained largely unchanged, but the passage of time, accelerated abruptly in the transition from monarchy to republic, brought new pressures to bear. From Rome (and then Fortaleza and Salvador) came neo-orthodox reform and hierarchical displeasure at the role of lay Catholic preachers *(beatos)* and other itinerants. Coastal elites in cities where the Church presence was strong tended to accept these reforms, but the rural population, fearful of the growing effort by outsiders to change their lives, reacted negatively. Most hostile to the reforms were the backlands *matutos* (a colloquial term for countryside rustics, analogous to *caipiras* in the South; *guascas* in Rio Grande do Sul; or *catingueiros,* inhabitants of the backlands' *caatinga* region). The *matutos* preserved their Portuguese peasant traits, especially their devout Catholicism, whereas *caboclos* and blacks tended to embrace spiritism derived from Bantu and Yoruba worship. Penitential lay Catholic missionaries, often laymen like Father Ibiapina, who abandoned his normal life to wander through the backlands preaching morality and the immanence of the final judgment, powerfully influenced villagers, especially in remote places where priests rarely visited. Catholicism, as well, provided blacks with martyrs and saints, including Anastásia, an eighteenth-century slave who, after being unjustly accused by her master's jealous wife of seducing him, was forced to wear an iron mask for the rest of her life.

Folk belief in supernatural intervention reduced the need in the region to rely on alternative political and legal mechanisms for social control. In the Brazilian case, because rural men and women believed that misfortune was the result of the failure to accept one's predestined lot in life, and accepted additional suffering in the form of droughts or disease as divine retribution, subjugation was accepted, usually without protest. Backlanders expected punishment when they did not fulfill duties *(obrigações)* to the saints or to God after assistance had been petitioned through a vow *(promessa)*. This is not to say that the faithful faced life with complete resignation. They fought tenaciously to surmount obstacles, wrestling with the earth at the same time that they called on individual saints to mediate between the secular and the sacred worlds. Existence involved constantly restating one's faith in the power and goodness of personal deities.

Devout backlands folk prayed constantly for divine intervention, groveling on dirt floors in rustic churches and chanting for salvation. We have noted the strenuous devotion to particular saints. They were believed to be able not only to cure disease but to cause afflictions, which then could only be removed through vows and pilgrimages to specified shrines or holy places believed to be inhabited by the particular saint's presence. Men and women offered heroic vows in exchange for favors; when the vows failed, the pious blamed themselves and pledged more self-denial and suffering. For many humble men and women, even daily devotions were expressed with such concentration and fervor that outsiders were astonished.

Prayers and pilgrimages were habits, ways of expressing intense wishes. The phenomenon derived from medieval roots native to the Iberian peninsula. Offerings—food products, knitted pieces of clothing, candles, rosaries of wood or *uricuri* shells, carved wax relics, and more elaborate ex-voto images (sculptured representations of injured or deformed body parts) were deposited at pilgrimage shrines, as if part of a personal transaction between supplicant and saint. These offerings were not mechanistic gestures; rather, they permitted exteriorization of anxiety and heavy emotion. Da Cunha attributed one fetishistic rite to the charismatic aesthete Antônio Conselheiro himself: the "kissing" of the images at the end of the long, drawn-out daily prayer service in Belo Monte, after "having run the gamut of litanies, said all the rosaries, and intoned all the rhyming benedicites." Starting with Pious Anthony, the altar boy, then taken up by Conselheiro and finally by every congregant in turn, every crucifix, saint's image, veronica, and cross in the Church would be passed along from hand to hand, from mouth to mouth, accompanied by "the indistinct drone of half-stammered exhortations" and "stifled exclamations of the throng."[17] Such graphic descriptions dismayed city readers and reinforced their discomfort about backlands life.

Flagellant practices—*Imitatio Christi*—introduced by Jesuits and Franciscans in the sixteenth century, survived and took on a life of their own in many backlands communities, where they became focal points for group associations. More than anything else, this strong penitential tradition explains the passivity with which Canudos residents accepted their lot. People were thin because their diet was restricted but also because of the *culto de fome,* the practice of almost continual fasting as a penitential act to mortify the body. Everyday backlands religious practices contained aggressive elements as well. *Ermitães* (shrine hermits), in exchange for payment, incanted "black" prayers, casting spells against enemies in a Catholicized variant of animism and black magic.

Rural and urban poor alike frequently used marijuana—variously called *diamba, rafi, maconha,* or *fumo d'Angola*—especially in the São Francisco region and the Northeast coast. Herbalists knew about the properties of other, more powerful mind-altering substances, and probably introduced them to communal ceremonies and occasions. Healers also prescribed natural remedies—salt for healing and apotropaic rites, boxwood, the poisonous seed of the cashew fruit—for cathartic ends, not nature worship. Then there were miracles and miraculous citings, usually experienced after the unexplained restoration of health, often after a return from a pilgrimage to a religious shrine. Claims of miracles were part of the popular cultural system, and were often welcomed by the Church. The commotion raised by miracles brought respite from the monotony of everyday life in "remote, patriarchal communities," and brought instant prestige and importance to the humble sufferer able to attest to the miraculous.[18]

Denigrated for their "mestizo religion" and for their heritage of "a multitude of extravagant superstitions which are no longer to be found along the seaboard," backlanders exhibited behavior which confirmed the prejudices of those judging them. They were ridiculed as being profligate. Rural families often ran to more than a dozen children. One woman, at forty years of age, was said to have borne thirty children, of whom eleven survived.[19] Forms of reaction varied but remained consistent with the stoic "vale of tears" outlook on life. Day-to-day hardship was accepted, although when a long-standing condition changed abruptly, local inhabitants mobilized spontaneously in protest. This was the case in the Quebra-Quilo eruptions throughout much of the rural interior of the Northeast, after the government introduced new regulations that had the effect of challenging the traditional way of doing business at the weekly markets. The rioters, it could be argued, smashed the weighing machines not in sullen ignorance, but precisely because they understood that government regulation, however "fair" to consumers, would bring new government control. What coastal officials deemed reformist and progress-minded, the backlanders saw as a violation of their autonomy. Individuals were not thought to have the right to complain about their own condition, whether rich or poor, because that was God's design.

Backlanders refused to marry on Sundays, and girls marrying on Sant'ana Day, in late July, were believed to risk dying in childbirth. The member of the couple who got into bed first, it was said, would determine the sex of the first child; the one who left the bed before the other in the morning would be the first to die. Wedding parties—even in austere Canudos—were greeted with rifle shots into the air, fireworks, cheers, and elaborate feasting. One prescription, that a banquet had to be held no matter how humble the bride and groom, had the effect of giving even the poorest members of the community something a bit special in their lives.

Backlands townspeople, somewhat more circumspect and formally Roman Catholic in their outward behavior than inhabitants of rural areas, also clung to old beliefs about magic and miracles. Throughout the region, women carried fetishes and amulets with their rosary beads and crucifixes. Simple folk carried out elaborate forms of penitential vows to erase infirmities or spells of misfortune. In the Bahian *sertão* south of the São Francisco, residents practiced rites linked to a death cult, first developed in the early 1700s, in which initiates involved themselves in acts of flagellation for seven-year periods. People sought countermagic *(juju)* and healing ceremonies *(catimbó)* to complement natural remedies. *Catimbó*, a form of white magic, involved ingestion of "holy smoke" permeated with the son of God *(onde Jesus encostou)*, singing, and shaking of hand rattles *(maracás)* harboring protective healing entities.

Outsiders, as might be expected, considered these things to be atavism at its worst, the result of a "miscegenation of beliefs." Secular positivists leaped to identify such influences as survivals of the fierce inquisitorial religious fervor exported three centuries earlier from Portugal. Since, in the backlands, time had "stood still—[backlands] society ha[d] not been affected by the general evolutionary movement of the human race"—it was easy enough to dismiss *sertanejo* religious practices as extravagant superstitions, "stigmata of their underdeveloped mentality."[20] This attitude was reinforced by the fact that, under the Empire, folk medicine was tolerated as "just another part of slave and *caboclo* culture," but under the 1890 republican Criminal Code, spiritism, *catimbó*, homeopathy, and all "natural medicine" were prohibited, with prison and fines for transgressors.

The backlands *matutos* were closely influenced by the Ultramontanist Catholic revival and therefore linked institutionally to the outside world, unlike most other rural groups. A portion of the *matutos'* traditional independence, moreover, disappeared after 1900 when they were increasingly drafted for corvée labor *(sujeição)* on *fazendas,* an obligation rising out of the cycle of uncollected debts to landowners. With their new *agregado* status, their reputation declined. *Matutos* came to be seen as "degenerate," men who lived by *vadiagem,* "hanging out" and making do day by day.

Yet backlands rural inhabitants enjoyed a relatively better image than the *caboclos* of the coastal plantation zone. To some extent, this image reflected the elite's prejudices on the subject of race. "The *sertanejo*," the president of the Brazilian Academy of Letters wrote some years later, "lacks Negro blood; rather, he is a product of Portuguese genes mixed with Indian blood and conditioned by the environment." "There is less ignorance and primitivism there," he added, "a legacy of their pastoral activities and the wide and deep resource of natural decency."[21] More recent (and more scientific) studies have revealed that the black presence in the backlands was greater than originally thought, especially in isolated places sought out by fugitive slaves or other migrating blacks in the nineteenth century and earlier. An anthropologist working in the Potengi-Encruzilhada region in the São Francisco Valley noted unusual usage of words of African origin, and classified three-quarters of the local inhabitants as *pardos*. Another investigator claimed to find the remnants of an African *quilombo* in the Serra de Borborema in neighboring Paraíba.[22]

The Church hierarchy endorsed the Vatican's demands for orthodox religious observance, and the bishops condemned socialism and were hostile to trade unionism. The Church thereby lost opportunities to make inroads among Brazil's growing urban working-class population. Ultraconservative prelates like Rio de Janeiro's Cardinal Leme related well to conservative elites, although after the successful Liberal Alliance coup in 1930 and after Getúlio Vargas's affectation of a populist style of governing, the Church went along with his combination of corporatist and socially liberal reforms with the understanding that although Church and state remained formally separated, Catholic chaplains returned to the armed forces, government leaders participated in the celebration of commemorative masses, and the Church acted as if Catholicism had regained its pre-1891 position.

In the hinterland, devout folk Catholicism not only persisted but, especially as the close of the nineteenth century approached, caught millenarian fire in the form of powerful social movements such as the one at Pedra Bonita in Pernambuco, in which thirty children, twelve men, eleven women, and fourteen dogs were sacrificed, and the later one, far more lasting and successful, led by the excommunicated priest Cícero Romão Batista. In the mid-1890s in the Bahian *sertão* there was the settlement of the holy city of Belo Monte at Canudos, led by Antônio Conselheiro. Canudos became a threat to coastal authorities, and in 1897 it was smashed and literally eradicated from the face of the earth by the last of a succession of assaults by the Brazilian army.

Other messianic movements erupted throughout Brazil, not limited to the Northeast, which elites considered most atavistic: in the Contestado, in Santa Catarina, thousands of *posseiros* (subsistence farmers), followers of a millenarian movement, died between 1912 and 1916. In Catulê, in rural Minas Gerais, a community of subsistence squatters, rural Catholics lacking in Catholic supervision who had converted to Adventism, accused four children of being possessed by the devil; police intervention resulted in the deaths of their leaders and the imprisonment of many of the community's adults. Decades later, in Santa Brígida near Jeremoabo in the Bahian *sertão,* a mystic arose, claiming to be the reincarnation of Conselheiro and Padre Cícero; he attracted more than 2,000 followers to his community, which was devoted to moral living, hard work, and abstinence, just as in Canudos. What made Padre Cícero so extraordinarily popular not only with his followers during his lifetime but among millions of ordinary northeasterners long after his death in the mid-1930s was the fact that at crucial moments in his life, he always renounced his temporal powers in order to remain on the side of the poor and the humble. Behind the scenes, however, he was an astute politician, and he adroitly allied himself with powerful interests in the backlands region.

The 1891 Constitution's provision ruling the country juridically secular was followed by the promise of religious freedom in 1937 and later charters, but the unwritten understanding between Church leaders and the elite was that Catholicism would tacitly prevail. This came about in part as the result of understaffed and underfunded conditions within the Church organization, which likely would have doomed efforts to pay greater attention to the poor, especially in the countryside. The number of parish priests during the colonial period and under the monarchy was always tiny in proportion to the population, another legacy of Brazilian slavery. In 1960, only 4,116 priests served dioceses, one-quarter of the number deemed suitable according to Church experts; although the number of seminarians increased to 6,500 in 1992, a full one-third of all priests in Brazil are foreign-born. Brazil-born priests tend to be from small towns in the interior, posing problems when they are assigned to large cities. Since the mid-1960s, as many as 4,500 men have left the priesthood to marry. All this points to a precipitous erosion in Church influence, especially in competition with alternative forms of religious expression that provided for practitioners reminders of Catholic symbolism.

By the late 1940s, many activist Catholics who before the war were heavily influenced by European corporatism and fascism now turned to the European Catholic Left and to the efforts by reformers in Rome to bring the Church closer to the needs of the faithful. A turning point came in 1952 with the establishment of the National Conference of Brazilian Bishops led by Dom Helder Câmara, during the 1930s a leader of the Brazilian fascist Integralist party, but now a champion of populist Catholicism and social justice. The Brazilian Church supported the creation of SUDENE, the regional development agency for the Northeast; and, during 1962–63, progressive priests and bishops allied themselves with students, labor militants, and others calling for land reform, literacy education for adults, and redistribution of wealth. The long-suffering Northeast was targeted as the prime recipient of Church reform efforts. Radio schools were established throughout the region through the Church's Basic Education Movement (MEB), which reached 180,000 peasants through radio programs and community-based groups whose teachings stressed not only reading but raising the social consciousness of the rural poor through the methods of Paulo Freire and other proponents of what was called liberation theology. Freire administrated his program through the extension service of the University of Recife, but the program—along with the entire thrust of the Catholic Church in the direction of social reform and education—was abruptly closed down by the military coup d'état of 1964.

There were some precedents within the Church for grassroots activities, but they had traditionally been conservative. During the 1920s, for example, priests often organized groups of students to spend Carnival and other popular festivities on religious retreats, so that the youths would not be exposed to frivolity and sexual exhibitionism. In the following decade Catholic women organized to help poor women nurse their infants under sanitary conditions, and to instruct the women in simple handicrafts. This was done as a charitable gesture, not in any way more deeply fixed in the lives of the poor. On the whole, Brazilian Catholic groups differed little from their Argentine counterparts, which were accused, by an angry labor organizer, of intolerable "passivity and a truly lamentable inertia."[23] During the heady 1950s, the Church split sharply along ideological lines, one group remaining socially conservative, the other plunging into liberation theology. This creed acknowledged the Church's revolutionary role, teaching that only through land reform and redistribution of income could Brazil progress in a moral way. The Church of the 1960s bristled with confidence and activity, creating base communities dedicated to teaching individual self-respect and the right of people regardless of social class to a decent life. Archbishop Dom Helder Câmara, by now a symbol of progressive Roman Catholicism, emerged as the leader of this left-wing movement, and earned the label "communist" among those opposed to his social preachments.

The 1964 military coup and its aftermath brought the fortunes of the liberation theology wing to an hurried end. The liberal wing of the Church's CEBs, or Catholic base communities, continued to organize, bringing literacy classes and an emphasis on raising social consciousness to the poor, but these base organizations dwindled, cut off from their former links to political figures and to left-wing groups. Buffeted by the change in the political climate under the authoritarian regime, the CEBs in the end were limited in their success to groups of deeply Catholic individuals, rarely touching the far larger lower-class population. Some liberal clerics, notably Cardinal Paulo Evaristo Arns of São Paulo, continued to speak out, attacking the deepening dictatorship and its abuse of human rights. Hardline anti-communists did not care, and a large number of progressive priests were arrested and tortured, just as other citizens were. In the exhausted atmosphere on the 1980s, facing remarkable growth among evangelical Protestant sects especially among the urban lower class, the Church changed again. Jettisoning its progressive baggage, the Church began to adopt a charismatic face, turning to deeply felt belief in Jesus accompanied by the same energetic presentation of ritual as the Protestants and the Afro-Brazilian spiritists, who were always potent rivals for the attentions of nonwhites and were also newly popular in the cities among trend-seeking members of white affluent urban groups.

Given its staffing shortages (only 7,630 priests in all of Brazil in 1993 led by a hierarchy of six cardinals and 378 bishops and archbishops; in São Paulo, one cleric for every 16,000 parishioners, compared with an estimated 100,000 evangelical churches across thirteen denominations), the Church now turned to radio and television to deliver its message. At Valinhos, outside of São Paulo, technicians constructed the largest and most modern television facility in Brazil. Afro-Brazilian choreography, music, and raiments were incorporated in a celebratory mass held in São Paulo's cathedral led by the archbishop Cardinal Paulo Evaristo Arns, dubbed an "*axé* mass" by the press. This was an effort on the part of the Church to take advantage of its long-standing relationship with blacks who were nominally Catholics in spite of their preference for spiritist cults. In Salvador, the annual mass celebrated since 1979 to honor Ilê-Aiyê was prohibited in 1993 by the new archbishop, Dom Lucas Moreira Neves, a black *mineiro* (from Minas Gerais) and a distant relative of Tancredo Neves, the popular president-elect who died before taking office in 1984. In defiance, Ilê-Aiyê's president, Antônio Carlos dos Santos, accused the archbishop of racism against his own people. Most Salvadoreans agreed with Antônio Carlos: for decades, the loose syncretism between Catholicism and spiritism has always existed; recently, Catholic priests have participated in *candomblé* ceremonies. The Church has not been happy with the situation. Earlier in 1993, Dom Lucas had reprimanded one of his parish priests for celebrating the baptism of Zeca Veloso, infant son of musician Caetano Veloso and actress Paula Lavigne, and blessing the child in the name of Jehovah, Olorum (the Yoruba god of the skies), and Oyo (the name of a spirit).

Evangelicalism

Evangelicalism, too, has made significant inroads into the traditional dominance of Roman Catholicism. Protestantism, except in the South, where it was brought to Brazil by German and other European immigrants decades ago, is a relatively new (and rapidly growing) option for people reared in the Christian tradition but estranged from the day-to-day demands of mainstream Catholicism. More than any other activity of the devout, it offers to the afflicted a tool for material survival. To meet the formidable challenge of evangelical Protestantism, Brazil's Catholic hierarchy has abruptly endorsed charismatic expression, turning away from the message of the CEBs and seemingly endorsing the evangelicals' emphasis on personal salvation, not social reform. Pentecostalism, on the other hand, being far more rigid in its demands on its faithful, clashed with *candomblé* and the other African cults popular with lower-class blacks, providing the opening to the Church to seek an association of convenience, although on the whole the Church continued to lose ground to both evangelical Protestantism and *umbanda*.[24] The Pentecostals were no less active than the Catholic Church in the use of media: more than 400 low-cost videotape cassettes in the Christian VCC series *(Vídio Cassete Cristão)*—including a program with instructions on how to conduct baptisms—have been marketed with great success.

Introduced into Brazil at Belém in 1911, Pentecostalism spread first through the Northeast and later to the South. Like the Catholic ecclesiastical base organizations, the CEBs, Pentecostalism supports strategies that tend to work better in modern society than the strategies offered by traditional religions. The CEB's main innovation is its motivation for political participation and mobilization, whereas the Pentecostal innovation relates to the transformation of the individual's own life. Both the Catholic CEBs and the Pentecostals express a process of religious rationalization and a path to action. They stress cultural and political autonomy and attempt to build psychological self-worth. Pentecostal churches emphasize fundamentalism; hard work; personal and daily prayer; tithing; marriage within the group; faith healing; and avoidance of such worldly activities as revelry, personal adornment, and lasciviousness. Religious Protestants shun Carnival, gathering in secluded retreats to wait out the celebration, which they consider pagan. Women have played a major role in Pentecostal activities, especially in the Northeast.[25] Charismatic and nontraditional sects—Holy Rollers, Seventh-Day Adventists, the Church of God, Rosicrucians, and Jehovah's Witnesses—as well as home-bred variant sects and also Mormonism, have flourished. Stress is placed on education and on honesty, and on community service. The heavy emphasis on Bible reading boosts literacy. Evangelical Protestantism's restrictiveness seems strikingly odd for the country known as the Land of Carnival: as Emílio Willems observed, these forms of religious expression represent value systems that are in the "sharpest possible contrast with a number of values of Brazilian society."[26] These kinds of belief systems, even if they are dogmatic in comparison to the relaxed tradition of Brazilian Catholicism, offer pragmatic guides for individuals aspiring to social mobility. Condemning drinking, smoking, and other vices, while stressing moral rectitude, keeps the faithful out of debt and focuses their efforts on self-help. This highly personal social milieu boosts self-confidence; the activist role played by evangelical pastors adds a sense of urgency and psychological support.

It has been asserted flatly not only that evangelical Protestantism has replaced Roman Catholicism as Brazil's most widely practiced faith but that the significance of the fact is that it proves that the old Brazilian order, based on rigid hierarchy and social immobility, has broken down. Ten million new believers have joined in the last decade as active parishioners, making evangelical doctrine part of their lives. Some Catholic leftists in Brazil, in fact, see the hand of the U.S. religious right behind the influx of dollars and personnel, but it is undeniable that the inroads made by the evangelical movement are Brazil-based and genuine. "Pinning the gringo label" on the growth of Protestantism cannot change the fact that the Catholic Church has been steadily losing its appeal, with an estimated 600,000 converts to Protestantism annually.

In 1992, nine out of every ten of the 673 new churches opened in Rio de Janeiro among its 5.4 million inhabitants were Pentecostal. By contrast, only one Catholic parish has been created since 1989. The evangelical movement started in Brazil in 1911 with the arrival of missionaries representing the Assemblies of God Church, but Pentecostalism remained marginal until the 1960s. Now, thousands of nominal Catholics flocked to become *crentes,* faithful believers obliged to live austere, moral lives, dress according to a rigidly conservative moral code, and seek personal salvation in charismatic religious expression. Of every seven *carioca* evangelicals, six live in the poorer central or northern neighborhoods of the city and belong to one of nearly 4,000 evangelical temples. In the Baixada Fluminense, a cauldron of poverty and violence, nearly 20 percent of inhabitants consider themselves Pentecostal. Protestantism, observes the English religion writer David Martin, is "the only institution in urban Brazil to care genuinely about the poor migrants flooding the cities." Rio de Janeiro's cardinal, Dom Eugenio Salles, agrees in a fashion, conceding that "these migrants find in the evangelical temples a religion close to the Catholicism of the rural interior."[27]

The number of practicing Protestants in the population jumped from 4 percent in 1960 to 20 percent, or 30 million Brazilians, after 1990. The pope drew 500,000 people for a mass in 1980 when he visited Brasília; in 1991, 100,000 came, but 400,000 others attended outdoor Protestant prayer meetings held in Rio, São Paulo, and Salvador by Edir Macedo, a popular television evangelist. On any given Sunday, more Protestants than Catholics attend church, with the widest margins in lower-class neighborhoods. Reacting to the passive Catholicism offered over generations, poor Brazilians have embraced evangelical sects led by hard-working, blue-collar ministers promising personal salvation and economic betterment through the application of pro-capitalistic virtues and personal austerity. Storefront evangelical churches often open adjacent to hospitals run by the state, offering faith healing and sometimes exorcism. Congregants seem to have the same needs as members of and visitors to spiritist sects: personal assistance in problems of everyday life.

The Reverend Caio Fábio D'Araujo, a Presbyterian pastor who heads the Brazilian Evangelical Association, offered his reasons for the explosion of interest in Protestantism after the arrival of Pentecostals: "The Pentecostal message touched the most essential part of Brazilian culture, which is both spiritual and pragmatic. If you talk about spirits to a Catholic priest, he will look condescending and not understand. The Evangelical will connect. He will look you in the eye and say: 'This is the Devil and he is destroying your life.'"[28] Protestant churches, moreover, have a large number of black pastors and deacons; the Catholic Church has remained overwhelmingly European, with only a handful of black priests.

Afro-Brazilian Religion

Historically, Brazil's lower classes have never been orthodox, monotheistic Christians, although to avoid persecution, non-European cults adopted outward Catholic symbols, especially representations of New Testament saints. African slaves brought to Brazil religious beliefs and practices centered around fetishes, prepared objects believed to be endowed with magical powers. Many used anthropomorphic representations of deities *(orixás)*, of Yoruban or Dahomeyan origin, each one representing one of the forces of nature. Over time, different cults established themselves in different regions. *Candomblé,* for whose faithful the achievement of a state of trance represented divine intercourse with the gods and rebirth, flourished in Bahia among the large Afro-Brazilian population. *Xangôs* predominated in Pernambuco. In Maranhão, a transitory zone between the *sertão,* the Amazon, and the Caribbean with the largest concentration of blacks outside of Bahia, the cult called *minas de crioulas* flourished. *Catimbós* dominated in other parts of the Northeast, and were brought to the lower Amazon by migrants. During the 1930s, the most celebrated *xangô* priestess from Óbidos to Paraitins, who was consulted by the high society of Pará, including the wife of the governor of Amazonas, was a woman from Ceará. In Rio de Janeiro and São Paulo, *macumba,* brought to Brazil by Bantu-speaking peoples of the Congo River basin and Angola, and less ceremonially elaborate than the Yoruban (Nagô) cults, came to predominate along with *umbanda,* a synthesis combining fetishism, Catholicism, and animism, popular not only among the poor but among the middle class, a product of the fusion of two movements—the "whitening" of black culture and the Africanization of imported French spiritism. Emphasizing possession, *macumba* is akin to charismatic Pentecostal sects. Less African but rooted in indigenous practices and deities were the *caboclo* cults, many of which also acquired aspects of spiritualism.

Afro-Brazilian religious leaders manipulated the supernatural to solve worldly needs. Practices and even the names of saints and gods varied widely from region to region. The deity corresponding to the Roman Catholic "Senhor" (God the Father) was called "Ganga Zumba" in Salvador and Recife. In coastal Bahia, the goddess Oxum was paired with the Virgin Mary, celebrated as "Yemanjá" in Bahia and Rio de Janeiro, and also known as "Sereia do Mar" in Recife. The deity called "Odé" in Pará was called "Omulu" and also "Sapatá" in coastal Alagoas. *Sertanejos* in southwestern Brazil believed in the existence of special manlike grizzled monsters called *pé de garrafa* ("bottle foot"), believed to practice witchery. Millions of poor Brazilians accept the existence of the *mãe d'Agua* (water mother), a fatal temptress who lures men to watery deaths, a figure akin to the Sereia do Mar. In the Amazon, it is believed that there are male counterparts to the water mothers, called *bôtos*. Rural Brazilians often believed (and continue to believe) in werewolves and other devils. Northern chapbook literature is filled with them.

Like the backlands penitential Catholics, the followers of spiritist cults were encouraged by their zealous personal faith to concentrate on the here and now. Omulu was the *orixá* (a Yoruba intermediary between heaven and earth) of communicable diseases, assisted by subordinate deities *(exus)* such as Exu Pemba (specializing in venereal disease), Exu Tata Caneira (narcotic addiction), and Exu Carangola (mental distress and hysterics). This movement had little in common with the city-based spiritism which by late century had gained a hold on a certain portion of the affluent classes. African-derived spiritism was strongest in the slave-holding regions of monocultural agriculture on the coast and to some degree further beyond, in pockets inhabited by former slaves and their descendants.

In addition to the spiritist religions brought to Brazil by African slaves, European spiritist mediums became wildly popular in elite circles following their introduction in the 1860s. The two most influential were Kardecism, the scientific-minded philosophy invented by the pseudonymous Alain Kardec (Hippoltye León Denizard Rivali), and reincarnationism. These forms of spiritism were also linked to homeopathic medicine. Emphasizing mediumistic healings, they drew the fire of the Catholic Church but eventually found a niche between formal Catholicism and what elites considered to be the "lower" religions of Afro-Brazilians.[29] Meanwhile, in regions where the numbers of slaves were highest—in Bahia, mostly along the coast as well as in the capital—the African-derived cults flourished. More faint instances of cult worship penetrated the *sertão*, although *matutos* borrowed from the Bantu-Yoruba panoply of spirits, especially the *orixás* invested with healing powers. But in the hinterland, folk religious practices borrowed from Amerindian beliefs, mostly animism in the form of anthropomorphic hawks, jaguars, turtles, songbirds, and wandering supernatural personages (werewolves, headless she-mules, and the Devil in all guises); *boitatás*, able to protect or to destroy pasturage; *caaporas*, mounted demons crossing the plains on moonlit nights; and the diabolic Saci, attacking belated travelers on Good Friday eves.

Yoruba ritual, holding sway over the greatest numbers of Afro-Brazilians, as well as other African and indigenous forms of spiritist expression, not only substituted *orixás* for the saints and icons of Roman Catholicism but represented itself as possessing two levels of understanding: that held by the believer, and a deeper, hidden knowledge, protected by its priests, priestesses, diviners, and herbalists. Knowledge makes ritual powerful. Spiritism, with its hidden, protected knowledge, grants the members of its community the secret power of unprecedented force.[30]

The Afro-Brazilian religions that have thrived in Brazil for centuries are cults of spirit possession, and are rooted in a nationwide network of religious houses, or *centros*, especially in the major cities of the coast. There are differences between the older, African *candomblé* and its twentieth-century variant, *umbanda*, which subordinates African spirits and deities to Western religious symbols and which situates blacks (symbolized in its ritual by the slave) at the bottom of its hierarchy of spirits. *Candomblés, macumbas*, and their sisterly expressions of ritual power provide a major coping mechanism for the devout, a form of cultural resistance for its practitioners, especially working-class black women. These women have greater access to status, power, and authority in *candomblé* language and religion than anywhere else in society. No matter what temporal figure may seek to exercise his authority, believers know that a deeper devotion must be reserved for the voices of deep knowledge within the occluded spiritist world. On the surface level of public ideology, festivals of deities represent collective renewal and empowerment, the closing of one part of the calendar, the opening of a new. But beneath the surface of these events a deeper drama takes place, involving witchcraft known only to the priestly class, paralyzing the faithful with awe and power. In this arena, efforts by the Catholic (or any other Christian) Church to make greater inroads are doomed to failure. The secret power of the African religion, on the other hand, serves as a masterful coping mechanism, protecting its believers from the rough buffeting of the day-to-day world and intimidating those who would drift away from the traditional secret world.

An important question about the impact of Afro-Brazilian religion among the poor, who are mostly nonwhite (or, in the term increasingly used in Brazil, *negro*), is whether these forms of religious expression inhibit (or contribute to) the development of autonomous racial pride. The traditional literature agrees with this, arguing that the popularity of such Afro-Brazilian spiritist sects as *umbanda,* along with surviving cultural attitudes denigrating nonwhite racial characteristics, serves to idealize whiteness and helps to construct a vehicle for white hegemony. *Candomblé* and its related sister religions of African origin have been diffused through a process of secular adaptation to the metropolitan areas of the South to which thousands of migrants have come.

Once the religions of the marginalized, an illicit form of cultural survival, they have grown to the point where they collectively represent a universal religion open to members of all races and to all socioeconomic levels. In São Paulo's case, this change has been relatively recent: as late as the early 1940s, there were more than a thousand Kardecist spiritist places of worship but no *candomblé terreiros* (centers) at all in that city. Since then, millions have come to São Paulo from the Northeast and from the interior of the state as well as from rural areas of neighboring Minas Gerais. Curiously, Afro-Brazilian religions were introduced not primarily by these migrants, but via *umbanda* transmitted from Rio de Janeiro as well as from Kardecism. The presence in *umbanda* of *pretos velhos, crianças, exus,* and *caboclos,* models of behavior to practitioners, was borrowed from European-inspired spiritism, and it filled a great need in the tumultuous world of São Paulo's urban explosion. In a manner akin to the northeasterner's devotion to his or her personal saint, at the center of the Afro-Brazilian religions was the relationship of the individual to the *orixás,* givers of assistance in exchange for offerings and demonstrations of homage.

The steady growth of *umbanda* and *candomblé,* combined with the counterculture of the 1960s and the influence of the black power movement in the United States, awakened blacks in São Paulo and other southern cities (as well as members of the middle classes alienated by the stress of life under the authoritarian regime) to new ways to express personal feelings and to seek help. *Terreiros* sprouted all over the metropolitan region, visited by individuals seeking solutions to their personal problems. *Candomblé* hierarchy became an extended family, with participation by women as well as by men, and therefore offered a positive counterforce to the impersonal aspects of industrialization and urban sprawl. *Candomblé* cult leaders, the *mães* and the *pais de santo*, functioned as agents for the faithful, helping them receive material as well as spiritual benefits. These ritualized fictive kinship patterns provided strong psychological reinforcement for efforts to preserve old values, and helped build a sense of community, even if the *terreiros* were often persecuted by police under the dictatorship.

Candomblé, unlike Catholicism, centers its attentions on life in the present, helping believers to attain earthly goals and to improve their lives, rather than dealing with questions of morality, sin, and the afterlife. Unlike Pentecostalism, *candomblé* does not impose behavior or forbid practices deemed harmful; it does not insist upon austerity, and it is not puritanical. As such, it is a natural and free-flowing relationship that brings self-esteem and feelings of relief to devotees.

There are critics as well. Blackness in *umbanda,* some argue, is reserved mostly for *pretos velhos,* old black men and women who died while still slaves and therefore submissive and conformist, at the lowest point of the spiritist hierarchy, while similar figures in *candomblé* respect the old black men and women and are paid homage, especially on May 13, the anniversary of the abolition of slavery. Other *umbanda* deities include the *exus,* scoundrels and petty thieves who in life were marginalized and nonconformist, "bad" Negroes—exactly as slaveowners saw them. The racial identification of the observer determines whether an Afro-Brazilian symbol is taken in a positive or a negative light; in real life, *umbanda* often plays a very positive and reinforcing role.[31]

Umbanda is not merely a lower-class phenomenon, although it evolved out of *macumba* rituals brought over from Africa by slaves. Its following among members of the professions, the bureaucracy, and even members of the police is very strong. Its own firm identity evolved around 1930 in Rio de Janeiro, when it incorporated European and Asian spiritist practices; by the 1980s it had several million adherents and more than 20,000 cult centers *(terreiros)* in the city alone. Thirty thousand persons participated in the Yemanjá festival in the port city of Santos in 1975, and more than 3,500 buses were used to transport the faithful from São Paulo and other locations. *Umbanda*'s popularity extends beyond the lower classes to tens of thousands of persons on every level of social and economic status. These individuals visit *umbanda* ceremonies to obtain spiritual aid, often to solve specific problems. Some visitors experience spiritist possession; others rely on spirit consultants, full-time *umbanda* practitioners who act on behalf of the visitor-client. Some people come seeking relief from illness, or economic misfortune, or family problems. Clients receive spiritual relief (cleansings, exorcisms, herbal remedies, and religious obligations) and also, in certain cases, loans, access to favors, or jobs. Some of the wealthier *centros,* Diana Brown notes, provide medical and dental care, psychiatric aid, legal services, and food and clothing. Interventions are individualized, but also derivative: thus persons coming from strong Catholic backgrounds find Catholic prayers and figures of saints, always with a dual African character (Ogum is St. George; Yemanjá, the goddess of the waters, is identified with the Virgin Mary; and so on), and either the Catholic or the African nature of the deity is emphasized depending on the particular *centro.* Negative spirits, in fact, often are portrayed as agents of the Catholic underworld, as devil figures.

Umbanda also borrows from other religious traditions, including Kardecist spiritism. More than anything else, what people who visit *umbanda* centers want is personal help from supernatural patrons; this custom is a survival, in many ways, of the traditional patron-client relationship so important in social relations in Brazil. Since many patrons of *umbanda,* especially from the prestige-conscious middle class, deny their participation in the cult, it is difficult to measure levels of participation. But there is little doubt that *umbanda,* as well as all related spiritist religions, plays a major role in the lives of millions of Brazilians.

What is perhaps most characteristic of the practice of popular religion in Brazil is the eclectic, open approach of the faithful. Many individuals drift from one religion to another, or combine them. Many consider themselves faithful (if not observant) Catholics, while at the same time visiting *candomblé* centers. Others borrow from several different religions, choosing what feels good or suits their purposes. Priests at Aparecida do Norte, the enormous shrine in São Paulo's Paraíba Valley, have long been accustomed to finding evidence of penitents on pilgrimages also making *candomblé* sacrifices outside the church. Devotees drift from one cult to another.

During the last few decades many new cults have emerged, some of them hallucinatory in nature. Most of them seem to be characterized by a racially integrated membership, with middle-class whites taking the lead. Black and *pardo* followers tend to be from lower economic groups. One of the more successful sects is Santo Daime, headquartered in Rio de Janeiro's Floresta de Tijuca, where it holds an outdoor tabernacle. Cultists dress in white, wear biblical sandals, and sit with women segregated from men and flanked by a nave covered with flowers. Male ushers with felt stars sewn on their shirts enforce behavior: no crossing one's legs, for example. Followers inhale a drug made from an Amazonian plant, whose effects last as long as ten hours. There is singing, mundane ceremonial music, and sermons about nature and peace. Thousands of initiates join this cult every year; the novitiates take it very seriously.

Another branch of spiritism which lives in the shadows but which is extremely active in the lives of large numbers of Brazilians, mostly in cities, is *quimbanda*, the darker form of spiritism dedicated to casting spells on one's enemies. This is a form of witchcraft in which mediums practice sorcery using a variety of potions, incantations, and other means to conjure up the evil eye, and to cast spells on persons designated by clients who come to the practitioners willing to pay for such services. Witchcraft has also long been practiced in the countryside.

Intimidating Rituals

In urban Latin America, where the gap between the very rich and the very poor is very great and where, in many cases, rich and poor work or even live in close physical proximity, such encounters occur frequently. A *porteiro* (doorman), dressed in a frayed uniform and carrying his starchy lunch in a tin box, may arrive as early as 5:00 or 6:00 A.M., after walking down hundreds of steps from his favela house, or after a two-hour bus ride over bumpy roads from the periphery of the city. When the doorman is then asked by an impatient, immaculately dressed professional man or woman to carry something, to run back for something forgotten, or to hastily clean off the dust accumulated overnight on a car, he is expected to react humbly, without complaint. Many such employees, fearing the loss of their jobs, react by adopting an air of near-total silence, often interpreted by employers as docility. Sometimes this seeming docility is internalized, and becomes part of the person's personality, exhibited even outside the employment framework. In other cases, the doorman (or the domestic servant, restaurant dishwasher, or crossing guard) goes home and becomes another person—aggressive, tyrannical, or abusive. These behavior traits are not seen by the employer class, because the private lives of the poor are well hidden, rendered all but invisible except for moments when this aggressive behavior crosses back over the boundary, as when a *marginal* (marginalized man or woman) breaks the law and is arrested for drunkenness or stealing.

This situation is exacerbated by the attitudes of some persons of higher status. Roberto DaMatta has captured the elite's expectation of deference and special treatment in identifying the ritual importance of the phrase *"Você sabe com quem está falando?"* ("Do you know who you're talking to?"), the embodiment of the ritual that plays out when someone powerful is challenged by someone of lower status, such as in the case of a policeman confronting someone who has parked illegally, blocking traffic. Even physical size can be a factor in this kind of exchange: traffic cops are usually small and thin (in contrast to the burly members of the military police, or the police *delegados* who deal with crime), in contrast to the wealthy, who can be fit and athletic. Even if the offensive big shot is short and paunchy, his use of intimidating language makes perfectly clear what DaMatta terms the "radical and authoritarian separation between two social positions that are objectively or conceptually differentiated in terms of the rules of classification of Brazilian culture."[32] This behavior reflects the true nature of social distance, and belies the myth endorsed by Gilberto Freyre and others of the Brazilian as cordial and tolerant of others. It also takes other forms. For example, it is a common practice among affluent teenagers to cut ahead in line, or to cheat in school, because they are privileged.

The use of the intimidating ritual question goes back in Brazil's past. The *mulato* novelist Afonso Henriques de Lima Barreto satirized the use and abuse of titles in his World War I–era novel, *Recordações do Escrivão Isáias Caminha*. In this novel about the imaginary republic of the United States of Bruzundanga, which Roberto DaMatta identifies as Brazil, he writes about the entrance examinations required by the prestigious professional schools of the country: "Passing the preliminaries, the future leaders of the republic, the United States of Bruzundanga, take courses of study and end up more ignorant and presumptuous than they were when they entered. They are the sort who loudly boast, 'I have a degree. You are talking to a man with a degree!'"[33]

Whether intentionally or not, people in high positions intimidate. Being a *filho de papai* (the father's son, implying nepotism) counts for a great deal in Brazilian life. Verbal and behavioral reminders of status, in fact, have in many cases grown in use in recent decades, as traditional marks of social position—examples for men include cream-colored linen suits worn by true whites of seignorial class, fountain pens, and walking sticks—went out of fashion. As a researcher in Brazil, I found this out the hard way. Waiting on line at a bakery counter in Ipanema on a Sunday morning during the military dictatorship, I was rudely pushed back by a man wearing shorts who bolted ahead of me. I muttered something about *"falta de educação"* (lack of manners) and beckoned to the clerk to do something about what was by any account a blatant violation of propriety. The clerk looked away, as did everyone else on line. As I walked away after my purchase was finally made, another person who had been standing on line with me whispered to me that I'd better be damned careful. The man who had cut into line was a colonel in the military police, he told me, who usually sent a servant to buy things for him while he waited in his car.

I also remember Asís, the doorman of a residential apartment house on Recife's Boa Viagem. An emaciated *caboclo* who had been born in the *zona da mata* a half hour from the city but who had been evicted from his plot of land, he lived with his family in a lean-to that could not have been more than fifty square feet in size, at the back of the elevator shaft. When residents of the building approached, Asís would lower his gaze to the pavement, avoiding eye contact in the manner slaves learned to do on the streets of colonial and nineteenth-century Brazil. There was a chute near the elevator on every floor into which maids threw refuse, and Asís, several times a day, would tip back the dumpster on the ground floor and take out anything in the garbage that was edible or that could be scavenged. Sometimes Asís permitted ragged children from the neighborhood to enter the dumpster room with him. One day, I saw him being confronted by the head of the building's *condomínio,* the residents' association, and ordered to stop "abusing" his position by taking the garbage. *"Mais amor e menos confiança,"* ("Show respect and less impertinence"), I heard the man say. Asís groveled and promised to obey. Within a month or so, one of Asís's small children died. In addition, rats infested the grounds of the building. Then Asís and his family disappeared; another doorman took his place. It turned out that when Asís asked the *condomínio* president for an advance from his salary to pay for the burial of his child, he was fired on the spot.

Many have dealt with the stresses of daily life by drinking. The coming of modern change to Arembepe, with a paved highway reducing the commuting time to Salvador to fifty minutes, brought with it a proliferation of *cachaça* bars to the village, accompanied by a breakdown in community solidarity. Men who used to socialize outside the Catholic chapel on the beach now downed a shot or two at a local bar when they returned from fishing, before going home. The entire system of whole-community interaction that had been present before 1960 was irrevocably changed. Crime also increased. Robbery, formally a "highly stigmatized type of antisocial behavior," now became commonplace, a by-product of the increased impersonality of life in the village and its new population of transients. Nor did everyone benefit from the economic boom. Not only in Brazil but across Latin America in the 1990s, prosperity has not affected the poorest members of society, still characterized by large disparities between rich and poor.

Notes

1. Marie-Ghislaine Stoffels, *Os Mendigos na Cidade de São Paulo: Ensaio de Interpretação Sociológica* (Rio de Janeiro: Paz e Terra, 1977), 152–53.
2. Marilene Cabello Di Flora, *Os Mendigos* (Rio de Janeiro: Agir, 1977), 118–31.
3. Albert Camus, *Diário de Viagem,* trans. Valerie Rumjanek Chaves (Rio de Janeiro: Editora Record, 1978), 119–20.
4. Dean Graber, "Real Brazil: October 1995," *Real Brazil* 1:1 (1995), 3.

5. Jorge Saba Arbache, "Salários Indiretos e Segmentação do Mercado de Trabalho no Brasil," E-mail text sent 1 July 1995, University of Brasília.

6. Stela Lachtermacher, in *Jornal do Brasil,* 8 July 1993, Negócios & Finanças section, 1.

7. Cláudia Shüffner, in *Jornal do Brasil,* 8 July 1993, Negócios & Finanças section, 1.

8. See Maurício A. Font, *Coffee, Contention, and Change in the Making of Modern Brazil* (Cambridge, MA: Basil Blackwell, 1990), 109.

9. Richard Crutchfield, "Small Is Beautiful (if Enormously Problematical) in Northeast Brazil," *American Universities Field Staff Reports,* East Coast South America Series, 20:1 (Brazil), December 1976, 16.

10. James Brooke, *New York Times,* 12 October 1993, A5.

11. "O Sertão Virou Fumo," *Veja* 24:41, 9 October 1991, 48–51.

12. Daniel Touro Linger, *Dangerous Encounters: Meanings of Violence in a Brazilian City* (Stanford: Stanford University Press, 1992), 7–8.

13. John Krich, *Why Is This Country Dancing?* (New York: Simon and Schuster, 1993), 188.

14. Gerard H. Béhauge, ed., *Music and Black Ethnicity: The Carribean and South America* (New Brunswick, NJ: Transaction Publishers, 1994).

15. Luiz Mott, "Acotunda: Raízes Setecentistas do Sincretismo Religioso Afro-Brasileiro," *Revista do Museu Paulista* 31 (1986), 124–47.

16. See Ruben George Oliven, "The Production and Consumption of Popular Culture in Brazil," *Studies in Latin American Popular Culture* 4 (1985), 144 (143–51).

17. Euclides Da Cunha, *Os Sertões* (Rio de Janeiro: Francisco Alves, 1901), 152–53.

18. Judith Devlin, *The Superstitious Mind: French Peasants and the Supernatural in the Nineteenth Century* (New Haven: Yale University Press, 1987), 70–71.

19. Limeira Tejo, *Brejos e Carrascães do Nordeste: Documentário* (São Paulo: Scopus, 1937), 55; *Veja,* 15 April 1970, 84.

20. Gustavo Barroso (João do Norte), "Populações do Nordeste," *Revista da Sociedade de Geografia do Rio de Janeiro* (1926–27), 48–50, 66–67.

21. Alfonso Trujillo Ferrari, *Potengi-Encruzilhada no Vale de São Francisco* (São Paulo: n.p., 1961), 174.

22. Ivaldo Falconi, "Um Quilombo Esquecido," *Correio das Artes* (João Pessoa), 1949, n.p., cited by Clóvis Moura, *Rebeliões da Senzala: Quilombos e Insurreições guerrilhas* (Rio de Janeiro: Ed. Conquista, 1972), 220.

23. José E. Níklison of the National Labor Department, cited by David Rock, "Antecedents of the Argentine Right," 1–34, in Sandra McGee Deutsch and Ronald H. Dolkart, eds., *The Argentine Right: Its History and Intellectual Origins, 1910 to the Present* (Wilmington, DE: Scholarly Books, 1993), 23.

24. See John Burdick, *Looking for God in Brazil: The Progressive Catholic Church in Urban Brazil's Religious Arena* (Syracuse: Syracuse University Press, 1993).

25. See Joanne L. Pepper, "The Historical Development of Pentecostalism in Northeastern Brazil, with Specific Reference to Working-Class Women in Recife," Ph.D. diss., University of Warwick, 1991.

26. Emílio Willems, "Protestantism as a Factor of Culture Change in Brazil," *Economic Development and Cultural Change* 3 (1955), 321–33, cited by T. Lynn Smith, *Brazil: People and Institutions,* 527–28.

27. David Martin, *Linguas de Fogo: A Explosão do Protestantismo na América Latina,* cited by Eliane Azevedo, "Fé Explosiva," *Veja* 25:51, 16 December 1992, 82.

28. Rev. Caio Fábio D'Araujo, cited by James Brooke, in the *New York Times,* 4 July 1993, A8.

29. See David Hess, "The Many Rooms of Spiritism in Brazil," *Luso-Brazilian Review* 24:2 (1987), 15–34.

30. Andrew Apter, "Reconsidering Inventions of Africa," *Critical Inquiry* 19:1 (Autumn 1992), 87–104, esp. 97.

31. Diana Brown, presentation to Conference on Black Brazil: Culture, Identity, Social Mobilization (Gainesville: University of Florida, 2 April 1993).

32. Roberto DaMatta, *Carnivals, Rogues, and Heroes: An Interpretation of the Brazilian Dilemma,* trans. John Drury (South Bend, IN: University of Notre Dame Press, 1991), 137.

33. Both books were reissued in 1956 by Editora Brasiliense, São Paulo. Roberto DaMatta, *Carnivals,* 154–55.

6

Diversions and Assertive Behavior

In spite of stressful lives often lacking in material comforts, Brazilians seem to emphasize their carefree and optimistic side. National culture—at least in its public manifestations—manages to cast off hardship and enjoy life enthusiastically. Nowhere is this more evident than as a function of the Brazilian calendar, filled with tiring workdays and long hours but also, almost more than any other country in the world, crammed with holidays, festivities, and seasonal celebrations capped by the annual exuberance of Carnival.

In the days of slavery, forced labor was broken only by Sunday as a day of rest—and this not always observed—and by the days given to observances of religious origin, especially Carnival (from the medieval Latin *Carne-vale,* or "flesh to be shed") in the days preceding Lent. By the late nineteenth century, this pattern had been expanded to the larger population and broadened to include not only Catholic festivals but also civic commemorations. During the twentieth century, the arrival of soccer as the national sport added still another set of days during which the playing of critically important matches galvanized national interest among almost all social groups. For World Cup play every four years, in fact, virtually all work ceases during important matches, followed by wild street celebrations and frenzied euphoria when the team wins. These events, Robert DaMatta observes, are played out in zones of encounter and mediation, when rational, normal time is suspended and a new routine must be innovated and repeated.

The Brazilian social world is ritualized at Carnival time, when its national soccer team plays, when processions (or military parades) wend their way down the main streets of cities. The calendar anchors these events,

145

three of which stretch for several days—Carnival before Lent; Holy Week preceding Easter; and Independence Day (September 7), which is surrounded by a week of civic and military festivities, the *Semana da Pátria.* The national focus during these celebrations becomes holistic, suspending, if for brief moments, the acute sense of social division that characterizes Brazilian society, even if the events are celebrated strictly according to proper hierarchy.[1] Whether the bread-and-circuses nature of the way Brazilians rich and poor are specifically permitted to rest and to blow off steam according to the religious, civic, and sportive calendars functions as a conscious safety device by managers and officials is dubious. In any case, the effect remains salutary. Brazilian celebrations, exuberant national rituals, have historically bound together members of disparate social groups and canceled, if temporarily, the rigid unspoken rules of segregated Brazilian society, which prescribes behavior and language in a world where everyone knows his or her place.

As a country in which Roman Catholicism has been either official or quasi-official, Brazil recognizes all the important religious holidays. Moreover, in the tradition of civic pride and nationalism, it also celebrates many days on the civic calendar, some of which are national, others regional or statewide. These rituals alike share the same characteristic: people use them to forget the difficulties in their lives. Some occur nationally; others, especially those celebrating a patron saint, are local. Some have become notorious: Ouro Prêto's saint's day attracts so many drug addicts and other undesirable types that it has been dubbed "the Festival of the Policemen."[2] In some localities, celebrations have become institutionalized ways of blotting out day-to-day existence, what Brazilians call *realidade do dia-a-dia.* Saints' days are celebrated throughout Brazil. Some (Santo Antônio, São João, and São Pedro) are universal; others depend on the locality and its patron saint or saints. The number of holidays in Brazil is among the highest of any country, and the impact of holidays on everyday life (not to mention on employee productivity) is enormous. Public celebrations, especially for the poor, reveal an astonishingly independent spirit and resistance to imposed "colonial" behavior and practice.[3]

Consider Salvador, Bahia's capital, one of the poorest urban centers in the country. Bahia, where the legacy of African slavery was strongest and where African spiritist religion has survived more tenaciously than anywhere else, in the Afro-Brazilian cults of *candomblé* (related to the *santería* of Cuba and South Florida as well as Haitian *vodun*), *tambor de Minas, jurema, xangó,* and other African-derived religions, offers full-time employees more days off from work than virtually any other place on earth. The cycle starts on December 31, when not only do public employees stay home from work to prepare for the New Year but thousands of the devout, many of them Afro-Brazilians, participate in the maritime procession of Senhor Bom Jesus dos Navegantes, a festivity brought over from Portugal in about 1750, involving hundreds of boats and other craft on two successive days, coming to be blessed. The city throbs with life. In Rio de Janeiro, members of all the spiritist *terreiros* in the city come to the beach dressed in white for the rite of Yemanjá, the Yoruban goddess of the sea—although her formal holiday comes a month later, in the first week of February, when the rite is celebrated in Salvador. The celebrants launch small boats and enter the waves, over which are strewn flowers. New Year's Day is spent by many on the beaches, since January marks the beginning of the hottest part of the summer.

For three days following January 3, Bahians observe the Festival of the Kings, commemorating the visit of the Three Wise Men to the infant Jesus. There are masses, processions, and an enormous outdoor party. Then comes the even more frenetic Festa do Bonfim, in honor of Oxalá, the African counterpart of the region's patron, St. Anthony. The festival peaks on January 14, when an immense procession of women and girls dressed in *candomblé* garb, as well as much of the population of Salvador, accompanied by music and fireworks, arrives at the Bonfim church to wash the chapel. A mass and an enormous public celebration follow. During the late nineteenth century in Salvador, Bonfim was celebrated not only in January but every Friday throughout the year. A cleric, Monsignor Brito, complained in 1893 that the celebration occupied his parishioners for the entire month of January, during which time they virtually did not cease celebrating. The only time the revelers stopped was when they moved to the Brotherhood of São Joaquim, to a celebration of the inauguration of its new building.[4]

In mid-January on a movable date, the Festa de Ribeira occurs, and percussion *baterias* and amplified carnivalesque music thunder through the city. This is no religious celebration at all: the event is simply a local tradition as a prelude to the Carnival season. When *orixás* are celebrated, each one is associated with its own tempo, and every samba rhythm has as its subtext the call to one or another spiritist deity. Four additional religious festivals fall at the end of January: Saõ Sebastião, on January 20, merged into the feast day of his African equivalent, Oxum (known as "Katendê" among some African sects); Nossa Senhora da Guia, celebrated on the Sunday following the Festa da Ribeira; São Lázaro, paired with the *candomblé* spirit of Omulu, with a major festival at the São Lázaro church; and São Gonzalo do Amarante, centered on a solemn mass. Finally, there is a regatta at the Porto da Barra, a touristic event staged late in the month, for which some municipal employees receive time off. By the last day of January, municipal and state employees since December 31 have already had between five and seven days off, respectively, not counting Saturdays and Sundays.

The first week of February brings the Festa de Yemanjá, filled with Carnival music to honor the "Mother of Waters." A few days later, a mini-Carnival follows in honor of the church of Itapuã, on the Praça Dorival Caymmi. A similar celebration is held at the Igreja de Nossa Senhora da Luz, starting about two weeks before the first day of Carnival. Then, on dates calculated by counting back from Easter, comes Carnival itself, the major event of the Brazilian calendar, celebrated so exuberantly in Bahia that the state grants five vacation days in contrast to the three days ceded officially in the rest of the country. The entire population of the city participates, some congregating in the old city or in the Farol da Barra, some remaining in their neighborhoods. There are *afoxés, blocos, cordões, batucadas,* and continuous dancing night and day, preceded by the washing of churches in Porto da Barra, Tororó, various places in the city, and Cruz da Redenção in Brotas. In the late 1980s, a sixth day was added to the official celebration, for the coronation of the Rei Momo, Carnival's rotund king, the modern version of the Greek god of debauchery and practical jokes. When it is genuinely celebrated, and not just a tourist event, Carnival frees men and women from the restrictions of everyday life. In Taubaté, all men dress as women for a day. Fools dress as wise men, servants as masters. Celebrants of all social classes rub elbows in the street, hiding behind masks. It is a momentary abandonment to fantasy, an unspoken negation of the status quo.[5]

Additional saints' days are celebrated during this period, but they tend to be dwarfed by the steady buildup to Carnival. Sometimes drumbeats and percussive sounds are heard weeks before Carnival, building up to almost a frenzy. The day devoted to São Brás, for example, is celebrated on February 3. São Brás is considered the protector of throats, and people suffering from throat ailments go to mass and seek blessings from the priest in exchange for a promise of penitence.[6] The supplicant usually takes the entire day off on such days, and sometimes children are held out of school, if school is in session. March and April bring additional celebration almost surpassing January's intensity. There are Ash Wednesday, Ember Days (with the procession of Nosso Senhor dos Passos), and Holy Week: Wednesday of Darkness, Thursday of Anguish, Friday of Passion, and Hallelujah Saturday, or Judas Day, when effigies of Judas are burned, hanged, and scourged throughout the countryside. In the interior these rites used to be known as *foliões cavalgadas,* and they were full-blown ceremonies with music, theater, and processions. A major religious procession in Salvador on the Sunday following Easter reenacts the Stations of the Cross and leads celebrants to the Terreiro de Jesus at the heart of the old city. The anniversary of the founding of the city is celebrated on March 29, but most functionaries go to work. On April 21, all Brazilians celebrate the birthday of the national hero, Tiradentes.

May brings three holidays, one on May 10 in honor of the patron saint Francisco Xavier, featuring a mass and an official ceremony at the municipal council, and Pentecost, with a religious procession on the Largo de Santo Antônio always led by a child. May 13 is a nationwide holiday commemorating the abolition of slavery by Princess Isabel in 1888, and is celebrated both civically and religiously. Afro-Brazilian cults hold their annual Inhoaíba festival on the same date. Some of the ceremonies date back to the decade of abolition, when a sisterhood of freed slave women developed the "Feast of the Good Death," commemorating the death and assumption of the Virgin Mary.[7] June 10, Corpus Christi, is a major municipal holiday, with São Jorge's image borne on horseback in full military dress and heavy armor. June also celebrates the saints' days of St. Anthony, St. Peter, and the Sacred Heart of Jesus. St. Anthony's (Santo Antônio's) Day is celebrated with a special mass, but most observers do not take the rest of the day off. São João's day follows on June 24, a state holiday in Bahia in which federal employees also are given the day off. São João is marked by fireworks and very loud noisemaking, as well as by traditional outdoor parties for children, sometimes following *caipira* (rustic) themes. July 2 is state independence day, commemorating the day on which Bahia accepted Dom Pedro I's rupture with Portugal in 1824, and the Visitation of Nossa Senhora, celebrated with a procession. Indulgences may be secured on this day. July 21 is allotted to the Guardian Angel of the Empire; July 25 to St. James; and July 28 to Santa Anna, Mother of the Mother of God. August brings São Roque Day, which is coupled with the day of Afro-Brazilian deity Obaluaê, so that the celebration occurs simultaneously in mainstream Roman Catholic churches and among practitioners of *candomblé*, as do Assumption Day, on August 15, and the Most Holy Heart of Mary Day, on August 25. Armed Forces Day is also celebrated in August, as a public holiday.

Then comes September 7, National Independence Day. The armed forces play a major role, organizing parades, ceremonies, and other forms of patriotic celebration. Three weeks later Bahians celebrate the days honoring São Cosme and São Damião, the twins Cosme and Damian, with masses and special dinners served in private homes. The Bahian Fair, which occurs in September, sometimes brings with it municipal holidays or release time for schoolchildren. October 6 is the day of the Most Holy Rosary, with a night-time procession; October 9 is the feast of São Pedro d'Alcântara. October 12 brings a national holiday celebrating Nossa Senhora da Aparecida, Brazil's national saint. November 1 is All-Saints Day, and November 2 is the Day of the Dead—occasions when virtually everyone in the city visits the cemeteries where their loved ones are buried or the ossuary niches in which their bones repose. Cemeteries are awash with bright-colored flowers, and the life of the city virtually comes to a halt. November 2 and 15 are also national holidays. Bahia adds two more, on movable dates, São Nicodemus and Dia da Baiana, formerly called "Dia da Baiana do Acarajé," a religious festivity mainly involving Afro-Brazilian women. December, to round out the calendar, sees Santa Bárbara Day, in honor of the patron saint of markets and matched with *candomblé's* Iansã, accompanied by fireworks, a large procession, and municipal bands. There is a state holiday at mid-month, in honor of Nossa Senhora da Conceição, linked with a *candomblé* deity and marked by the Church with an elaborate procession involving images of the infant Jesus, Santa Bárbara, Joseph, and Mary, accompanied by bands playing Carnival music. Finally, there is Santa Luzia, also at mid-month, which is patronized by the military police and given to pilgrimages and fireworks. Christmas follows on December 25, and many government offices stay closed thorough New Year's.[8]

The elite's attitudes toward Carnival always revealed their wariness of common people. In the 1870s, for example, in Salvador, editorial writers began to attack what they called the "savage, gross and pernicious" *entrudos,* whose celebrants overstepped the unwritten boundaries of behavior by dousing bystanders with foul mixtures of flour, water, and sometimes urine and by playing other rough tricks on fellow celebrants. In response, the police chief invoked stern countermeasures, including the organization of deputized posses. Foreign observers as early as 1815 were shocked by seeing women participate in these "little wars" as well as men.[9] Black youths also took part, but they took care to attack only other blacks; white youths, of course, attacked anyone in their way. The leveling character of Bahian Carnival did not extend to relations between the races. "Proper citizens" responded to the rising outcry against what they called the uncivilized and barbarous nature of Carnival by retreating to theaters and private clubs. There, they staged lavish and expensive masked balls, decorated with materials imported from Europe, held safely out of contact with the common people, tens of thousands of whom had come to the capital from different parts of the region and who remained in the noisy streets. Paper confetti was substituted for thrown liquids. Not all Carnival conventions were dropped, though: at many of the masked balls, men dressed as women, as (in the Portuguese of the day) *damas travestis.* Once in a while, a gesture was made in the spirit of generosity. At the masked ball at Salvador's Poly-theama, in 1887, the leader of the elite Carnival club Fantoches mounted the stage and presented emancipation documents to two female slaves. "The act," the *Jornal de Notícias* commented the next day, "was received with general enthusiasm and concluded with the playing of the National Anthem."[10]

Following abolition in 1888, black street Carnival clubs played such major roles that elites complained that they were taking over the celebration. The clubs included Embaixada Africana (African Embassy) and Pândegos d'África (African Clowns), the most famous, organized in the early 1890s; Chegada Africana (African Arrival), between 1895 and 1897, and Guerreiros d'África (African Warriors), after the turn of the century. Newspaper editors complimented these clubs for their efficient organization and for the good behavior of their members. For a few years thereafter, Bahian Carnival came to represent a model for the rest of the country: spirited, open to all, and within the unwritten rules of the festivities (whites dressed as Europeans; blacks as "savage" Africans), egalitarian. In 1904, however, things changed again when an editorial appeared demanding the prohibition of African drum corps *(batuques),* the use of masks after dark except at formal balls, and any act critical of or offensive to distinguished people. The chief complaint was that the Africanized Carnival clubs were extolling primitivism in the place of civilization, producing great noise, and distorting the traditional samba. A year later, in 1905, the "shameful" *Afro-batuques* were banned by the chief of police. The Africanized clubs remained outlawed in most cities for nearly three decades, until they reappeared during the 1930s (in some places, notably São Paulo, they survived out of sight of the police, in poor districts where police rarely entered).[11] The reason that the *batuques* (later called *afoxés*) offended so many was that unlike their predecessors, the African-theme clubs of the 1890s, they were formed by "less decorous," "less civilized," and "poorly adapted" blacks, in the language of the day. Salvador's black population continued to grow through the 1930s and 1940s, in part owing to a constant influx of migrants from the cacao zone in the southern part of the state, whose economic boom had peaked in the late 1920s. After 1950 the number of migrants leveled off to 15,000 per year, two-thirds from the interior of the state.[12] Wags named Salvador the "Negroes' Rome." Carnival institutions evolved differently in Salvador, perhaps because of its heavily Afro-Brazilian population. The enormous samba schools in Rio de Janeiro, for example, with up to 3,500 participants, never demonstrated the same ethnic fraternity and identification as their counterparts in Salvador.[13]

Rio de Janeiro's twelve Carnival samba schools, all housed in favelas or working-class districts in the city's North Zone, date to the late 1920s. The first one, "Deixa Falar" ("Let 'em talk!"), founded in 1928, was located near an elementary school; this, possibly, is the origin of the term "samba school." Each of the twelve associations put up to 3,000 dancers and 500 drummers as well as floats and musicians, all in costumes costing the members—mostly lower-class *favelados*—up to $1,000 each. These days there are municipal and other subsidies, and record contracts, but the costs are still enormous. The origin of the word *samba*—the percussive dance rhythm to which Carnival pulses for four days or more—is thought to be from the Ngangela word *kusamba*: to skip, to express oneself joyfully.[14] Free urban blacks danced samba as early as the 1870s in Bahia. A Bahian woman, Tia Amelia, brought samba to the slums of Rio de Janeiro; her son, Donga, composed the first recorded samba, "Pelo Telefone," its words wryly poking fun at the links between the police and illegal gambling. Samba flowered during the 1920s and after; it became Brazil's national music.

Neither then nor now, however, did the black musicians (including Cartola, Carlos Cachaça, and Moreira da Silva) who became popular culture icons make much of a living from samba, although the dance anchored Brazil's tourist industry for generations. The musicians lived in seedy parts of the city and received little or nothing in royalties. In the 1980s, musician John Krich claimed that the only reason the remaining samba immortals, members of the Velha Guardia da Portela, which is akin to New Orleans's Preservation Hall Jazz Band, got any decent bookings at all was that the group was fronted by white singer Christina Buarque, the sister of composer and singer Chico Buarque de Holanda.

But time (and exposure to foreign broadcast media) has eroded these slights. In the mid-1990s, for the first time, national television networks and their local affiliates have followed the American practice of hiring non-Caucasians as newscasters and correspondents. Blacks, previously rarely given nonstereotyped roles in television, have won some breakthroughs, especially in theater, and television in general has begun to reflect the laid-back, relatively color-blind attitudes of life in the streets.

One of the most exceptional characteristics of mundane Brazilian life is its capacity to retain appreciation of life even with hardship. An example is found in Andrea Vila Nova's oral-history life story of seventy-nine-year-old Waldir dos Santos, an ex–gold miner for the English-owned Saint John d'el Rey Mining Company in Minas Gerais, which presents a portrait of a man hardened through decades of backbreaking toil, working eight-hour shifts in dark mining tunnels starting as a teenager in the 1920s. Waldir's father, an alcoholic actor, died of cirrhosis; his mother, at one time an actress, could find work only sweeping streets. As a child Waldir got meningitis but recovered; a friendly village pharmacist treated him out of charity. His schoolteachers beat him severely (he says matter-of-factly) because he was poor; children from comfortable families were never touched. He attended school for five years and then went to work in the mines.

Waldir's brothers and sisters and many of his peers died from disease, malnutrition, or in industrial accidents. Those who were crippled had to beg. His family lived in a tenement, sharing cooking facilities and living, in his word, in "promiscuity"; they later had to move to a shack hard by a local cemetery and then, in 1928, to the slums of Belo Horizonte, the capital.[15] Yet his recollections are not filled with bitterness or disappointment; they paint rich stories of appreciation for decades of festivities, music, and warm relationships. Unlike what might be expected in the case of an American or a British miner in similar circumstances, Waldir's memories easily overlook the grimness of his past, focusing instead on its pleasures, and acknowledging, almost without a second thought, the ways that people helped one another. What does Waldir remember most? As a boy he had a collection of Buffalo Bill comics, and a children's history of France, also written as a comic book. He read them with relish. He describes his youth:

> In Belo Horizonte I learned to dance . . . because we had friends there from Nova Lima [who came to the city and who helped us]. There were four girls and, I think, four boys. They were fun-loving, and they went on Thursdays and Saturdays to a club in a handsome building downtown on Av. Brasil, near the Church, and they took me with them. I was 13, 14. . . . I loved dancing, and I became good at it. . . . When Fredie [sic] Astaire films came, I went just to watch his steps.

Two years later, Waldir returned to the Morro Velho mine and started working. He was so exhausted at the end of his shift that he sat, sobbing. The tunnels reeked with arsenic. The work was dangerous. The foreman beat the miners, often boys as young as fourteen, when they bumped their carts or otherwise displeased him. Anyone who complained was fired. The company employed spies to be sure that no one would steal, and its word was law. Yet the English-owned company also provided workers' housing, and in time, after he married, Waldir was able to live in one of the cottages. First he lived with an aunt, and then with an uncle, part of the extended family networks that cushioned life's burdens. Waldir took courses and got a better job, as a stonemason's helper. The wages were meager, but he felt on top of the world. "I was earning almost as much as a mason," he exulted. From age sixteen to age twenty-five he lived a life he describes as "bohemian," filled with drinking and friends in the "zone." Radios played boleros and tangos; the cabarets had record players. The young prostitutes would go with their *coronéis* (customers) and, after they were paid, would dance and make love with Waldir and his friends for free.

During Carnival, Waldir danced all night without sleeping, even though the Morro Velho miners had to work despite the holiday. The community pulsated with the rivalries among the samba schools. Carnival bands played, almost without stop, for three or four days. Waldir was in heaven. His boundless energy paid off for him in his work, as well. By 1945 he was a full-fledged stone worker, and two years later, because he had learned English from the foremen, he was moved to an office job, working as a translator. He married in 1946 after a courtship of two years. In 1952 he left the company for unexplained reasons and became a construction worker. He never complained. He never joined any union, always attempting to preserve his independence.

Waldir and countless others lacking day-to-day empowerment were able to overcome stubborn obstacles with imagination and verve. The genius for improvisation flavors Brazilian life and makes the oppressive nature of its political culture bearable. Inmates in São Paulo's Juquery asylum, considered a model hospital but regimented like a military facility, fought back by wearing flowers in their uniforms and hiding away objects from their earlier lives, to preserve their individuality.[16] It is telling, however, that most marginalized Brazilians have not often stepped over the line, as was the case of Italians in debtors' prisons during the eighteenth century who manipulated the system by making frightful allegations as a weapon to improve their own situation.[17] For most Brazilians, the goal has been not to win but to survive from day to day. Sometimes, however, even the most ingenious coping strategies have failed. The next chapter looks at the measures taken by some Brazilians who feel pushed to the wall or who no longer feel obliged to fight back by playing within the accepted rules, written or unwritten.

Notes

1. Roberto DaMatta, *Carnivals, Rogues, and Heroes: An Interpretation of the Brazilian Dilemma,* trans. John Drury (South Bend, IN: University of Notre Dame Press, 1991), 4, 26, 33.

2. John Krich, *Why Is This Country Dancing?* (New York: Simon and Schuster, 1993), 126.

3. Cf. Richard Price, *Alabi's World* (Baltimore: The Johns Hopkins University Press, 1990).

4. Quoted by Jaime de Almeida, "Há Cem Anos, O Quarto Centenário: Dos Horríveis sacrilégios às Santas Alegrias," *Estudos Históricos* (Rio de Janeiro) 5:9 (1992), 14–28; 25.

5. Allison Raphael, "Carnival in Rio: Myths and Realities," pamphlet, Institute of Current World Affairs, New York, 6 April 1976.

6. Ineke van Halsema, *Housewives in the Field: Power, Culture and Gender in a South-Brazilian Village* (Amsterdam: CEDLA, 1991), 63. São Brás Day is celebrated mostly in the South, but is also observed in Bahia.

7. See Sheila S. Walker, "The Feast of Good Death: An Afro-Catholic Emancipation Celebration in Brazil," *Sage: A Scholarly Journal on Black Women* 3:2 (1986), 27–31.

8. Calendar furnished by Bahiatursa. Courtesy of Consuelo Novais Sampaio, 12 January 1993.

9. Henry Koster, *Voyages dans la Patrie Septenrionale du Brésil, Depuis 1809 Jusqu'en 1815,* vol. II (Paris: Delaunay Lib., 1818), 213.

10. *Jornal de Notícias* (Salvador), 21 February 1887.

11. Ari Araujo, *As Escolas de Samba: Um Episódio Antropofágico* (Petrópolis, Rio de Janeiro: Ed. Vozes, 1978), 36.

12. Oceplan/Pandurb, *RMS: Evolução Demográfica (1940–2000)* (Salvador: Prefeitura Municipal do Salvador, 1976), cited by Jefferson Bacelar, *Etnicidade. Ser Negro em Salvador* (Salvador: Ianamá [PENBA], 1989), 74.

13. See Ana Maria Rodrigues, *Samba Negro Espoliação Branco* (São Paulo: Huitec, 1984).

14. J. Krich, *Why Is This Country Dancing?* 73.

15. Oral history testimony of Waldir dos Santos, transcribed by Andrea Vila Novo, Nova Lima, Minas Gerais, August 1994–September 1995.

16. See Maria Clementina Pereira Cunha, *O Espelho do Mundo: Juquery, A História de um Asilo* (Rio de Janeiro: Paz e Terra, 1986), esp. 83.

17. Sabina Loriga, "A Secret to Kill the King," in Edward Muir and Guido Ruggiero, eds., *History from Crime* (Baltimore: Johns Hopkins University Press, 1994), 88–109.

7

Beyond Coping

When people realize that striving to cope leaves them exhausted and losing ground, they are moved to resist the system that constricts their existence. In most cases, as James C. Scott and others have noted, these forms of struggle and resistance stop short of outright defiance because ordinary, powerless people know too well the penalties inflicted by society against deviants and rebels. Often, they resort to more mundane weapons: foot dragging, apathy, dissimulation, desertion, false compliance, stealing, feigned ignorance, arson, sabotage—"Brechtian" forms of class struggle, in Scott's words, that have in common the fact that they require little coordination or planning; they represent a form of self-help; and they typically avoid direct confrontation with authorities.[1]

Not only do people driven to resist do so in conflict over property, jobs, access to resources, and other material needs, but they struggle over symbols, over self-image, and over the way they are treated in everyday life. Weapons in this daily war between rich and poor, the entitled and the marginalized, include gestures, mannerisms, calculated contempt, character assassination, stereotypes, nicknaming, and gossip. Resistance to hurtful slights, and to any harmful ways of keeping people down, are expressed in symbolic forms of everyday life and by individual choices among different forms of behavior; some of which, when they challenge the status quo, are perceived as challenges to the system. It is the lot of Brazilians that historically many actions or behaviors that were not intended as aggressive attacks on the system were taken that way by those whose interests were affected.

Many affluent Brazilians, including members of the middle class, rarely see the world of the common people because they are insulated by their private schools, private clubs, elegant residences, and state-of-the art security. Poor Brazilians endure innumerable daily humiliations by social superiors, economic hardship, slights, and insults, which are expelled in what David Cleary terms the "more or less controlled" release of the *desabafo* during Carnival and in street fights *(brigas)* that occur spontaneously, fueled by hurt feelings and by alcohol.[2] This is not to say that upper-crust Brazilians do not engage in *brigas* among themselves; indeed, when a man kills his lover, or when one elected official assaults another, only rarely is the guilty party punished. Lower-class Brazilians do not have this immunity. Aggression remains the principal way to vent one's inner anger and frustration in Brazilian society, one of the few ways to move beyond mere coping in a universe where very few options exist at all.

Migration

Rigid limits on social mobility have historically spurred migratory pressures in search of better lives, despite tremendous prejudice against newcomers from rural areas prevalent through the present day. The South's booming economic development since the 1940s has fueled this pattern, offering manual labor jobs for the building of hydroelectric power systems, factories, and tremendous housing and apartment construction in the major cities. The aggregate impact of the migrations has been enormous. Fernando Henrique Cardoso called São Paulo "the largest northeastern city." Had he not said this before an audience in Recife, he could have been accused of being as insensitive as journalist Paulo Francis, who during the Fernando Collor debacle said that Brazil's political problems stemmed from the stranglehold of northeastern elites.

After World War II, improvements in Brazil's road network and the construction of better railroad links from Salvador south, permitted, for the first time, migration without intermediate stops from the most remote areas of the interior to the cities of the Center-South. The favelas and shantytowns in which migrants finally settled became kinds of rural islands amidst the urban tumult, perhaps another reason many migrants stayed in their shantytown communities. After 1965, women played an increasing role in migrations as opportunities for employment increased for them in the service sector while manual labor jobs for men did not rise, and indeed fell after the severe recession of the mid-1970s caused by the Organization of Petroleum Exporting Countries (OPEC) petroleum crisis. In the late 1950s, the country built a new national capital in the wilderness. Thousands of *pau de arara* trucks, clad in wood with narrow benches holding from forty to sixty people, wended their way south over thousands of kilometers of dirt roads to Belo Horizonte, Rio de Janeiro, and São Paulo. These trucks sometimes overturned, with many fatalities. Once they arrived, rumors about available employment often turned out to be false or outmoded, and even when jobs were available the workers were always fired when the heavy jobs were done. So Brasília's modernistic neighborhoods of residential apartments, government ministries, and handsome churches soon became surrounded by a permanent circular shantytown of more than a million residents, migrants from the North, the builders of the city who were condemned to favela existence once construction stopped. Now wage workers when work became available, these migrants lacked the protection of their former patrons. They could not plant gardens to raise chickens and vegetables. Their lives remained nearly as hopeless as they had been in the countryside.

The main reason for migration within Brazil has been the terrible periodic droughts that have struck the interior *sertão* of the Northeast with increasing impact over the years, owing to the always larger population in the region despite substantial outmigration. Records of devastating dry spells, sometimes with no rain for years, go as far back as 1710–11. Starting in 1723, no measurable rain fell until 1727. Traditionally, when severe drought struck in the Northeast, families waited stoically until no hope remained, then trekked to the coast or to other urban places in expectation of food, water, and shelter. Provincial and state officials expected this, and often forced the refugees to camp outside the cities they were bound for, to prevent the spread of disease and to minimize the disruption caused by the dislocation. In more recent times, open trucks carrying goods on interstate roads over long distances made migration to the South easier; whole families now abandoned their stricken villages not only to escape from drought but in search of hoped-for permanent industrial employment. These migratory patterns are well documented. The social costs of these migrations are also evident: high proportions of the newcomers to the cities come from the sectors of the population that are least able to adapt and to deal with life in the burgeoning metropolitan centers.

The 1992–93 drought afflicted nearly 10 million people. Federal drought relief funds totaling $180 million went to supply water, not to create jobs or pay for social needs. Sugar cane production dropped by more than half, forcing employers to lay off thousands of workers. In Paraíba, 400 rural workers invaded the market at Bananeiras in search of food, threatening to pillage unless the mayor cooperated. He did, distributing food packages from a truck in the town square. In four other Paraíban cities, sackings did take place; as many as 500 seized the municipal building in Cajazeiras, demanding relief. Forty more sackings were reported in neighboring Pernambuco. The civil defense agency in Alagoas investigated widespread claims that drivers carrying water in tank trucks contracted by the state to be given to the needy were selling it. The companies were accused of not sending out nearly as many water trucks as they had been paid to send. The reservoir supplying water to Fortaleza, the capital of Ceará, was operating at 12 percent of capacity with 3,597 cases of cholera reported.[3] The state of Piauí's minister of social action complained that only one-third of the funds allocated to his impoverished state had arrived in six months. Eighty-four cities reported mob violence and looting in search of food just during a two-week period in March. Agricultural producers entered SUDENE headquarters in Recife, holding its employees (including its chief) hostage for nine hours and demanding to be heard by the president of the Republic. President Itamar Franco agreed to see them, and a day after their meeting, public works funds started to flow north. Drought victims themselves ate cactus to survive and waited for the drought to end, as they have done for at least 800 years in the region. Others, less patient, fled to the South, where police tried to turn them back. One canvas-topped truck bearing thirty-five refugees from Sobradinho, Bahia, 2,500 kilometers distant, was stopped on the Rio de Janeiro–Niterói bridge when a military policeman noticed a head poking out from under the canvas. "Chico Pinga," one of the exhausted and hungry would-be migrants, had stuck his head out because he had never before glimpsed the ocean. The state of Rio de Janeiro paid for bus tickets to transport the truck passengers to São Paulo.[4]

Somewhat less known is the pattern whereby individuals, often driven by a high degree of motivation and courage, have on their own set out from rural villages or small cities and moved to larger urban places, sometimes going to live with family members, in other cases striking out on their own. Household composition, of course, was always affected by the amount of physical space available and the cost of food. In many cases, especially given that, in the Brazilian extended family, kinship was sometimes supplanted by other factors, persons not closely related or not related at all ended up in the household. Kin relations in lower-class households had to be flexible to suit the demands of stressful lives. When things became crowded, families typically permitted young unmarried men to choose whether they would leave to seek their fortunes elsewhere or stay to contribute income. Children were permitted to stay since their needs were modest; but as soon as they were able, they had to produce incidental income. Adolescent girls married early or voluntarily left the home, even if this led to their being considered whores if they ended up living on their own in another locale.

In spite of the fact that most women striking out on their own were ostracized, economically unproductive females were spun off from lower-class family units as soon as possible, owing to limitations on physical space and scarcity of housing. They then had to earn wages as maids helpers while they were young girls, later on as full-time domestics or prostitutes. Carolina Maria de Jesus's life followed this pattern: born out of wedlock in rural Sacramento in Minas Gerais, she was taken out of primary school after two years so she could work alongside her mother. When her mother died, she migrated by herself to a larger town and, during the depression-ridden 1930s, then to São Paulo, the largest and most impersonal city in Brazil. Carolina succeeded at first by performing hard work as a maid for wealthy families, and eventually was hired in the homes of several prominent residents of the city. When she started bearing children, however, she suddenly became unemployable, even though she had developed good relationships with some of her employers, discussing politics and current events with them. She was forced to build a shack in Canindé favela and to provide for herself and her family by scavenging for paper, glass bottles, and tin.

Migration of individuals followed this pattern because it was the young adults, especially the young women, who were more readily able to find domestic work. Except in the direst of times, older and especially elderly persons tended to stay where they were. Not all migrations involved long distances: many persons, as in Carolina Maria de Jesus's case, came from adjoining states, or from the interior of the same state. The material and psychological differences between, for example, Sacramento in rural Minas and the city of São Paulo were so significant that migrants like Carolina might as well have emigrated from the moon.

Packing up a family's possessions and migrating to the coast or to the South represented less of a strategy for coping than a desperate, one-time search for a better life. Ceará, Pernambuco, and Bahia typically lost up to a third of their populations during years of severe deprivation. Seasonal migrations, however, were one way to seek at least temporary improvement for residents of destitute areas. Most such moves were determined less by deliberate individual decisions than by the evolution of agricultural labor systems following emancipation of slavery dependent on intensive work during harvests. For rural folk living as squatters or renting land, another motivation was the prevalent method of agricultural production based on ages-old slash-and-burn techniques. Throughout Brazil, agricultural renters completed their harvest and moved on to a new *roça* (site). Moves had to be made in time to fell trees and permit the earth to dry before the next rainy season. Millions of renters have migrated seasonally for decades, usually for distances. Brazil's vast stretches of unused land made this practical. The resulting facility of the rural poor to migrate in this manner struck foreign visitors as remarkable, although the Brazilian elite saw in the frequent moves evidence of instability and disorganization embedded in the lower-class personality. The nomadic existence of Amazonian rubber gatherers during the 1920s so impressed a team of North American scientists that they attributed to the gathers a "migratory instinct."[5]

Seasonal migrations flow back and forth from the interior to the coast throughout Brazil's North. Thousands flock to the *mate* fields of Mato Grosso, many of them Paraguayans who cross the border. Seminomads care for cattle in Matto Grosso, Goiás, and throughout Amazônia. Thousands of migrant workers harvest the cocoa output in southern Bahia, hired on a daily basis by *empreiteiros* (plantation overseers). Seasonal migration is the basis for manual labor on the sugar plantations stretching from Bahia to through Rio Grande do Norte. Workers move from the semiarid cotton-producing areas of the near-backlands to the better-watered coast, then return later in the year. Tens of thousands come to work the cane harvest. Sometimes they take their families; other times, not. Those that do carry their children with them from job to job. They live in temporary, thatched shelters and toil for three months, and then they go back to the harsh interior. Why do they return? In 1937, Limeira Tejo offered a psychological explanation:

> The *retirantes* arrive in the cane fields but their thinking is not detached from their scorched lands. In the lowlands they are always restless, always sensing the lack of something, always prepared to begin at any moment the return journey. A notice of rainfall in the thorn bushes is sufficient for them to abandon all and return. They are strongly bound to their world. . . .
>
> In the dry country, man is castigated by climatic inclemency, but he has the compensation of immense personal liberty, giving rise to a proud race, to an almost savage independence, undisciplined, without submission to work, without a systematized life. . . . In the lowlands, on the contrary, there develops a repressed type of humanity. Its soul does not expand in that tie which the man of the *caatinga* [backlands] has with his land. . . . The man of the cane fields asserts his personality by turning inward, creating new emotional worlds . . . where he can regain his liberty. For this reason, the lowland is an intolerable world. . . . To return to the *caatinga* signifies the return to his liberty of movement. . . . [6]

Resistance, Militancy, and Violence

Although Brazil's labor union history is filled with struggle against stubborn employers, elite hostility, and government repression, except in the very early years when syndicalist activity was carried out by fiery immigrants moved by socialist and anarcho-syndicalist passions, labor unions were led by intellectuals and by others not of working-class origin, although in the name of the working class. Before 1930, unionism was, in the words of a prominent politician, "a matter for the police." There were some successes, notably when labor union goals converged with political interests, as in the case of the 1917 strike in Porto Alegre: because the incumbent machine needed worker votes, the government supported the union's demands. Two years later, a second general strike was suppressed by the police, as all such efforts were suppressed in other cities. That 1919 strike, marked by radical union demands, led to permanent state-worker animosity in Rio Grande do Sul that ultimately led to Getúlio Vargas's election as governor.[7]

The total breakdown of the Comintern's popular front, the Aliança Nacional Libertadora (ANL), or National Liberation Alliance, is a case in point. The ANL failed to win any support from the peasants and working class that it championed because ANL leaders, following closely the line of the not-so-clandestine Brazilian Communist Party (PCB), saw Brazilian reality in the abstract. ANL leaders were nearly all from the comfortable and well-connected class; they rarely had contact with the poor, certainly not in rural areas. Nevertheless, the language of their newspapers and propaganda broadsheets rang with Marxist slogans and diatribes against oppression. The descriptions of underclass misery were accurate and sympathetic, and their depictions of maladies like racism courageously punctured prevailing myths, but the left-wing ideologues who led the ANL never learned the vocabulary of the working classes, whose members, when they could read, must have been puzzled at constant references to Lenin, to "capitalist trusts," and to the "international proletariat."[8]

When the Moscow-based Comintern ordered the ANL to raise the flag of revolt against Getúlio Vargas's government in the name of antifascism and to establish workers' soviets, and when the PCB leadership and their ANL protégés blindly followed suit, the uprising was confined to barracks mutinies led by PCB cadres in Natal, Recife, and Rio de Janeiro, which were quickly smashed. Only in Recife was there a brief moment when workers raised their hands in support of the rebellion, and they were quickly crushed. Some ANL members privately saw what was coming, and stepped back. The principal ANL organizer was Roberto Faller Sissón, a career navy officer from a well-connected family, an incurable revolutionary romantic. "The Aliança," wrote Barreto Leite, a friend of Castelo Branco and later a Brazilian ambassador, in a letter to Luis Carlos Prestes, the legendary PCB chieftain, "exists mostly in Sissón's head."[9] The real planning was likely done by Comintern agents, one of them a Soviet national who had infiltrated the Brazilian political police.

Not only did the hapless local Communists and fellow travelers have to dodge the police and guard against military informers in their ranks, but they had to watch with vigilance the shifting leadership and topsy-turvy policies emanating in Stalin's Soviet Union. Their theorists were forced to fit Brazilian class structure and other realities into the "semicolonial" mold prescribed by V.I. Lenin. These "strategies of illusion," as Paulo Sérgio Pinheiro calls them, fell woefully short of any rational analysis of fast-changing events. Brazilian leftists were trapped by the requirement that they accept the universality of Marxist-Leninist theory, and they foolishly persuaded themselves that the Brazilian people were "seething with revolutionary spirit." They ignored the fact that the Communists had no rural following and only minimal influence among factory workers in a few cities. Blindly, they believed that a Communist-led mutiny within the armed forces would create the conditions necessary for revolutionary action. They expected that the masses would rise up in solidarity. They were sorely mistaken.[10]

For decades in Brazil, intimidation and violence have been used as weapons to enforce social control. Since mechanisms to ensure a coherent order include values and consensus, the threat of being branded dissident, and therefore the threat of exclusion from privileged circles, has been felt by the elite as well as by the lower classes, but personal violence has usually been reserved—at least until the late 1960s under the repressive military dictatorship—for those lacking the protection of their status, family connections, or wealth.[11] Violence has also, of course, been employed by individuals against others, and not disproportionately by the poor. These acts of violence have included banditry, murder, assaults, and mistreatment of women, children, and the vulnerable—all despite Brazil's larger pattern of pacific interpersonal relations.

During colonial days, placid, isolated country villages always faced danger from roving highwaymen or bands of thugs, but they never had very much to steal, and people were certainly were not afraid to venture out at night. Because everyone knew everyone else in a village, women were relatively safe from sexual attack, since rapists would be instantly identified and dealt with savagely. With the arrival of paved roads and economic diversity, though, things swiftly changed. Outsiders poured into villages within driving range of big cities, buying up land and constructing summer or vacation houses. Managers of factories and other personnel now resided in such places year-round, creating overnight a new elite. These newcomers brought with them loaded guns, since they knew that they would be the likely targets of robbers. The better the roads and the more closely linked formerly remote places became to the outside, the higher the sense of real fear of assault, robbery, and death.

Violence took secular, outward forms. Noblemen fought duels; members of the lower classes brawled in the streets. Much of this violent behavior, however, was ritualized. Noblemen preparing to avenge their honor could expect to be pulled aside by friends before the duel actually began. Many threats of violence among all classes were empty, although to be sure many were not. Once drawn into the fray, men sometimes fought to the death lest they lose face and be humiliated as cowards. Sociologists differentiate between "theater cultures" (Mediterranean Europe) and "sincerity cultures" (northern Europe) but point out that, paradoxically, in sincerity cultures individuals must practice even more self-deception than in the other kind, since theater cultures "cultivate the self-awareness they value less."[12] The literature of early modern Europe is filled with discussions about how to cultivate seemingly natural behavior, to give the illusion of effortless spontaneity, how to wear "masks" and "cloaks" to cover true motives. Well-bred Italian women were encouraged to develop a sense of *vergonha,* or shame, since such a sensitivity would keep them from shameful behavior, or, as Peter Burke points out, from the appearances of shameful behavior, "which was what really mattered."[13] One was not supposed to look behind facades, although people did this all the time, as recorded witness testimonies in court records show.

Encroaching political and economic change in the late nineteenth century broke down traditional patron-client bonds in northeastern Brazil and saw violence erupt in many different ways. Some brigands accommodated to the changing power structure by aligning themselves with either incumbent or opposition political factions; others saw themselves as independent actors, Robin Hood–like champions of the downtrodden even if their actions did not follow from their claims. Romanticization aside, this would-be social banditry represented less class consciousness and conflict than an adaptation to, and not a protest against, the local power structure.[14] They did, however, made their mark with flair. Many *cangaceiros* (backland bandits) put brilliantine in their hair and splashed perfume on their unbathed bodies, "so their distinctive odor became one of their trademarks," Billy Jaynes Chandler reminds us.[15] The legendary bandit Lampião openly negotiated with politicians and in 1926 was hired by federal and state government officials to pursue and capture the Prestes guerrilla column, members of the nationalistic crusade that had raised the banner of revolt against the civilian regime of the First Republic. Less patriotic than practical, he accepted because of the lure of government weapons.

Every unit of the federation since 1889 maintained state police forces, many linked to the national armed forces and heavily armed, the members of which were called soldiers. São Paulo invited a French military mission in 1906 to train its own state Força Pública (police force);[16] during the 1920s that same police militia maintained its own air force. Under the military dictatorship in 1969, the state police were placed under the control of the Brazilian army, to be headed by an army brigadier general on active duty. The long-standing state police mission, in the words of political scientist Paulo Sérgio Pinheiro, "to defend and protect the ruling classes from protest by the lower classes," was consolidated, with state police units taking charge of policing urban areas and charged with the task of combating subversion and Brazil's "internal enemy." When eruptions occurred among the lower classes, retribution was swift and ruthless. The black sailors who mutinied in November 1910 in Rio de Janeiro harbor against excessive flogging, bad food, and other bad conditions surrendered and were promised fair treatment. Instead, nine were shot; twenty-two others were thrown into an underground cell on the Island of Cobras, where sixteen died of thirst and suffocation.[17]

Collective revolts against established authorities were few and far between. From 1595 to 1694, armed escaped slaves successfully defended an autonomous maroon society at Palmares, in the sugar-growing region of the Northeast, until it was crushed by authorities. What was popularly called the "rebellion" at Canudos during the 1890s was not a revolt but a massacre of a peaceful, settled population of devout men and women.[18] The Contestado was a revolt of sorts, but most of the movements challenging the hegemony of the elite tended to be political forays organized in the name of the general population but really representing the interests of a faction or a coalition of factions, as was the case of the so-called 1930 Revolution. In the central interior of the state of Goiás, however, during the period between 1940 and the 1960s, there were conflicts that, taken together, were known as the Revolta de Formoso, or the Revolta de Trombas. These rebellious squatters, Janaína Amado shows, based on their historical experiences and their everyday lives, developed extremely complex notions of being "somebody," and being a "peasant." They were the first large-scale revolt of squatters in Brazil, a kind of conflict that in later decades has spread to many parts of interior Brazil, especially to the distant Amazon frontier.

The migrants who had come to Formoso in the 1940s, when it still was an isolated frontier region, were very poor, usually illiterate, lacking in any skill except the driving goal of obtaining the use of land for farming or mining. They were not a deviant or a marginal group; they were like every other rural landless Brazilian except that they had trekked to the Formoso region. The people they found occupying the land were *grileiros*, ranchers and farmers with dubious claims to the land but with the stamp of legitimization granted by local judges with whom they had forged connections. After the squatters refused to budge, the *grileiros*, aided by the militia, drove them out after four years of bloody campaigns and open warfare. In 1958, after appealing their case to state authorities, the squatters received a favorable ruling, permitting them to stay in the region undisturbed. Actual titles for land were distributed by the government in 1962, and the movement's leader, José Porfírio de Souza, was elected to the state chamber of deputies, the first peasant to be elected to any post in Brazilian history. This initiated a period of peace in the region that lasted until 1964.

A few days after the 1964 military coup, however, federal troops invaded the area and remained for years, arresting the former squatters and driving away many others with threats of violence. Some of the movement's leaders organized to defend their interests, but they were arrested and tortured in a massive government offensive in 1971. José Porfírio de Souza was released from federal prison in 1972 and allowed to return home, but he never arrived, becoming one of the *desaparecidos* (disappeared ones) of the military dictatorship, presumed murdered. Only in 1981 did the Supreme Court rule in favor of the squatters, but by then the region had been transformed into large *latifúndio* units, with very few of the original migrant settlers remaining.

The use of torture as a form of coercion was not limited to the landowner-squatter issue. For decades, Brazilian police authorities, as well as the armed forces, have regularly subjected citizens to brutal and violent treatment. The practices were cruel. In the old days, under Vargas, for example, routine arrests of suspected criminals produced beatings, deprivation of sleep, and feedings of salty and spicy foods without water. Suspected communists, of course, received harsher treatment, ranging from extraction of fingernails with pliers to electric shocks to flogging and other tortures to the point of death. Women prisoners were systematically raped and constantly mistreated. Felinto Müller, the Rio police chief who proudly corresponded with Nazi leaders and who visited the Reich to observe Gestapo activities, gained notoriety for the brutality of his subordinates.

After 1964, and especially after 1968, the use of torture by agents of the military regime was much more systematic and technologically sophisticated. Victims were taken to killing centers, usually rented houses, where body parts were amputated and grotesque punishments inflicted during interrogation sessions; in the end the victim, if he did not die from this treatment, was injected with serums used by veterinarians to kill horses. The bodies were then dismembered and disposed of in pieces. More than

4,600 persons were stripped of their political rights; 10,000 more fled into exile, mostly to Europe, the United States, and Canada, and 144 officially "disappeared" as part of the anticommunist campaign directed not only at radical activists but also at journalists, intellectuals, union leaders, students, and even Catholic priests, all in the name of national security. Thousands of persons were detained without formal charge, often in secret prisons. Inmates were subject to beatings, rapes, and mock executions. Others were administered electric shocks in the anus or genitals while their heads were held under water until their lungs nearly burst. Some were driven to insanity, and many died under torture. After the successful Operação Araguaia in northern Goiás, prisoners under torture were shown slides projected on the wall of the severed heads of some of their former comrades.

In São Paulo, an elite military police shock unit called the Rondas Ostensivas Tobias de Aguiar (ROTA) was established in 1972 to combat terrorism. These forces, sent out in groups of four heavily armed men in a patrol car, became the "vanguard of political repression by Brazil's military government." The military police's de facto impunity was formalized in April 1977 by an amendment to the 1969 military constitution guaranteeing the military police unlimited leeway. Vigilantist activities carried out by military police during the decade of the 1970s included illegal breaking and entering, beating, the systematic use of torture, and death. Many felt that many citizen deaths, claimed officially to be the results of shootouts with the police, were actually due to summary executions, since in the entire period during which 129 people were listed killed by the ROTA in this manner, not a single ROTA policeman died.[19] After the publication of *Rota 66*, an exposé of vigilantism, its author received death threats by telephone and felt obliged to leave Brazil, taking up domicile in New York. Allegations also surfaced that ROTA policemen in the wealthy Jardins section of the city of São Paulo would from time to time stop drivers of luxury cars, take their house keys, and rob their houses. Some of the victims then were stripped of their cash and personal effects, beaten, killed, and dumped into the river with stones tied to their legs. Six ROTA policemen were interrogated after anonymous callers reported their names. In response, the public prosecutor received phone calls threatening his life.[20]

During the height of the dictatorship, urban guerrillas not only robbed banks but sequestered diplomats and foreign ambassadors. By the 1980s, kidnapping of family members of wealthy and prominent families had become so prevalent that most lived in armed camps, traveled incognito (or by private helicopter), or fled Brazil entirely. The number of ransom kidnappings in Rio de Janeiro rose from 39 in 1989, to an average of 87 in 1990–91, to 122 in 1992 (before the end of the year). Zózimo Barrozo do

Amaral, the chic society columnist for the *Jornal do Brasil,* moved to Miami, along with Kiko and Bebel Malzoni (owner of Bob's, a fast-food chain). Dozens of other *colunáveis,* wealthy and socially prominent *cariocas,* also moved to Miami or to Paris (as did Fernando Collor de Mello's former in-laws). More than 50,000 residents of Rio de Janeiro were reported to have bodyguards, one of them, José I. Peres, the owner of various shopping centers, reportedly spent $50,000 a month on security. Foreign firms and banks faced mass requests for transfer out of Rio de Janeiro.[21]

To counter these acts, the police and military response was overwhelming, although in comparison to the Argentina's vicious "dirty war," during which nearly 10,000 Argentine citizens were arrested with formal charges, taken to prison, tortured, and killed, Brazil's record during its military dictatorship between 1964 and 1978 involved many fewer victims but was no less brutal. Thousands were tortured in centers run by competing police and military entities: the Navy, the Air Force, the Army, various National Security groups, as well as by detectives of city police forces, especially the notorious DOPS-CODI, the independent secret police agency.[22]

During the transition from dictatorship to civilian government, and with the threat of leftist terrorism and kidnappings contained, the military police and their backers shifted their venue by declaring crime to be a problem of national security and by employing the same methods waged against radicals in the 1970s against the *povão,* the "large public," meaning the lower class. To be sure, there were overlapping areas: urban guerrillas staged bank robberies to seize money to buy weapons and to support their movement; apprehending these assailants and preventing acts of armed robbery was a natural enough task for urban shock forces. The 720-man ROTA even well into the *abertura* period continued to police the streets of São Paulo, committing 129 quasi-legal executions during the first nine months of 1981, supplanting a rate of death squad murders estimated at an average of more than one per day. During the first half of 1981, there were 40,264 people in the capital who were detained for "investigation"; 21,956 more were held in rural parts of São Paulo state.[23]

In the early 1990s, Rio de Janeiro and São Paulo surpassed Lagos and Johannesburg in per capita murders, with the numbers rising each year and many additional homicides not reported. The atmosphere encouraged vigilantism and crude repressive measures by authorities. Not only suspected robbers or drug traffickers were targets. The 1993 annual report of the Brussels-based International Confederation of Free Trade Unions (ICFTU) designated Latin America as the most dangerous region in the world in which to belong to a labor union. During the 1920s and the 1930s, Brazil (with Argentina) would have topped the list; in 1992, out of 123 reported murders of trade union officials, only two were Brazilian, with the greatest incidence of violence in Guatemala, El Salvador, Colombia, and Peru. In 1994, one of every 700 residents of Rio de Janeiro was a victim of homicide.[24]

In 1992, 1,259 verified cases of persons killed by the state of São Paulo military police for "resisting arrest" were reported, an average of 3.7 per day, or one every six hours. This did not include the 111 prisoners killed in the massacre at Pavilion 9 of the House of Detention at Carandiru in October, the largest such killing of inmates in more than twenty years. Observers noted that Governor Luiz Antonio Fleury and other officials used certain phrases in their statements about criminals—"bandits with their beards in the soup" and "bandits who don't deserve roses"—as code messages to inform policemen that killing was condoned. Supporters of the use of police violence, however, could point to the fact that criminals usually were much better armed than lawmen, and that as a result of the strong-arm tactics, the number of policemen killed in the line of duty dropped by 16 percent from 1991 to 1992.[25]

A major share of Brazil's drug trafficking has been directed by convicted criminals serving penitentiary time, known as the "Red Command" (Comando Vermelho). Through the use of couriers called "carrier pigeons," relatives and members of the heads of the drug-trafficking syndicate who are permitted to visit the leaders of the Red Command in prison, orders and instructions are transmitted to confederates still at large. Starting out in Rio de Janeiro's penitentiaries, the Comando Vermelho group has allegedly made contacts with counterparts in São Paulo, becoming so powerful that, like the Mafia, they order with impunity the deaths of enemies outside prison walls. Drugs are purchased from producers in Bolivia or Colombia rather than through intermediaries. Every kilogram of cocaine sold by Comando Vermelho operatives netted a profit of $27,500, a comparatively small amount in North America but a fortune in Brazil.

In a system organized originally within prison walls, each drug lord serving time used a protégé on the outside to act as his intermediary. Newspapers were able to name names—the Comando Vermelho chief controlling the Morro da Mineira was Altair Domingos (Naí), assisted by Ricardo Chaves de Castro (Fú) on the outside; the imprisoned chief of the Morro do Pavão near Leblón was Róbson Roque (Caveirinha), and his protégé on the outside was Fábio Soares Cabral (Fabinho); and so forth. "Justice" is summarily administered. Virtually every favela boss exercises his authority in violent ways. In Rocinha, those who cross traffickers are punished with blows to the head with clubs. Men who beat women are forced to walk seminaked through the favela for a week, wearing a bra and panties. Rapists are lynched.

In Borel favela, which has shacks housing 13,000 residents and over-looks Tijuca in Rio de Janeiro's North Zone, Cláudio da Silva (Tatinha), serving a twelve-year sentence, does business from his cell, while his brother, Nelson da Cunha (Bill), runs Borel. A "fat *mulato*" (according to the newsmagazine *Veja*), Bill became famous for capturing and torturing twenty-one local *pivetes,* personally supervising vicious acts of beating while he passed around beer to onlookers. After the beer bottles were empty, they were broken over the heads of the bound victims, who were accused of selling books of stolen checks in the favela and other petty crimes challenging the monopoly of Bill, the favela boss, who announced that he would kill the three oldest youths personally. The other victims were then ordered to place their hands atop a wall; each was then shot in both hands. All but the three detained by Bill were released; while their muti-lated hands were being treated in local hospitals, not a single one was willing to tell what had happened to them while they were being interro-gated. Residents of Borel interviewed later on the whole expressed their satisfaction at the punishments. "Given that there is no justice outside, someone has to punish these *moleques* (urchins) in the favela," one told a journalist.[26] The governor, Leonel Brizola, responded to the news of the events by claiming that the perpetrators, seemingly immune to police arrest, had borrowed the notion of mutilating their victims' hands from reading the Koran, claiming that the act was a version of the Arab practice of cutting of the hands of thieves.

Comando Vermelho leaders have used helicopters to stage spectacular prison escapes. The Comando is considered so powerful that the government of the state of Rio de Janeiro negotiated directly with drug dealers in Vila Nova Park in Duque de Caxias, in the notorious Baixada Fluminense, to be able to continue construction on the second leg of the Red subway line from the city, for which officials had appropriated $100 million. The traffickers de-manded guarantees that their business would not be interrupted, and offi-cials reportedly provided satisfactory assurances. Officials denied this, of course, and went out of their way to claim that the Comando Vermelho's powers have been exaggerated by the press.[27] São Paulo's Military Police Intelligence Agency claimed in March 1993 that Comando Vermelho gangs had become involved in bank robberies and armed attacks on luxury apart-ment houses, had made legitimate purchases of gas stations and lottery parlors, had infiltrated the numbers racket, and had illegally imported arms from dealers in Europe and the United States. Officials admitted that they had lost control of most of Rio de Janeiro's 400 favelas, prompting Presi-dent Itamar Franco to use the army to coordinate police efforts to arrest suspected drug traffickers and to intercept suspects fleeing from the city.[28]

Individuals caught up in the struggle for day-to-day survival react in different ways. Carolina Maria de Jesus, the mother of three who was ousted from her jobs as a maid because she could not care for her children in her patrons' houses, and who was forced to live in São Paulo's Canindé favela, reacted psychologically by adopting a fierce protective shell. She shut out the ugliness of favela life by cultivating a reputation that combined elements of a scold, a crank, and a person brave enough to call the police when trouble broke out. More commonly, marginalized children living in city streets and living as small-time robbers or as runners for drug dealers cope with their reality by sniffing glue or by becoming drug addicts themselves. When a psychologist asked some of the child delinquents why they sniffed glue every day to get high, one replied: "Well, have you got a better suggestion?" Another said bluntly: "I sniff glue so I won't feel anything when I'm beaten."[29]

Responses

The growth of government at all levels meant that the lives of ordinary people were increasingly likely to be touched directly. To administrators, introducing the metric system, an innovation from continental Europe, not Great Britain, was a logical step in Brazil's efforts to compete in world markets. The "French" system, as it had been called by the Liberal party government of the Marquis of Olinda, had been introduced in 1862 and given a period of ten years to be fully applied. By so doing, Brazil was in fact a very modern country: Germany, in contrast, only substituted metric measurements for a traditional system of more than 3,000 weights and measures in 1968. Viscount Rio Branco, a mathematician and the president of the Imperial Council of State in the emperor's absence in 1871, not only enacted the Free Birth Law, presaging the death knell of Brazilian slavery, but carried out instructions for final implementations of the metric system. After September 1872, any failure to use this system would result in jail or high fines. Implementation for the rural Northeast, however, was delayed until mid-1874, a recognition, legislatively, of the slowness officials knew characterized the isolated regions of Brazil, which they considered backward as well.[30]

More than a hundred armed riots protesting the metric system erupted in marketplaces throughout the backlands of the provinces of Paraíba and Pernambuco during the three-month period from November 1874 to January 1875. Many of these riots resulted in wanton destruction, not only of the new weights and measures but of notarial tax records, which were used as the basis for tax collection and for finding names of men who could be drafted into the militia. This "Quebra-Quilos" revolt was not the only popular manifestation against the government. Widespread resistance to governmental acts had occurred sporadically for decades. In 1851, the imperial decision to transfer the registration of baptisms and funerals from parish priests to civil authorities provoked riots throughout the region. Other acts that had been misunderstood (or understood too well) included the first major national census in 1872; the regulations requiring slaves to be registered with municipal officials; and the Law of Military Enlistment, enacted in September 1874, making it easier for men to be seized and impressed into service. New municipal taxes were instituted in Paraíba in mid-1874. Relations between Church and state were also strained as a result of Dom Pedro II's laxness in enforcing neo-orthodox pressures from the Vatican, and government officials in the Northeast blamed local missionary clergy for stirring up the population.

Virtually every Brazilian city with urban transit systems experienced periodic antiproperty riots in protest of fare hikes, often resulting in the shattering or burning of transit stations, trains, buses, and trolley cars. Starting as far back as the nineteenth century, but escalating in ferocity after the Second World War, especially during periods of regional drought and falling standard of living, Brazil has experienced thousands of attacks on streetcars, buses, ferries, and trains, and thousands more on food warehouses, retail food shops, and supermarkets.

Since many of the rioters were residents of shantytowns, officials stepped up their pressure. In Rio de Janeiro, where tens of thousands lived in favelas perched on the city's hills and stretching north for miles, heightened fear of *favelados* led to the policy, starting in the late 1950s, of evicting favela residents and destroying their shantytowns. This was done in many cases to make room for high-rise apartment buildings and luxury hotels. Land in Rio has always been costly, and some favela sites commanded magnificent views of the sea or of the city. Some 140,000 *favelados* in eighty favelas were displaced. They were not thrown out into the streets: most were resettled in one of the twenty-nine new housing projects owned by the municipality. Many social workers and urban planners applauded the evictions, seeing them as a necessary step toward housing the urban poor in solid structures with electricity and running water, part of a process of rehabilitation and urban renewal that had been started in the early 1960s under the tutelage of the U.S. Agency for International Development (USAID) and President John F. Kennedy's Alliance for Progress.

Opponents, however, accused planning officials of wrongheadedness at best and of corruption and cynicism at worst, since the upper-class and commercial interests, not the *favelados,* benefited most from the evictions.

They pointed out that the new housing projects were in most cases hours from the source of jobs in the city, and that even if some of the resettled *favelados* were willing to travel several hours each day, they could not afford the bus fares, which added up to a substantial portion of the minimum wage. Opponents also pointed out that *favelados* were moved (sometimes forcibly, herded onto trucks by soldiers with machine guns) to their new housing even before the projects were completed, and in all cases before the promised new factories (few of which ever materialized), health posts, schools, and grocery stores were ready.

The debate between urbanologists and bureaucrats did not filter down to the men and women whose lives were being affected by the new policies. Unlike the experiences of Lima, Santiago, and other cities, in Brazil the urban poor rarely created squatter settlements from mass action. The favelas grew passively, by accretion, over time. Almost always they sprang up on empty land where the property owner was unlikely to make trouble after asking for (and receiving) cash payment, a few days after the initial settlement. Sometimes political parties lent their support to the *favelados* in exchange for electoral support. Favela growth followed the same patterns as the rest of urban society, with social differentiation based on income and status within the favela. "Wealthy" favela residents sold the use of electric lines and water spigots. Most *favelados* lived in shacks of wood, zinc, or tin, but some lived in two- or even three-story brick houses. Sociologist L.A. Machado da Silva observed the growth of a favela middle class in his study of Rio de Janeiro in 1967.[31]

Popular mobilization in opposition to obligatory resettlement occurred only twice. The first time was when Pasmado, a large favela in the middle/upper-class Zona Sul, was condemned in 1963. A coalition of neighborhood associations was organized to fight the decision; residents were instructed not to cooperate with the resettlement process. Police arrested Pasmado residents considered ringleaders.[32] The same thing happened at another Zona Sul favela, Ilha das Dragas. In response, police dragged out recalcitrant residents and jailed the entire board of directors of the Ilha das Dragas association. In the face of the official actions, and in the light of the general atmosphere of intimidation under the military regime, the coalition turned over its leadership to new directors willing to cooperate, and no further hindrances to resettlement occurred.[33] There was never any real change. Although the creation of the favela residents' associations in 1961 by the government was portrayed as a progressive measure, in reality the measure was primarily a device to control the favela bloc vote. After authoritarian rule canceled most elections, even this became a moot point, and the associations were allowed to wither.[34]

Favelados were aided in their efforts to beat the resettlement system by the fact that authorities had poor information on where *favelados* actually lived. Maps were inaccurate and addresses often approximate. *Favelados* gave wrong information whenever it suited them. As soon as news circulated that a favela was on the list to be condemned, the local housing market reacted. Some non-*favelados,* desiring public housing or other leverage with social agencies, immediately rented a room or a shack in the favela destined to be torn down. Original residents could then either elect to move or to turn their shacks over to others as a business proposition. People with spare rooms rented them out. Prices for shacks in the poorest condition in Catacumba favela, following the announcement in late 1968 that its residents would be resettled, shot up to the equivalent of six minimum wages. Condemned favelas mushroomed overnight as people moved into existing shacks, or built new shacks on adjoining land, however precarious. Catacumba spread horizontally to almost double its size; the Praia do Pinto favela, unable to expand horizontally because of the terrain, grew vertically.[35]

Families who were interviewed by resettlement officials taking surveys responded in ways calculated to benefit them. When two adults in a family earned income, they typically would declare themselves as heads of separate households, so they would be allocated two houses, thus manipulating the system. *Favelados* inflated their monthly income because they knew that "better" housing would be allotted to families earning more. It took at least six months before the preparatory interviewing and the final eviction to take place. Each household had been classified and assigned to a public housing unit according to the results of the interview process. It then took weeks or even months for the favelas to be emptied, especially when coercion was not necessary to force everyone out at once. Members of the residents' association had their belongings moved first, carefully; everyone else had their possessions thrown, together with other people's, into trucks. Empty favela shacks were guarded until they were bulldozed so that they would not be stripped of their building materials or simply reoccupied by newcomers.

Officials hoped that the resettlement process would permit *favelados* to become homeowners over time by paying off government-sponsored mortgages. The system, however, did not work as it was planned. Once they received occupancy of their new homes, *favelados* designated as heads of households clamored to prove that their incomes had fallen since their classification, so that their monthly rent or mortgage payments would be lowered. People offered to work in exchange for favors. Some managed to switch the houses that had been offered to them because of a crack in the wall, dampness, or other problems. Since nearly everyone had complaints, officials responded to those who worked out private deals with them.

Although rents and taxes were low, based on the minimum wage, the former *favelados* did everything in their power to reduce their obligations. Some refused to sign the permit of occupancy or to pay the required occupancy tax, daring, as it were, officials to evict them. Knowing that any punitive action would take months to carry out, occupants deliberately stopped payment until the bureaucrats caught up with them. Some rented out their units, although this was not permitted. Such rent was used to make mortgage payments. Others so inclined tried to sell their units at a profit. For non-*favelados,* the housing projects were far preferable to the old system, since social and housing workers were much more amenable than landlords, so property values in some cases went up considerably and made selling attractive to the resettled *favelados,* anxious for even a small profit even if it meant moving back into some other favela.

These conditions in Rio de Janeiro peaked during the middle 1970s and then dissipated as government priorities shifted away from public housing. More recent times have seen new urban forms of aggressive behavior in the form of *invasões* (invasions), the seizure of vacant lots and lands and derelict buildings to set up housekeeping. Favelas themselves are called *invasões* in Salvador because so many of the city's shantytowns were built on land occupied by the poor. In the mid-1980s, a reform group, the Movement in Defense of Favelados, linked to CEBs and other left-wing Roman Catholic groups, organized in São Paulo to fight for legalization of squatter-occupied lands that were publicly owned. In turn, the city administration offered a plan whereby part or all of 386 existing favelas would be improved. Bureaucratic obstacles impeded any real progress: the water utility, for example, demanded that the paths separating shacks in the favelas, often as narrow as 80 centimeters, be widened to 3 meters before they would bring water into the favela. The electric company, Eletropaulo, made similar demands. After numerous futile efforts to resolve the dilemma, the focus shifted to the state government, and the favela reform organization combined forces with the Workers' Party (PT) to form a new Unified Movement (Movimento Unificado). Protest marchers in June 1984 demanded that the governor support a cap on water and electric charges not to exceed 1 percent of the official minimum monthly salary for each utility, and demanded that public land to be leased to *favelados* for a period of ninety years. The governor, Franco Montoro, refused. A second march in January 1985 failed as well. Despite earnest intentions and careful marshaling of data on all sides to confront the issue, little was accomplished, even when the PT's Luiza Erundina was elected mayor.[36]

Although Mayor Erundina radically altered municipal priorities by concentrating on health care, education, and the needs of the poorest citizens, her party was voted out of office. The new municipal government returned to the old ways, emphasizing construction projects mostly benefiting businesses and the affluent. Nor did the electoral victory of populist Leonel Brizola in Rio de Janeiro lead to significant change, and many hostile industrialists and business leaders fled from the region, exacerbating the long-term economic decline in Rio's fortunes. Across Brazil, the cycle of official violence against marginalized citizens accelerated. In Rio, more than a quarter of the members of the city's police forces admitted to having been invited to participate in death squads. Inside the favelas, drug bosses acted with increasing audacity, acquiring near-absolute power on their turf and enforcing public order on their own terms to keep police out. They often shot youths in the hands for participating in robberies. Death squads committed thousands of summary executions.

In March 1991, residents of the Rio de Pedras favela in Rio de Janeiro, heartened by the electoral victory of socialist governor Brizola, seized and occupied an unfinished luxury high-rise condominium development half a mile from the exclusive Barra de Tijuca beach. The development was valued at $100 million, and its owners had gone into receivership in 1983. Rio das Pedras houses 80,000 poor people, many of them wage earners unable to pay for nonfavela housing. The developer's debts had been resolved, but inaction on the part of the Central Bank had held up the resumption of construction when the *favelados* took matters into their own hands. Among the pressures motivating the *favelados* was the rising cost of slum living in Rio de Janeiro, where rent charged for a shack cost three times the official minimum wage. The invaders took over 980 half-finished luxury apartments and were applauded by the newly inaugurated governor, who vowed at a press conference to "put the slum-dwellers in the condominium complex and [the] developer . . . in the slum." Less polemical observers blamed the government for its inaction and declared the unfinished condominium project a "monument to government paralysis."[37] In the end, the *favelados* were coaxed into leaving with promises of public housing elsewhere, and the specific crisis was defused while other invasions, albeit on a smaller scale, continued. São Paulo continued to average two invasions daily, with more reported in Rio de Janeiro.[38]

Street Violence

In Rio de Janeiro, waves of random gang attacks on pedestrians and beach goers began in October 1992, so-called *arrastão* (dragnet) attacks. The first such events occurred when the chic beachfront of Ipanema was invaded by vicious bands of favela youths, swarming out of buses in five separate groups, and assaulting, robbing, or knocking down anyone in their way. "It was like a cloud of locusts," said an eyewitness, a resident of Arpoador beach between Copacabana and Ipanema. The first wave centered on a gang fight between members of Vigário Geral and Parada de Lucas from the North Zone, on one side, and Vila Operário, from the notorious Baixada Fluminense, outside the city. A half-hour later, about a hundred *favelados* from Penha and Olaria assaulted beach goers in Ipanema. Then a group of fifty youths attacked one part of Copacabana and a second band of eighty attacked further down the beach. Finally, twenty *pivetes,* adolescent muggers, attacked the handcraft market at Praça General Osório, in Ipanema, a locale frequented by tourists. Police were almost nowhere to be seen during the two and a half hours of the attacks.[39] It may not have been coincidental that the police massacre that left 111 inmates dead at the Carandiru prison in São Paulo—the largest in Latin America—occurred in the same month. Spurred probably by the role of sensationalist television programs that relished this kind of coverage, the practice of *arrastão* spread overnight to other cities. In Belém, 200 persons were arrested during one "dragnet" attack, 80 of them youths who were arrested as juvenile delinquents. In Riberão Preto in the state of São Paulo, eighteen youths were seized when they coursed through bars on the principal streets of the city, stealing watches and tennis shoes. São Paulo's Praça da Sé, in the heart of downtown, was paralyzed for several days by a wave of collective assaults committed by bands of adolescents escaped from FEBEM, the city's institution for orphans and homeless youths.[40]

Brazil's street gangs, dubbed *tribus* (tribes) by journalists, differed only superficially from gangs in Los Angeles and Manchester, but in the context of the Brazilian experience, where the poor and unemployed have been docile for hundreds of years, their appearance was unexpected. Several varieties of youth gangs emerged. Those based in favelas, such as the ones that invaded Rio's beaches, were considered to be involved in criminal activity and drugs, and to be connected to the Comando Vermelho, the primary organized crime group in the large cities. Others, made of mostly of working-class youths from employed families, such as São Paulo's Mancha Verde, liked to incite violence and to fight, but were not otherwise criminal or predatory.

The third kind of gang was made up of *funkeiros,* their name derived from "funk" music, which had been imported from the United States over the past twenty years and were prevalent especially in the city of Rio de Janeiro and in favelas in the surrounding region. These were *favelados,* usually black, who worked at odd jobs during the week to permit them to buy clothing and to attend funk dances on the weekends in the favela dance halls, magnets for young people. Until late 1992, the *funkeiros* stayed in their favelas, but in October 1992 they started traveling to more affluent neighborhoods. "Funkeiros come down from Rio's *morros* (hills) to terrorize the *bacanas* (affluent kids)," a newspaper headline warned.[41] Typically, the *funkeiros* hung out, brawling with their rivals over claims to territory, and competing for young women by chanting war cries and carrying out acts of daring and stylized brawling. These gang members termed themselves *galeras*.

A particularly wild melee broke out at the Escola de Samba Império Serrano, in Madureira, where 4,000 people gather every Sunday to dance and to listen to live music. During the time that the *galeras* stuck to the favelas, at least twenty youths were killed and another forty-nine ended up seriously wounded, but the police did nothing, even though high-placed police officers claimed that the *funkeiros* were connected to organized crime personages who controlled crime in favelas and prisons. Nightclub owners throughout the region defended sponsoring the lucrative and wildly popular funk music dances—"They are the only form of diversion for favela young people," one explained—but politicians, of course, got into the act once the gangs stopped fighting in the *morros* and began to cross socioeconomic lines.[42] Rio's governor Brizola proposed confining the favela youths to their neighborhoods if the disturbances continued; César Maia, the mayor, proposed to call in federal troops to handle future disturbances. Some individual *funkeiros* protested, saying that if the police removed the drug-related elements and prevented fighting at the dances, there would be no threat. Homeowners disagreed: the specter of black youths from the North Zone of the city cruising through the city in search of trouble was enough to ring the alarm.

Even more ominous was the sudden appearance on Brazilian soil of working-class hate groups, notably Nazi skinheads *(carecas* or *cabeças-raspadas),* spreading the gospel of "white power" by distributing photocopied brochures (perversely dubbed *fanzines*) calling for death to Jews and Northeasterners. Imitating their comrades abroad, skinheads in São Vicente, São Paulo, marched to celebrate the 103rd anniversary of Adolf Hitler's birth and later to commemorate Heinrich Himmler's birthday. *Fanzines* published in Santo André advertised videotapes on Hitler's life and explained how to become involved in neo-Nazi groups in Argentina, Chile, France, Germany, and Italy. Articles demanded the forcible concentration of northeasterners in work camps. Mostly between the ages of twenty and thirty, Brazil's homegrown skinheads were most heavily concentrated in São Paulo, Paraná, and Rio Grande do Sul. They claimed not to use drugs, they practiced muscle building, and they distributed anti-Semitic literature.

They also exalted the Ku Klux Klan, harassed homosexuals, and favored what they call *"oi"* music, a kind of heavy metal. Groups of skinheads calling themselves "nationalists" attacked Jews in the streets and professed alliances with the revived Brazilian Integralist movement, a relic of the pro-Fascist late 1930s, headed in São Paulo by Anésio de Lara Campos Júnior, the half-brother of PT Senator Eduardo Suplicy. Rio de Janeiro's skinhead association claimed to differ from the skinhead associations of other states because its leaders denied being racist, even to the point of recruiting blacks. Rio's skinheads were just as prone to physical violence, and there were several skinhead groups, not only the one spoken for by those rejecting the white-power banner.[43]

In September 1992, "white-power" skinheads invaded the headquarters of Radio Atual, a São Paulo radio station featuring a weekend program of Northeastern music. The invaders fired gunshots and painted swastikas and "death to northeasterners" slogans on the walls of the building under siege. In response, spokesmen for São Paulo's Jewish Federation, members of the Brazilian Bar Association, some unions, and others met with police officials to demand countermeasures. A smattering of politicians, including the PT's Eduardo Suplicy and then-mayor Luiza Erundina, herself a Paraibana, spoke out, but few others spoke out against the outrages. Brazil's Interpol representative pledged to investigate to what extent funds were being received from neo-Nazi groups elsewhere, especially Chile. There was less doubt among federal police officials, who admitted that funds had been received from neo-Nazi groups in England (from the group calling itself "Condemned 84," in Ipswich); from a Dutch group, "Streetwise"; from the "Junta de Defesa Nacional" in Lisbon; and from the Klan in the United States.[44] In Porto Alegre, the Jewish Federation demanded police protection for its synagogues and cemeteries after a wave of desecrations. In the aftermath of the death of a black student beaten and stabbed by thirty *carecas* in Santo André, one of the ministers of the Brazilian branch of the Nation of Islam threatened that for every "black brother" who died, a white racist would die as well. São Paulo's secretary of justice responded by calling the Nation of Islam's claim of police inaction against the Nazis a "total absurdity," warning that the black militants were trying to turn São Paulo into a "racial far-West."[45]

A Catholic University of São Paulo anthropologist studied the ABC-region skinheads and found them to be distinct from the more publicity-conscious Nazi, white-power skinheads who attack Jews, northeasterners, and other outsiders. The homegrown skinheads, she found, face problems rooted in the marginalization of lower-class life. Interestingly, many come from *crente* families, whose evangelistic Protestantism demands moral be-

havior, hard work, and sacrifice. Those she interviewed were strongly opposed to the use of drugs, and seemed to find in their gangs' structure a
form of protection against the daily violence of their lives. Seeing themselves as economic victims, the skinheads are receptive to clichés about
imperialist intrusions in Brazilian life; therefore, they tend to consider
themselves nationalists. Conservative ideologically, they consider domestic
politicians thieves, and therefore do not respect the political system. White-
power groups around the country, the anthropologist found, represent a
dissident minority of the working-class skinheads, whose leaders are from
higher socioeconomic levels and who are more likely to be of German,
Polish, or Central-European descent. She claimed that being hostile to
northeasterners was not a domestic version of the European animosity toward immigrants, although she agreed that northeasterners are hated by the
local skinheads because, like immigrants, they compete with local working-
class youths for jobs.[46]

Mortal Neglect, Death, and Suicide

Not strategies for coping but acts of hopelessness and profound depression
are acts causing willful death, including suicide. Nancy Scheper-Hughes
has shown that even maternal love dries up in cases of suffering rural
women who become so listless that they neglect their sickly infants, permitting them to die. Not only do Brazilian infants of poor mothers die at one of
the highest rates in the world, but Scheper-Hughes's path-breaking recent
study in the northeastern Alto do Cruzeiro revealed an even more shocking
fact among chronically starving young women: an accommodation to infant
death that begins with pregnancy, which is seen by the mother not as a
beginning of new life but as a possible new death. When they saw signs that
their infants were weak, these mothers gradually disengaged from their
fragile infants, reducing their intake of food and water and producing starvation and dehydration.

How did these women become so apathetic? There was an existential
insecurity prevalent in their community of shantytowns, one so powerful
that it caused residents to divert their scant resources from buying food, for
example, to purchasing folk medicine remedies and tranquilizers for the
local condition described as "nerves." By resigning their infants to death,
the women of Alto do Cruzeiro were unknowingly following the old pattern
in the region of infant abandonment, forced upon families by the grinding
poverty that threatened the family unit itself by producing too many mouths
to feed. The Northeast Catholic Church's historically strong opposition to
artificial methods of birth control and the inability of priests and health

workers to teach these hapless men and women to apply the so-called rhythm method has created a reality in which withholding of infant nurturing has become the only strategy of coping available to the shantytown residents.[47]

Women seeking abortions, illegal in Brazil, in recent years have resorted to taking misoprostol, an antiulcer drug that causes uterine contractions violent enough to induce uterine bleeding, and that is widely available at $6 a dose. Forty percent of misoprostol users are the poorest Brazilian women, living in slums or favelas. Other abortions are induced by police in large cities: sometimes when they capture a pregnant teenager, they kick her in the stomach, a practice known as "the heavy one."[48] An estimated 1.5 million Brazilian women have abortions each year, the same number as in the United States, whose total population is 255 million—100 million more than Brazil. Dilation and curettage was the fourth most frequent medical procedure conducted in Brazilian hospitals in 1991, performed on 342,000 women. Most of these cases resulted from incomplete abortions brought on by the self-prescribed antiulcer drug. Individual state governments have acted to restrict or ban the use of misoprostol, but it remains available. Women not wishing to use the dangerous drug also resort to more traditional methods, including surgical removal of fetuses by unlicensed midwives.[49]

Suicides in Brazil are mostly registered in urban areas, so our view of the problem is incomplete. Before 1960, taking poison was the preferred method among both men and women; more recently, men have turned to the use of guns, while women still use sleeping pills or poison, both readily available in pharmacies.[50] Suicide has been a particularly acute problem among indigenous Brazilians as their numbers fall. The 8,000 Kaiowá (Caiowáa), living in misery on a tiny (3,000-hectare) reservation in Mato Grosso do Sul, the state's third largest city, offer a sad case study. They share a reservation divided by a road to Ponta Preta, on the Paraguayan border, with members of two other tribes, Guaranís and Terenas, themselves remnants. Rudimentary social services are provided by FUNAI, the national Indian Service, and by the Presbyterian Church and the Seventh-Day Adventists. The residents have been driven from their land, which is now used to grow soybeans for export and to graze cattle, and they utterly lack hope. Their chieftain, Marçal de Souza, was shot in the head by a gunman in November 1983 because he protested. It is widely believed in the region that the man who ordered the killing was Líbero Monteiro de Lima, an absentee landowner. Suicides among the Indians, long a problem, subsequently increased dramatically in the wake of family disintegration, poverty, generalized disorientation, and knowledge of continual mistreatment from intruders.

Among the Kaiowá and Guarani peoples, suicide is an ancient practice, an aspect of the religious belief in the coming to earth of the *ñhanderu,* the tribal deities. The high incidence of suicide among the indigenous population (and among the population at large as well) must be seen as a cry for help, a call for attention. Paradoxically, then, the death of so many Kaiowá is an appeal for life.[51]

Notes

1. James C. Scott, *Weapons of the Weak: Everyday Forms of Peasant Resistance* (New Haven: Yale University Press, 1985), xvi.

2. David Cleary, review of Daniel T. Linger, *Dangerous Encounters: Meanings of Violence in a Brazilian City* (Stanford: Stanford University Press, 1992), in *Bulletin of Latin American Research* 12:3 (1993), 344–45.

3. See Richard A. Gorell, "Families in Shantytowns in São Paulo, Brazil, 1945–1984: The Rural-Urban Connection," Ph.D. diss., University of Kansas, 1990.

4. *Folha de São Paulo,* 19 May 1993, 14; *Veja,* 24 March 1993, 78; *Veja,* 10 February 1993, 36.

5. T. Lynn Smith, *Brazil: People and Institutions* (Baton Rouge: Louisiana State University Press, 1954), 160.

6. Limeira Tejo, *Brejos e Carrascães do Nordeste* (São Paulo: 1937), 154–56, cited by T. Lynn Smith, *Brazil: People and Institutions,* 163–64.

7. Joan Bak, "Regional Variants in Brazilian Labor History," paper presented to MACLAS meeting, 2 April 1993, University Park, PA.

8. See, for example, *A Manhã,* the ANL's newspaper published in Rio de Janeiro, 21 August 1935, "Manifesto do Caravana ANL ao Norte do Brasil," 1.

9. Letter, Barreto Leite to Luis Carlos Prestes, Rio de Janeiro, 26 October 1935, PCB Archive, Rio de Janeiro. For a detailed history of these events, see the author's *The Vargas Regime* (New York: Columbia University Press, 1970).

10. Rollie Poppino, review of Paulo Sérgio Pinheiro, *Estratégias da Ilusão: A Revolução Mundial e o Brasil, 1922–1935* (São Paulo: Companhia das Letras, 1991), in *American Historical Review* 97:5 (December 1992), 1635.

11. See A.P. Donajgrodzki, ed., *Social Control in Nineteenth-Century Britain* (Totowa, NJ: Rowman and Littlefield, 1977).

12. Peter Burke, *The Historical Anthropology of Early Modern Italy* (New York: Cambridge University Press, 1987), 13.

13. P. Burke, *Early Modern Italy,* 14.

14. Peter Singlemann, "Political Structure and Social Banditry in Northeast Brazil," *Journal of Latin American Studies* 7 (1975), 60.

15. The quote is from Paul J. Vanderwood, *Disorder and Progress: Bandits, Police, and Mexican Development,* rev. ed. (Wilmington, DE: Scholarly Resources Books, 1992), 6, citing Billy Jaynes Chandler, *The Bandit King: Lampião of Brazil* (College Station: Texas A&M University Press, 1978), 176.

16. Paulo Sérgio Pinheiro, "Police and Political Crisis: The Case of the Military Police," 167–88, in Martha K. Huggins, ed., *Vigilantism and the State in Modern Latin America* (New York: Praeger, 1991), 168.

17. Marcos A. da Silva, *Contra a Chibata: Marinheiros Brasileiros em 1910* (São Paulo: Brasiliense, 1982).

18. See the author's *Vale of Tears* (Berkeley: University of California Press, 1992).

19. Paulo Sérgio Pinheiro, "Police and Political Crisis," 168–69, 179, 181.

20. *Folha de São Paulo,* 16 March 1993, 4; Caco Barcellos, *Rota 66* (São Paulo: Globo, 1992).

21. *Veja,* 16 December 1992, 22–25.

22. See the harrowing film directed by Lucia Murat, *Que Bom Te Ver Viva* (São Paulo, 1991), the story of several women who were captured and tortured at great length during the early 1970s.

23. Special Commission of Investigation, Legislative Assembly of São Paulo, interview with Colonel Arnaldo Braga PMSP, 9 September 1981, cited by Paulo Sérgio Pinheiro, "Police and Political Crisis," 179.

24. International Confederation of Free Trade Unions, *Annual Survey of Violations of Trade Union Rights* (Brussels: ICFTU, 1993); *New York Times,* 25 October 1994, A4.

25. *Folha de São Paulo,* 21 January 1993, 2

26. *Veja,* 2 December 1992, 22–24.

27. *Folha de São Paulo,* 17 December 1992, 1; 2 May 1993, n.p. (*Folha de São Paulo* clipping file).

28. *Folha de São Paulo,* 11 March 1993, 1; *New York Times,* 6 November 1994, A4.

29. Gilberto Dimenstein, *Brazil: War on Children* (London: Latin American Bureau, 1991), 28–29; John Krich, *Why Is This Country Dancing?* (New York: Simon and Schuster, 1993), 95.

30. Magnus Mörner, *Region and State in Latin America's Past* (Baltimore: Johns Hopkins Press, 1993), 54.

31. L.A. Machado da Silva, "1967: A Política na Favela," *Cadernos Brasileiros,* 9:41 (1967), 35–47.

32. Lícia do Prado Valladares, "Associações Voluntárias na Favela," paper presented at the twenty-eighth meeting of the Sociedade Brasileira para o Progresso da Ciência, Brasília, 1976.

33. Lícia do Prado Valladares, "Working the System: Squatter Response to Resettlement in Rio de Janeiro," *International Journal of Urban and Regional Research* 2:1 (March 1978), 12–25 (12–13).

34. See Robert Gay, "Community Organization and Clientelist Politics in Contemporary Brazil: A Case Study from Suburban Rio de Janeiro," *International Journal of Urban and Regional Research* 14:4 (December 1990), 649, note 3.

35. L.P. Valladares, "Working the System," 18–19. See also *Jornal do Brasil* (Rio de Janeiro), 28 September 1968, 1.

36. See Anne Boran, "Popular Movements in Brazil: A Case Study of the Movement for the Defence of *Favelados* in São Paulo," *Bulletin of Latin American Research,* 8:1 (1989), 83–109.

37. Paul Craig Roberts, "Siege in South America," *Washington Times,* 10 April 1991, 36.

38. Carlos H. Vasconcelos, "É Pau," *Classe Operária,* 6:79 (25 May 1992), 9.

39. *Veja,* 28 October 1992, 19.

40. *Folha de São Paulo,* 2 November 1992, 1.

41. *Folha de São Paulo,* 2 November 1992, 1.

42. *O Estado de São Paulo,* 26 April 1992, 1.

43. *Folha de São Paulo,* 26 September 1992, n.p. (*Folha de São Paulo* clipping file).

44. *Folha de São Paulo,* 25 September 1992, 1; 29 September 1992, 3.

45. *Folha de São Paulo,* 18 October 1992, n.p.; 9 April 1993, n.p. (*Folha de São Paulo* clipping file).

46. *Veja,* 29 October 1992, 9.

47. Interview, Nancy Scheper-Hughes by Naomi Schneider, January 1993, in *Imprints,* 7 (1), 1993 (University of California Press), 5; Sarah Blaffer Hrdy, review in New York *Times,* 30 August 1992, 11. See Nancy Scheper-Hughes, *Death without Weeping: The Violence of Everyday Life in Brazil* (Berkeley: University of California Press, 1992).

48. J. Krich, *Why Is This Country Dancing?* 95.

49. James Brooke, "Ulcer Drug Tied to Numerous Abortions in Brazil," *New York Times,* 19 May 1993, B7; based on information published in *The Lancet* (London), n.d.

50. Roosevelt Moises Smeke Cassorla, ed., *Do Suicídio: Estudos Brasileiros* (Campinas, São Paulo: Papirus, 1991), 49.

51. José Carlos Sebe Bom Meihy, *Canto de Morte Kaiowá* (São Paulo: Edições Loyola, 1991), 293.

8

Toward a New Civil Society

During the·1970s and the early 1980s, a consensus among observers of Brazilian politics held that the military regime would be difficult to dislodge because it saw taking power not as something for its own sake but as a mission to restructure society, and that it was supported in this quest by the industrialists and businessmen, the leaders of the new elite. Political scientists pointed to the "new professionalism" of Brazil's Superior War College; Fernando Henrique Cardoso argued that the root of Brazilian authoritarianism was a response to Brazil's condition of external dependency. When the armed forces moved to step back from power in the 1980s, scholars reevaluated their stance, arguing that the military had been less monolithic that earlier imagined. Others credited opponents of the military government with sensing that the "patrimonial state" had been weaker than supposed, and that the liberal-representative traditions had been suppressed but not eradicated. The military had preserved the trappings of democracy, and this, in turn, had kept the hopes for a return to civil society alive. In 1984–85, tens of millions of Brazilians took to the streets demanding direct presidential elections and a return to democratic practices that Brazil had not seen for twenty years.[1]

The return to civilian rule brought back into power the old power brokers who, in turn, ran up what Frances Hagopian terms "a staggering debt during a spree of wild clientelism in the late 1980s and early 1990s."[2] Yet despite these bumps along the way, by the mid-1990s signs of positive change were evident. The landslide election of social democrat Fernando Henrique Cardoso to the presidency in October 1994 buoyed financial markets and produced a wave of long-term optimism. Many progressives who had initially had favored the candidacy of the Workers' Party's Luis Inácio da Silva (Lula) defected to Cardoso's camp as the voting neared. The new president, a brilliant sociologist and former finance minister who, while manacled and hooded, had heard the cries of friends being tortured in a São Paulo prison during the dictatorship, and who had spent four years in exile in Chile, France, and the United States, in the words of novelist Jorge Amado, brought "an immediate and real change in Brazil's image."[3] Brazil's economic prowess and stubborn efforts by administrators to improve the effectiveness of social programs were beginning to show results.

Cardoso sought to entice foreign investment by promoting a "new Brazil" that respects human rights and is committed to free-market economics, including privatizing government-owned oligopolies in transportation, energy, chemicals, and mining. "Brazil has given up rowing against the tide of history, trying to obtain isolated advantages without entering the crux of foreign affairs," Cardoso told the press after returning from a European trip in September 1995. "We're living in a time when the notion of the Third World is a thing of the past, when we no longer have a complex about saying our most important partners are the United States, Germany, and Japan."[4]

Pegging Brazil's currency to the dollar stabilized prices three months before the election, permitting working-class families to put meat on the table regularly (for years, inflation had been so bad that within a few days of being paid, wage earners could no longer afford to buy meat). It remained trying for people to subsist on one, two, and even three minimum salaries, but working conditions for menial employees improved. Registration of domestic employees, evaded for decades, now became more commonplace so that servants could collect social benefits. Maids, in turn, were given representation by a labor union apparatus that traditionally ignored women, even when they made up a large share of the national wage-earning force.

One hopeful indicator was that Brazil's previously unchecked population surge was approaching stabilization. There were 156 million Brazilians in 1995, but the number was expected to level off at 200 million between 2020 and 2040. The largest cities, sprawling São Paulo and Rio de Janeiro, by the mid-1990s had already stopped growing.[5] This meant more room in schools and hospitals, respite for the stretched electric and water utilities, and prospects for higher wages as the relentless migratory stream of earlier decades, constantly depressing wages, began to diminish. Vargas's inefficient state-run social security apparatus, which covered 15 million Brazilians in late 1994, was supplemented by $6.4 billion in private pension funds.[6] Even the repressive military regime in many ways was far more of a welfare state than Getúlio Vargas's Estado Novo. Meanwhile, by 1995 the electorate exceeded 80 million, in contrast to the 6 million votes cast in 1960. Still, Brazilians on the whole remained poor, although affluent Brazilians, including the upper-middle class, lived in more luxury than most of their counterparts anywhere in the world. Five million children—25 percent of all children under five years of age—were classified as malnourished by the World Bank, the worst record in Latin America except for Guatemala and Haiti. In 1992, only *half* of Brazil's population was classified as economically active. Fewer than 20 percent completed four years in school; more than half of all adults were functionally literate.

Traditional politics did not seem to provide answers. Brazilians in the 1990s have fewer outlets to air their grievances than their parents and grandparents' generations. The demise of the old system of politics, in which mayors and even governors had accepted petitions personally delivered by constituents in need of favors, ended, as government became more impersonal, run by computers and bureaucrats. Pre-television-era politicians offered little substance, but they always showed proper personal respect to their constituents. This personal touch, so valued and so calming an influence, was swept away by the advertising circus atmosphere of nationally televised political campaigns. Cardoso's election presented a chance to stabilize the political process and to implement measures to carry out sweeping social change and to clear obstacles to free-market reform. His platform called for help for agricultural producers, including tax exemptions for basic foods; privatization; more than doubling federal expenditures (to $93 per person) for public health care; deregulation to attract external investment; more autonomy for communities in public education; and the lowering of the public debt. Past efforts, however, invariably clashed with entrenched powerful bureaucratic forces tied to the status quo. It remained to be seen how effective the new president's whirlwind initiatives would be, and whether his pragmatic deals with the political Right would hinder his effectiveness in fostering change.[7]

Civic Responsibility

Brazil has been governed under eight different national constitutions since independence, and it likely will have still another constitution in the late 1990s. Three (in 1891, 1934, and 1946) were drafted by constituent assemblies; two more (in 1967 and 1969), by the military. Most promised assurances to protect the powerless. The 1824 Constitution prohibited cruelty to slaves. The 1891 republican Constitution guaranteed habeas corpus; the latest, in 1988, abolished the death penalty. Even so, scores of Brazilians have been arrested and imprisoned without their civil rights being respected, and vigilante bands, often led by police, have murdered hundreds if not thousands of persons extralegally. After abolition, communities and states toughened their laws defining vagrancy. Leftists faced intermittent repression from the 1930s through the 1980s. Even after *abertura* and the restoration of civilian government, the right to privacy was ignored by private security companies who tapped telephone lines on demand. Laws against racism and discrimination were not enforced. The traditional practice of criminalizing the unemployed continued.

Economists argued that while the worldwide success of inflation stabilization combined with economic reform was incontestable, Brazil's resistance to reform remained a liability. "Politically impossible, the essential conditions are not satisfied," demurred Fernando Henrique Cardoso on becoming finance minister in 1993. The Massachusetts Institute of Technology's Rudi Dornbusch offered a four-step "shock treatment" to end the stalemate: rapid privatization, a freeze on wages and prices, budget balancing (and tax reform), and a targeted antipoverty program, on the basis of Carlos Salinas de Gortari's program in Mexico.[8] In late February 1994, Cardoso announced a novelty in the annals of world inflation: the URV (Unidade Real de Valor), an index adopted as a currency. With $33 billion in foreign exchange reserves in the Central Bank, analysts considered Brazil potentially able to fix its exchange rate and to end five decades of chronic inflation. As a result, foreign traders increased imports to Brazil by 50 percent during 1993 and 1994, even before the elections. Economists estimated that at least $23 billion would be invested in Brazil by the turn of the century, spurred by eased restrictions on foreign ownership of Brazilian industry.[9]

Brazil's earlier achievement in removing Fernando Collor de Mello from office showed that democratic principles still prevailed. Collor's exit was the first successful instance of impeachment in Brazil's 103-year republican history, an example of constitutionalism in action. Brazil faced the future, however, not assured that it would be able to sustain the high level of politicization it had achieved in 1984, in 1989, and again during the impeachment campaign. That political mobilization, of course, needed to be accompanied by political education and responsible behavior on the part of political leadership and by a commitment to the rule of law. The electoral legislation passed during the transition from military to civilian rule was responsible for the fragmentation of political factions into nineteen political parties represented in the 1986 Congress and no fewer than forty weak political parties operating in 1992–93. Worse, the 1988 Constitution perpetuated an overrepresentation of the small and rural states, places historically dominated, as in the case of Collor's Alagoas, by oligarchic clans, in that it granted each state, regardless of size, a minimum of eight deputies.

One of the challenges faced by Cardoso's government was the need to furnish meaningful powers to the judicial and the legislative branches of government and to create a more equitable system of checks and balances. Executive power is enormous. The chief executive names 50,000 new bureaucrats on taking office, in comparison to 3,000 in the United States. Thousands of state employees lose their jobs when a new governor comes to power. On the other hand, the federal bureaucracy, with its 2 million employees, represented a powerful obstacle to reform efforts. The Congress, too, played a dual role. Since the restoration of civilian rule, it had displayed significant power, especially fiscally; of the 1993 federal budget of 240 billion dollars, Congress held authority over only $9 billion dollars, merely 3.75 percent of the total.[10] But it remained divided into dozens of parties and factions, hopelessly divided and characterized by abruptly shifting alliances and political manipulation. Polls in 1994 showed that 70 percent of Brazilians favored constitutional change to open statist monopolies and imposed presidential control of the budget, but the civil servant bureaucracy—many of its members holdovers from the decade and a half of dictatorship—held firm, extending the historical impasse.

Prospects

This book began by noting characteristics that made colonial Brazil singularly different from the Spanish-, French-, English-, and Dutch-speaking colonies in the hemisphere. At the end of the twentieth century, Brazil remains markedly distinct. After Nigeria, it has the world's largest black population, a fact that has been unconsciously (and consciously) denied or ignored in all expressions of official culture. Brazil has become a Third World country surrounding a First World archipelago, the site not only of the protected neighborhoods of the wealthy, with their elegant shopping malls and private clubs in the cities, but also of the comfortable rural homes of landowners with their satellite dishes, stables of four-wheel-drive cars, and tennis courts.

Although Brazilians over the decades have sought to reform their country's institutions, few have sought to alter the underlying attitudes and behavior patterns standing in the way of deep-seated change. After all, if there is such a thing as inevitability in history, it is that those who think that they can ordain what will henceforth be will always end up finding themselves overcome by what has ever been.[11] This seems apt for Brazil. Its society is highly stratified, a condition that often legitimizes inequality and measures status by affluence and autonomy. Reinforcing this in Brazil's case is the shared value system held by "insiders": no matter how far one may stand from another in stated views about such things as political beliefs, even far-right conservatives and radical chic leftist intellectuals close ranks in accepting the comfortable advantages shared by educated and affluent Brazilians. Access to privilege in Brazil is not a matter of belonging to the right club, or to the right political party; it is inherited privilege (for some) and the effectiveness of one's connections (for others) that determines whether one is an insider or an outsider. And woe to the latter: society closes ranks against outsiders, an action that, as a kind of dirty secret, defies redress because its rules are applied silently, like the "gentlemen's agreements" that excluded Jews and blacks from jobs in many fields and from access to private clubs in the United States as late as the 1950s and beyond. Pessimists, as we have seen, doom any reform plan to failure if it does not break the economic and psychological impasse, derived from wage repression and institutions historically favoring the privileged, that had yielded structural impasse.

What are the ways in which this impasse might be broken? Some argue that capitalism should be fully imposed on the country's capitalists, that the private sector should be genuinely privatized. Under the existing state of affairs, this argument goes, reforms socialize losses while privatizing profits. True autonomy, with no safety net for the privileged, would reward entrepreneurship at all levels of the system, ensuring a level playing field and providing fairer access to economic advancement. This would then be followed by massive government investment in people and in infrastructure, backed by strong procedural mechanisms to protect against backsliding and privilege. Priorities would be changed: from costly therapeutic medicine to preventative public health; from traditional elitist education to new ways of teaching generic conceptual capabilities, mixed, no doubt, with strong doses of consciousness raising and with efforts to raise individual self-esteem, especially for those at the bottom.

Preference would be given for devices geared to raising the level of political mobilization, making government more representative and more responsible, ending the referendum character of presidential elections and the stranglehold of partisan political dealings. There would be massive investment in a wholly reformed system of public education, giving access to the free universities to the most meritorious, not the most privileged, and providing years more of schooling for every child. Private financing of election campaigns would give way to public financing; there would be forced breakups of the television network cartels; the programmatic aspects of political parties would be strengthened. The goal would be, in Roberto

Mangabeira Unger's words, "permanent political mobilization," an "organized frenzy" of political discussions, debates, recalls, referenda, and anything else geared to watch with vigilance for evidence of deception or special privilege or any lack of receptivity on the part of public servants.[12]

Less radical observers offered their own goals after a bilateral colloquium held in late 1995. Members of the U.S.-Brazilian Dialogue agreed that the establishment of a hemispheric free trade area would produce trade expansion, assure more stable and predictable market access, and improve international competitiveness. Economic integration, in turn, would lead to improvements in wages, working conditions, and environmental standards. Spokesmen for the group noted that Brazil and the United States, as the largest economies in South America and in North America, respectively, have a strong common interest in addressing economic and social issues. For the first time in decades, leaders from both Brazil and the United States stood in agreement on what course to follow.[13]

Politics and Social Responsibility

In the April 1993 nationwide plebiscite, which was marked by a telling 25 percent nonparticipation, voters endorsed a continuation of the presidential form of government, failing to support either a parliamentary system or a constitutional monarchy. The difference between presidentialism and parliamentarism, it has been noted by Alfred Stepan, is the difference between *mutual independence* and *mutual dependence* among governing institutions. Because the chief executive and legislatures under presidentialism are elected separately, with their own fixed mandates, that system creates the possibility of impasse (or gridlock, to use the U.S. term) out of a lack of effective vehicles for resolving disputes between the branches. Parliamentarism, of course, especially in systems with extensive regional differences (as in Brazil) and a history of political factionalism, threatens never to offer stability for a long enough period to permit effective governance. It involves mutual dependence, because the prime minister's government needs at least the passive support of a legislative majority.[14] This lessens the danger that a government will rule without majority support, but it raises other problems, all of which became academic at least for the short term when parliamentarism went down to defeat at the polls.

In 1993 Itamar Franco's government bid to reform the 1940 Civil Penal Code, not only to bring it up to date but to attempt to make the judicial system more responsive and efficient. One reform would be to adopt the American practice of probation, according to which persons convicted of crimes may receive, if warranted, release with the obligation to serve parole. This would help relieve the terrible overcrowding of prisons: 48,000 in São Paulo alone, with 113,820 more under prison sentence but not incarcerated. Another measure would be to raise judges' salaries, now only twice that of court clerks.[15] Another measure, untranslatable into law, would be to give support to judges who courageously punish criminals in spite of their power or connections. In June 1993, Rio de Janeiro judge Denise Frossard sentenced fourteen *banqueiros*—numbers racketeers involved in turf war murders, drug sales, and bribery of public officials, who used samba schools as their legal fronts—to six-year prison terms for criminal conspiracy, amid gasps of surprise from the press, the public, and the high-priced society lawyers who represented the defendants. The judge then moved out of her home to more secure quarters and received heavy security from the police. In prison, the racketeers immediately received unheard-of privileges, from meals prepared by their own cooks to the use of their cellular telephones. After all, the numbers game *(jogo de bicho)* is worth more than a billion dollars a year.[16] On the other hand, former President Collor remained unscathed by the corruption scandal that led to his resignation and was well along in his personal campaign to rehabilitate his image as a "regular guy" *(gente como gente)* falsely accused of stealing millions.

Signs have emerged that Brazilian sensibilities have reached out to embrace underprivileged groups. A study of ways to initiate affirmative action programs (in cooperation with the U.S. Embassy) was initiated in mid-1996. Another case in point was the widespread support for a group of descendants of runaway slaves, in Bahia's backlands Rio das Rãs, where ranchers, armed with land titles and backed by lawyers, attempted to drive out the black rural folk by bulldozing their homes, shooting their horses, destroying their fences, and running cattle through their crops. In an unprecedented act, federal prosecutors in 1993 asked a federal judge to protect all descendants of *quilombos* (settlements of runaway slaves) from such evictions.[17]

A number of individuals who a few years before could not have dreamed of rising above their menial conditions have, since the return of civilian government in the mid-1980s, attained success in the political arena. Foremost among this group is former favela dweller Benedita da Silva, who in 1992 was nearly elected Rio's mayor and in 1995 became Brazil's first black female senator. The urban poor have attained a political voice that would have been equally impossible. Genário Xavier da Silva, the president of Rocinha, the largest favela in Latin America with 200,000 inhabitants, is considered to control the votes of as many as 80,000 of its residents. The second largest favela, Jacarezinho, has been organized under the leadership of Josué Antônio de Matos, who is said to control 60,000 votes in his favela of 150,000 residents. Efforts to organize others of Rio de Janeiro's 480 favelas are proceeding. "Scalded cats are afraid of cold water," says Irineu Guimarães, head of the Rio de Janeiro Favela Association (FAFERJ), warning politicians not to forget their promises. Rocinha's political association in 1993 was negotiating with two potential presidential candidates, Mário Covas and Leonel Brizola, the governor of Rio de Janeiro State. "The election happens here," Covas was quoted as saying during his first visit to Rocinha. Favela political organizers relentlessly seek improved benefits, access to water and electricity at affordable rates, cheaper mass transit, and a broad range of assistance for the poor. For the first time in history, they may have achieved the numbers necessary to force politicians and officials to listen to them.[18]

Another success story belongs to Paulo César Melo de Sá, known by the shortened name Paulo Melo. Born in 1957 into a poor family in Saquarema, Rio de Janeiro, with eleven brothers and sisters, Paulo sold candies on the street to bring home money for food. His father, a stonemason's helper, never earned more than the monthly minimum wage, and usually less. At eleven, Paulo left home completely and lived in the streets of Rio for five years, washing cars, doing odd jobs, and keeping himself alive through his wits. When he was seventeen, he enrolled in a reading course offered by the government, and he completed his primary school equivalency diploma. He then studied at the secondary level and graduated.

In 1981, he began to work with street children with similar backgrounds to his. He founded the SOS Criança (Save the Children) Association, taking responsibility for the welfare of about 300 homeless children living in the vicinity of the Flamengo Aterro, Rio's waterfront causeway, which was dotted with parks and soccer fields, and served as a haven for the homeless. In 1991, he was elected to the Rio de Janeiro state legislature, where he rose to the post of vice-leader of the Partido Social Democrático Brasileiro (PSDB), becoming an outspoken voice for the rights of children and a vocal opponent of the police extermination squads that were murdering children with increasing impunity. He achieved this meteoric rise from street urchin to leading legislator in the space of less than a decade.[19]

There have been a small number of other voices arising from the black community as well. Rosa Maria Eipcácia da Vera Cruz, a mid-eighteenth-century woman, was kidnapped in Africa as a child and brought to the New World: some of her writings survive, although it was illegal for a slave to read or write. Maria Firmina dos Reis published the first abolitionist novel written by a Brazilian woman. Leila Rodrigues made a name for herself outside of Brazil speaking about racism against black women, although she did not win a public forum in Brazil. The sociologist Sônia Fátima da

Conceição, a professional social worker and a writer of short stories and essays about black children, has been given a forum through the publication *Cadernos Negros,* the product of a small black cultural association, Quilombohoje. What is interesting about Conceição's writings is that, although she is highly compassionate, she also maintains that responsibility for black abandoned children lies within the black community, something that no one else has ever said in public.[20] In 1991, Maranhão-born João Clemente Borges Trinta (Joãozinho Trinta) left Nilópolis's Escola de Samba Beija-Flor after leading it to five Carnival samba championships in seventeen years, turning full-time to his Flor do Amanhã project to help street children, at least 10 percent of whom were estimated to be HIV-positive.

Brazilians display high personal levels of toleration and acceptance of persons different from them. This trait makes Brazilian life unique: in the United States (it is said), laws forbid discrimination and government protects the disadvantaged, but on the personal level, disadvantaged people are pariahs, kept at a distance at all costs. In Brazil (it is said, in a cliché that seems for the most part accurate), society in general casts a blind eye to the fate of the disadvantaged, but on the individual level, other people relate to them warmly and with understanding. Consider the way gays are treated: in the United States, friendship networks of gays are usually with other gays; in Brazil, the lives of homosexuals are much more integrated with their families, and friendships tend to be much more mixed.[21]

A number of innovative programs have in a short period achieved breakthrough progress. In Curitiba, the capital of southern Paraná State, Mayor Jaime Lerner during the 1980s revived the city's handsome center core, turning downtown streets into pedestrian malls, opening a low-cost trolley bus transit system, and improving urban services. Northeastern Ceará, under Governor Tasso Jeressati and his successor, Ciro Gomes, achieved small miracles in public education and especially in health care, curbing the infant mortality rate despite the fact that more than 4 million residents of the state earn less than $1 per day. Infant mortality was cut by a third in four years.[22] Many of the jobs created in the state were the result of its open-door policy regarding foreign investment, particularly from Japan and Taiwan, a policy frowned on in the rest of Brazil, where nationalistic opposition to such investment persists. Nationwide, 250,000 Brazilian children die before turning five; 35 million workers earn less than $1 a day. In four years, Ceará cut the death rate of infants under the age of one by nearly one-third. In Brazil's $450 billion national economy, roughly the equivalent of China's, Brazil's infant mortality is 2.5 times that of China, even though Brazil's per capita income is 8 times China's. Such deaths occur nearly entirely among the very poor. For the affluent, mortality rates stand at European levels.

Ceará's governor created his Viva a Criança (Long Live Children) campaign in 1987, a decentralized program stressing preventative health education. Community workers, paid only the monthly minimum wage of $55, were recruited from among people displaced by drought. These wages barely permitted the health workers to escape misery themselves, but as state workers they also received other benefits. Many traveled on bicycles, carrying backpacks with first aid items. By 1993, 7,240 health workers were on the job, each one responsible for visiting about a hundred poor families a month. The cost of the program was meager, even for Ceará, one of the poorest states: $500,000 a month. The health workers instruct families in such things as dealing with lice and scabies, purifying drinking water, and making oral rehydration formula with salt and sugar. Government health clinics offered vaccinations and gave pre- and postnatal care to mothers; municipalities ran day-care crèches. Under thirty-five-year-old governor Ciro Gomes, in 1993 Ceará won UNICEF's Maurice Pate Award for child-protective efforts, the first time in its twenty-seven-year history that the prize went to a South American locale. Ceará's per capita revenue rose from 1986 to 1993 by 30 percent, while Brazil's as a whole declined by 4 percent.

As important as the dramatic impact on the health of Ceará's poor was the fact that, for virtually the first time in Brazilian history, men and women at the bottom—victims displaced by drought—were being incorporated into the system as health-care deliverers. Training drought refugees to become Brazilian versions of Chinese "barefoot doctors," even only for the low minimum wage, was a dramatic innovation within a system whose best effort over decades had been to create temporary make-work jobs, also for minimum wages. The opportunity for meaningful work for these people, unprecedented as it was, brought enormous psychological benefits. For the first time, Brazilians from a chronically poor, mostly rural part of the country were treated by government as human beings, permitted to share in social development.

In the wake of Ceará's success, similar efforts based on massive foreign investment have sprung up in other parts of the country. Industrial output in the 300-mile inland corridor between the state capitals of São Paulo and Minas Gerais is expanding at a rate of 10 percent a year. This is one of the largest growth areas in the world, comparable in the 1990s only to coastal China. Fiat has invested $1 billion, four times its total investment in the rest of the world combined. Fiat employs 18,000 people in shifts around the clock, and has attracted fifty-three car-parts manufacturers to the region. The Inter-American Development Bank is funding improved highways between the two capitals, a project that, when completed, is expected to spur another $10 billion in investment.[23]

In the blighted area of public education, a few bright spots have begun to shine through. In Resende, in the interior of the state of Rio de Janeiro, 160 kilometers from the city, administrators dismissed half of the district's 1,265 teachers so that the other half, more effective in the classroom, could teach unhindered. Salaries for the remaining 670 teachers were tripled to 10 million cruzeiros a month (June 1993). The dismissed teachers, however, were given desk jobs working for the municipality, simply adding to the bloated bureaucracy. The Resende district also extended the school year from 180 to 235 days, following the model of schools in Japan. Students falling behind were permitted to take extra classes to avoid being left back a grade, the traditional method which over the years caused millions of poor children to drop out because of the humiliation of being older than the other students in their classes. By 1993, 93 percent of Resende's students who had entered first grade made it through the eighth, as compared to the national average of 30 percent. In Iguatú, in the Ceará backlands, half the schools in the district were closed so that teachers could be paid more than the poverty-level minimum wage. A few districts have started to pay student tuition at private schools; other districts have paid tuition at local universities for older students willing to become teachers. In Recife, a pilot program in which firms and schools in affluent parts of the city "adopt" poor schools located in the slums brought better education in 1994 to 9,300 favela children. "It is important for [rich children] to understand the reality faced by others," the director of one of the elite schools said.[24]

Brasília's Governor Joaquim Roriz initiated a pilot program to replace a squalid shantytown with a public project of 1,000 freestanding concrete houses up to 150 square meters each, all in an unprecedentedly short time. The social welfare program of Roriz's government, the Programa de Assentamento da População de Baixa Renda do Governo do Distrito Federal, the largest such program in the country, reaches 600,000 residents living on less than the poverty level, one-third of the population of the capital city. Even members of the opposition Workers' Party (PT) have applauded Roriz's actions. We have introduced a "model of social justice," boasted the governor's Works Secretary, Roberto Arruda, "that avoids what happened in Rio de Janeiro and São Paulo, and that bypasses the utopia of the National Housing Plan (BNH)."[25]

Spurred by the creation of the National Food Security Institute, the tide seemed to be turning toward recognizing the problems of the poor and hungry. President Cardoso acknowledged the need to accelerate land reform in a country where 44 percent of the land is owned by 1 percent of landowners, and some 4.8 million rural families do not own the land on which they live and work. Decades-old government pledges to distribute land not put under cultivation have begun to be fulfilled, with 40,000 landless families resettled by the end of 1995, mostly in the South.

The effort to combat hunger gained momentum under the tireless leadership of Herbert de Souza, an activist sociologist. An easy target for witty political cartoonists and journalists because of his disheveled appearance, de Souza hammered away, much as Ralph Nader had done two decades earlier in the United States, and by the mid-1990s he had become nationally recognized as a public conscience against hunger. Signs emerged that public opinion was beginning to turn against corporations and institutions not willing to cooperate. The problem, de Souza and others pointed out, was neither the food supply nor the poor themselves, but the lack of purchasing power and jobs for the majority of the population. Unique in the annals of privately sponsored philanthropy, heretofore always restricted to individual states, in the early 1990s the antihunger campaign took on national proportions. The Bahian group Olodum, for example, sent a delegation to São Paulo in November 1993 to parade the streets to publicize the event. Rock musicians and other performers gave a fourteen-hour benefit concert in São Paulo, requiring that in lieu of paying admission, fans bring a package of five kilos of beans, five kilos of rice, a can of powdered milk, and a can of cooking oil. São Paulo's venerable Santa Casa de Misericordia auctioned off towels and T-shirts used by Michael Jackson during the entertainer's stay in the city to raise money for its efforts to aid the poor.

The antihunger campaign was only a start. Since Brazil has little tradition of individual or collective action to alter civil society, that part of everyday life not governed by the state has for generations remained uneven and informal. Despite the language of universal rights employed since the Vargas years, citizenship has not been extended to all; rather, government has maintained regulated, partial citizenship, denying rights to millions of Brazilians deemed unworthy of them. With no rooted notion of civil rights, and with law applied narrowly as the domain of the rich, democracy has remained a disjunctive concept; as a result, social justice (as well as the right to secure contracts and to acquire property) has been elusive. Lacking effective associations on the model of the American Civil Liberties Union, the Urban League, Common Cause, or other advocacy or public interest organizations, such work in Brazil has remained entrusted to a handful of principled individuals, defenders of lost causes, who somehow have managed to escape the broad brush of accusation that for most Brazilians historically has meant guilt by association.

One such man was Heráclio Sobral Pinto, the tireless Rio de Janeiro lawyer who in the 1960s and 1970s defended one after another of the members of the Communist Party and other radicals against charges, sometimes trumped up and sometimes not, of subversion. Another is Ivone Bezerra de Mello, a sculptor and member of *carioca* high society who gives her home telephone number to street children so they can call her in emergencies; who feeds them; and who sat with them on the steps of the Candelária Church after the 1993 police massacre, in case the vigilantes returned. Still another is Evandro Lins e Silva, eighty years old in 1992, one of the main prosecutors in the impeachment proceedings against Fernando Collor. "I consider myself," he said when questioned about his motivation, "a symbol of the indignation of the Brazilian people. I am the people's defender against moral degradation."[26] Boastful, perhaps, but indicative of a rarely expressed attitude in Brazilian public life, part of a national political culture in which the concept of citizenship does not, for the most part, include responsibility or obligation.

Brazil's emotional conquest of the 1994 soccer World Cup produced an outpouring of valedictory writing, much of which looked beyond the playing field to the state of affairs for Brazilians as a whole. The victory proves "that Brazilians, united and prideful, are capable of facing adversity," Luciano do Valle wrote. To be a Brazilian is not only the privilege of the big shots, he added. Being Brazilian requires pride in the present and in the past. The effort that succeeded in winning the *tetra* (its fourth World Cup championship), the journalist implored, must be applied permanently. Brazilians must take back their own country, he implied, addressing the agonies and banalities of day-to-day life.[27]

Although President Cardoso's initiatives were slowed by foot dragging by the traditional politicians on whom his coalition depended for support, he did not shy away from addressing the country's critical needs. The president also moved forward in the area of human rights, following a massacre of protesting landless workers in the state of Pará in early 1996 and the resignation of Herbert de Souza from the social action commission's advisory board headed by Cardoso's wife Ruth.

No one doubted President Cardoso's deep commitment to reform and to social justice. What made his job excruciatingly difficult, however, were the surviving legacies from the past. Inadequate monitoring and suspect practices led five state banks in 1996 to run up debts totaling $20.4 billion, requiring a government takeover and the most expensive bailout in history. Brazil's impressive economic growth in recent decades has flowed around large pockets of chronic urban and rural poverty—obstacles, according to sociologist José Pastore, which can only be reduced by specific structural change. What Brazil was achieving was dynamic economic progress acting to preserve the social structure as a whole.[28] Brazil today is better than yesterday; for a few, it is significantly better. But high rates of growth still need to be achieved both in mobility and in inequality. This is Brazil's dilemma as it faces the new century.

Notes

1. See Frances Hagopian, *Traditional Politics and Regime Change in Brazil* (New York: Cambridge University Press, 1996), 7–13.
2. F. Hagopian, *Traditional Politics,* 13.
3. Jorge Amado, quoted in *New York Times,* 3 October 1994, A4.
4. Quoted in *O Estado de São Paulo,* reprinted in *Real Brazil* 1:1 (October–November 1995), 4.
5. Simon Schwartzman interview in *Veja* 27:28 (13 July 1994), 7–8.
6. James Brooke, in *New York Times,* 10 September 1994, 17, 25.
7. See *Wall Street Journal,* 5 October 1994, A1–A8.
8. Rudi Dornbusch, "Economic Viewpoint," *Business Week,* 13 September 1993, 16 (including quote from Fernando Henrique Cardoso). See *Latin American Regional Reports–Brazil,* 5, RB-94–01, 13 January 1994, 4.
9. Norman Gall, letter to author, São Paulo, 17 March 1994. See Roger P. Hipskind, *The New Plan: New Money, New Politics?* (São Paulo: Fernand Braudel Institute of World Politics, March 1994); Dean Graber, "Real Brazil: October 1995," *Real Brazil* 1:1 (October–November 1995), 4.
10. "O Anão Fantasma," *Veja* 25:51 (16 December 1992), 32–33.
11. See Walter Goodman, review of Murray Kempton's *Rebellions, Perversities, and Main Events* (New York: Random House, 1994), in *New York Times Book Review,* 10 April 1994, 13.
12. Roberto Mangabeira Unger, presentation to "Wither Brazil" Conference, University of Miami Law School, 27 February 1993.
13. Inter-American Dialogue, *Statement of the U.S.-Brazil Dialogue on Hemispheric Trade and Financial Issues* (Washington, DC, May 1996), 1–5.
14. Alfred Stepan, "The Brazilian Impeachment and Beyond," *The Camões Quarterly* 4: 3–4 (Autumn–Winter 1992–93), 40–41.
15. *Visão* 41:19 (26 May 1993), 10–13.
16. *Visão* 41:20 (2 June 1993), 22–23; *Latin American Weekly Report,* WR 93–22 (10 June 1993), 257.
17. James Brooke, in *New York Times,* 15 August 1993, 9. The 1988 Constitution had promised to issue land titles to descendants of former runaway slaves.
18. "Favelas são Trampolim Político," *O Estado de São Paulo,* 16 December 1988, 10.
19. See Comissão Parlamentar de Inquerito, *Para Apuração de Responsabilidade pelo Exterminio de Crianças e Adolescentes no Estado do Rio de Janeiro* (Rio de Janeiro: Assembléia Legislativa do Estado do Rio de Janeiro, 1992).
20. See Carolyn Richardson Durham, "Sônia Fátima da Conceição's Literature for Social Change," *Afro-Hispanic Review* 11:1–3 (1992), 21–25.
21. Richard Parker, quoted in *New York Times,* 12 August 1993, A4.
22. Richard D. North, *Life on a Modern Planet: A Manifesto for Progress* (Man-

chester: Manchester University Press, 1995), 20; John Flint, "Pristine Chapels," *San Francisco Examiner Magazine* (15 October 1995), 47–48.

23. James Brooke, in *New York Times,* 10 August 1994, C1–C2.

24. *Veja* 27:27 (6 July 1994), 50.

25. "Exterminador de Favelas," *Istoé* 1239 (30 June 1993), 48–49.

26. Interview, Evandro Lins e Silva, *Visão* 41 (23 December 1992), 7.

27. Luciano do Valle in *Istoé* 1295 (27 July 1994), 71.

28. José Pastore, "Inequality and Social Mobility," in E. Bacha and H.S. Klein, eds., *Social Change in Brazil, 1945–1985* (Albuquerque: University of New Mexico Press, 1989), 171–95.

Index

Y

Z

Robert M. Levine has published sixteen books on Latin America, five of which have been translated and published there. He has chaired the Columbia University Seminar on Brazil and is past chair of the Committee on Brazilian Studies of the Conference on Latin American History. He is director of Latin American Studies at the University of Miami, Coral Gables. He was elected in 1995 a corresponding member of the Instituto Geográfico e Histórico in Rio de Janeiro. He has lectured in São Paulo, Goiânia, Natal, Rio de Janeiro, Curitiba, Recife, and Salvador. He is co-editor of the *Luso-Brazilian Review*.